Managing Spoiled Identity

# Muslim Minorities

*Editorial Board*

Jørgen S. Nielsen (*University of Copenhagen*)
Aminah McCloud (*DePaul University, Chicago*)
Jörn Thielmann (*ezire, Erlangen University*)

VOLUME 41

The titles published in this series are listed at *brill.com/mumi*

# Managing Spoiled Identity

*The Case of Polish Female Converts to Islam*

By

Beata Abdallah-Krzepkowska
Katarzyna Górak-Sosnowska
Joanna Krotofil
Anna Piela

BRILL

LEIDEN | BOSTON

This work was supported by the National Science Centre, Poland under grant 2017/25/B/HS1/00286.

The authors have no known conflict of interest to disclose.

The order of authorship does not indicate primacy – all authors contributed to this work equally. Correspondence concerning the book should be addressed to Katarzyna Górak-Sosnowska, SGH Warsaw School of Economics, al. Niepodległości 162, 02-520 Warsaw, Poland. Email: kgorak@sgh.waw.pl.

Cover illustration: Image by Aleksandra Malinow.

Library of Congress Cataloging-in-Publication Data

Names: Abdallah-Krzepkowska, Beata, author. | Górak-Sosnowska, Katarzyna, author. | Krotofil, Joanna, author. | Piela, Anna, author.
Title: Managing spoiled identity : the case of Polish female converts to Islam / by Beata Abdallah-Krzepkowska, Katarzyna Górak-Sosnowska, Joanna Krotofil, Anna Piela.
Description: Leiden ; Boston : Brill, 2023. | Series: Muslim minorities, 1570-7571 ; vol. 41 | Includes index.
Identifiers: LCCN 2022052269 (print) | LCCN 2022052270 (ebook) | ISBN 9789004529533 (hardback) | ISBN 9789004529540 (ebook)
Subjects: LCSH: Muslim converts from Christianity—Poland. | Islam—Poland. | Muslims—Poland.
Classification: LCC BP170.5 .A233 2023  (print) | LCC BP170.5  (ebook) | DDC 297.5/7—dc23/eng/20221102
LC record available at https://lccn.loc.gov/2022052269
LC ebook record available at https://lccn.loc.gov/2022052270

Typeface for the Latin, Greek, and Cyrillic scripts: "Brill". See and download: brill.com/brill-typeface.

ISSN 1570-7571
ISBN 978-90-04-52953-3 (hardback)
ISBN 978-90-04-52954-0 (e-book)

Copyright 2023 by Koninklijke Brill NV, Leiden, The Netherlands.
Koninklijke Brill NV incorporates the imprints Brill, Brill Nijhoff, Brill Hotei, Brill Schöningh, Brill Fink, Brill mentis, Vandenhoeck & Ruprecht, Böhlau, V&R unipress and Wageningen Academic.
All rights reserved. No part of this publication may be reproduced, translated, stored in a retrieval system, or transmitted in any form or by any means, electronic, mechanical, photocopying, recording or otherwise, without prior written permission from the publisher. Requests for re-use and/or translations must be addressed to Koninklijke Brill NV via brill.com or copyright.com.

This book is printed on acid-free paper and produced in a sustainable manner.

# Contents

Acknowledgements   VII
List of Figures   VIII
Notes on Authors   IX

Introduction   1
    *Anna Piela, Katarzyna Górak-Sosnowska, Joanna Krotofil and Beata Abdallah-Krzepkowska*

1  Setting the Scene: Islam in Poland   33
    *Katarzyna Górak-Sosnowska*

2  The Socio-Demographic Profile of Survey Respondents   51
    *Katarzyna Górak-Sosnowska*

3  Old and New Connections: Religious and Cultural Belonging Post-conversion among Polish Female Converts to Islam in the UK   71
    *Joanna Krotofil*

4  Polish Platonic Islamophobia   103
    *Katarzyna Górak-Sosnowska*

5  Language of Polish Female Converts to Islam   135
    *Beata Abdallah-Krzepkowska*

6  Converted Bodies: Interior Life and Embodied Religious Practices of Polish Female Converts to Islam   169
    *Anna Piela*

7  From a 'Salafi Bite' to the 'Middle Way'   200
    *Beata Abdallah-Krzepkowska*

Conclusions   240
    *Anna Piela, Joanna Krotofil and Katarzyna Górak-Sosnowska*

Glossary   244
Index   250

# Acknowledgements

Success has many fathers, an old saying goes. To paraphrase it, this monograph has many mothers. It could never have been written without the support, trust and engagement of Polish female converts to Islam who shared with us their life stories, invited to their meetings, and welcomed us as allies. At the individual level, our research has been facilitated by Agnieszka Amatullah Wasilewska in Poland, and Sandra Iman Pertek and Joanna Święcińska in the UK, and Monika Ben Mrad – the research assistant on the project. Dr. Michał Łyszczarz has supported the project by helping out with data collection and transcriptions, for which we are grateful. We also thank Aleksandra Malinow, who represents the community we studied, for the cover photograph. At the institutional level, we extend our gratitude to the Centre of Islamic Culture in Warsaw chaired by imam Nizar and Kobiety Wiary (Women of Faith) in the United Kingdom. Last but not least, our research has been supported administratively by Anna Senator and the Project Support Office at SGH Warsaw School of Economics. We are grateful for all their support.

It would not have been possible to publish this book without the support and patience from the Brill editorial team, especially Nienke Brienen-Moolenaar and Nicolette van der Hoek. We would like to also say thank you to the Department of Religious Studies at Northwestern University for offering Dr Anna Piela the opportunity to work on the project in their institutional space. The Expert Consultation Group supported us through the course of the project, and included prof. dr hab. Janusz Danecki (University of Warsaw), prof. dr hab. Halina Grzymała-Moszczyńska (Akademia Ignatianum in Kraków), Prof. Karin van Nieuwkerk (Radboud University), and Prof. Egdūnas Račius (Vytautas Magnus University). Other colleagues who supported us by reading and commenting extensively on our work include Dr Michael Woolf (Harvard University), Prof. Christie Traina (Fordham University), and Dr Dominika Motak (Jagiellonian University of Kraków).

The COVID-19 pandemic slowed down our research activities and delayed the production of this book. But the delay had another, much brighter reason – two babies, Ania and Zosia, were born to two of the authors in the course of the project. We would like to dedicate the monograph to them.

# Figures

1. Age at conversion by year of birth  53
2. Years in Islam by year of birth  53

# Notes on Authors

*Beata Abdallah-Krzepkowska*
has an MA in Arabic Philology (Jagiellonian University in Kraków) and a PhD degree in linguistics (Silesian University). She is an Assistant Professor at Silesian University, and publishes widely on the topic of Qur'anic semantics, for example most recently she published a chapter on the Qur'anic concept of soul in the book *The Soul in the Axiosphere from an Intercultural Perspective*. Her research interests focus on the language of the Quran, contemporary Islam and Islam in Europe. She participates in public education in relation to Islam and Arab word in Poland. Moreover, she is a research consultant for the Nahda Foundation which promotes cultural cooperation between Poland and Arab countries. | ORCID: 0000-0003-4370-8095

*Katarzyna Górak-Sosnowska*
is an associate professor and head of the Middle East and Central Asia Unit, SGH Warsaw School of Economics. She has a PhD in economics (SGH) and habilitation in the study of religions (Jagiellonian University in Cracow). Her research focuses on Muslim communities in Poland and Europe. She has published five monographs including *Deconstructing Islamophobia in Poland* (2014), and edited a book on *Muslims in Poland and Eastern Europe. Widening the European Discourse on Islam* (2011). Currently she is leading the "EMPATHY: Let's Empower, Participate and Teach each other to Hype Empathy. Challenging discourse about Islam and Muslims in Poland" project, funded by the European Commission: Directorate General for Justice and Consumers, 2022–2023 as well as the Polish team in the "DIGITISLAM: Digital Islam across Europe: Understanding Muslims' Participation in Online Islamic Environments" project (2022–2025) funded by CHANSE – Collaboration of Humanities and Social Sciences in Europe. | ORCID: 0000-0002-1121-6240

*Joanna Krotofil*
is an Assistant Professor at the Institute for the Study of Religion, (Jagiellonian University in Kraków). She has a MSc in Psychology, is a member of the International Institute for The Dialogical Self and a trainee clinical psychologist. She has published a number of articles and book chapters on the relationship between religion, identity and migration. In her first book, *Religia w procesie kształtowania tożsamości wśród polskich migrantów w Wielkiej Brytanii* [*Religion in the Process of Shaping Identity among Polish Migrants in the UK*], she explored, among other topics, experiences of Polish Muslim converts in

the UK. Her main research interests include the place of Islam in contemporary Western societies, in particular the processes related to shaping and negotiation of Muslim identity. She has published in the *Sociology of Religion, Religions*, and the *British Journal of Psychiatry*. | ORCID: 0000-0003-2308-5329

*Anna Piela*
is a visiting scholar at the Department of Religious Studies at Northwestern University, USA. She has a PhD in Women's and Islamic studies (York, UK). She previously worked as lecturer in Religious Studies at Leeds Trinity University and a research consultant with the Muslim Women's Council, Bradford, both in the UK. Her monograph, titled *Muslim Women Online: Faith and Identity in Virtual World* focused on religious authority of Muslim women fostered in various online communities. Her second monograph is titled *Wearing the Niqab: Fashioning Identity among Muslim Women in the UK and the US* (2021). She has published articles in the *Journal of American Academy of Religion, Religions, New Media and Society*, and several other journals. She is a member of the steering committee of the Islam, Gender and Women unit at the American Academy of Religion. Her website is at www.annapiela.com. | ORCID: 0000-0002-3589-1822

# Introduction

*Anna Piela, Katarzyna Górak-Sosnowska, Joanna Krotofil and Beata Abdallah-Krzepkowska*

This book brings to light the existence of a Muslim convert population in Poland, a post-communist country known for its fervent Catholicism, as well as a migrant Polish convert population in the United Kingdom, the primary destination for Polish emigration after the European Union enlargement in 2004. Poland is currently notorious for its right-wing government which promotes hostility towards religious and other minorities. This raises the question of why Polish women and men would openly adopt the stigmatized identity of a Muslim and risk vulnerability at many levels. This book addresses experiences of Polish female converts to Islam both in Poland and the UK, and frames the UK as a 'conversion-friendly' space for Polish women who may not have come into contact with Islam before leaving Poland. This is definitely an unexpected consequence of the largely economic migration post-EU accession. However, female Polish Muslim converts in the UK are doubly stigmatized due their Muslimness and Eastern-Europeanness. furthermore It applies a wide range of social science theory to explain the social consequences of conversion in this particular spatial-temporal context.

This book sets out to examine the 'spoiled' identities of Polish female converts to Islam living in Poland and the UK. We argue that for these women, conversion is accompanied by the development of spoiled identity, and analyse how our respondents manage the stigma. Their narratives are likely to challenge traditional dichotomies embedded in our thinking about cultures and religions and the ways we define the lines of division between 'us' and 'them', frequently mobilised by right-wing populist governments and their supporters. Their experiences offer an intriguing subject of research, as they decide to embrace Islam regardless of all the challenges, risks, and steep social costs they face as new Muslims.

## Conversion and a Spoiled Identity in the Polish Context

Conversion is a complex phenomenon entailing changes in many different aspects of life. It affects not only the convert, but also their social worlds. Being a female convert to Islam[1] situates women in a potentially challenging and vulnerable position. It forces them to re-negotiate their position within their families and communities in which they functioned before the conversion, as well as their new position within the Muslim community. By embracing Islam, many (although not all) Polish converts abandon the Catholic faith, considered by many as one of the pillars of the Polish identity, and usually do so in a publicly visible way. For women, becoming a Muslim is associated with profound changes in cultural norms and practices; the *hijab*, or the Muslim veil, is one of the most visible examples of that. Since Poland is one of the most ethnically and religiously homogeneous states in the now expanded EU, a new religion and associated practices cannot go unnoticed in converts' social surroundings. On the other hand, converts to Islam may be placed in a vulnerable position in the newly adopted socio-cultural environment. Their status as Muslims is sometimes questioned by 'heritage' ('born') Muslims who may perceive them as either unauthentic (less knowledgeable in Islam) or overzealous (since they converted out of conviction) (Roald, 2006). Our choice of women as research participants was dictated by two factors. First, women are much more visible as a Muslim convert community in Poland and globally. Although there are no statistics for Poland, in the UK, three-quarters of converts are women (Peppiatt, 2011). We assume that this is because Islam has something valuable to offer to women in particular, despite the stereotype of this religion as patriarchal. This book explores Polish female converts' perspectives on this subject. Secondly, as an all-female research team, we had an easier access to all-female Muslim spaces and gatherings, and so this reason was much more pragmatic.

The bulk of Western[2] research focuses on the spiritual aspect of the conversion (Mansson McGinty, 2003; van Nieuwkerk, 2006), that is the motivations

---

[1] We selected this term for its wider usability. However, the proper term would actually be 'New Muslim' as it is more inclusive and universal, covering not only the women who changed their religion (converted), but also those whose starting point was atheism or agnosticism.

[2] The terms "West" and "Western" used in this book are deployed with an awareness of the problematic and hierarchical vision of the world divided into "East" and "West," analyzed famously by Said in his now classic work *Orientalism* (1978). Listing countries or regions that are broadly considered to be a part of the West (most commonly Western Europe, the United States, Canada, and Australia) is not helpful without noting the problematic power dynamics of colonialism and neoliberalism. However, although much of contemporary social theory focuses on deconstructing "the topic, the authority, and the assumed primacy of 'the West'" (Young, 1990, p. 19), it is difficult to disentangle oneself from the East/West dichotomy because it has infused public discourse globally, and this is reflected in participants' narratives. In fact, as Bonnett (2017) notes, postcolonial studies has inexplicably failed to sufficiently examine perspectives of groups commonly constructed as "non-Western" on the notion of the West. Therefore, we borrow here from Patel's disclaimer (2009, p. 292)

and stages of the conversion (often using Rambo's seven-stage model (1993)[3] as the theoretical framework). In the last decade, there has been, however, growing research interest in the social functioning of converts to Islam as it involves transformed realities of gender, race, and class (for example, how it influences the way converts function in a variety of social contexts).[4] In this study, we approach female conversion to Islam from the perspective of identity management and relation to significant individuals and groups (significant others, SOs). Both at the personal (transformed individual identity), and the social level (group stigmatized identity) embracing a religion that differs from the mainstream creates a challenging psycho-social situation (Heatherton et al., 2007). The central question which therefore arises is how converts manage their 'spoiled' identity – to use the term introduced by Erving Goffman (1963) – in relation to their SOs. Here, the SOs to be investigated would be their family, other Muslims (both other female converts and heritage Muslims) and the wider non-Muslim society.

In order to facilitate a better understanding of this complex process, we posed the following research questions:

1) How are female converts to Islam socialized into a new set of norms and values?
2) Which elements of cultural-religious symbolic worlds do they choose to embody and express their new identity?
3) What resources and strategies do female converts to Islam use in order to cope with their spoiled identities and resultant social stigmatization?
4) How do they perceive and enact their role in communities (both Muslim and non-Muslim), in the wider society, and at the state and global levels?

---

stating that she uses the term "West" to denote "rich, industrialized, pre-dominantly white, Judeo-Christian countries that have hegemony in the global community and that exercise omnipresent colonial domination worldwide. However, we also understand the term to refer to a racialized, mythical construct defined in relation to 'the Rest' – that is, to nonwhite, often colonized nations." Hall (2007 [1997], pp. 56–60) offers a robust examination of the debates pertaining to the idea of "the West."

3 Rambo (1993) proposed seven stages of religious conversion: the context, the crisis, the quest, the encounter, the interaction, the commitment and the consequences. The model has subsequently been critiqued and built on (for example, Gooren, 2007; az-Zahra and Kumpoh, 2016). It weaves together earlier conversion models and disciplines where they emerged. Its weaknesses include a limited consideration of the role of theology, gender, and age in the conversion process (Gooren, 2007).

4 Some more recent literature discusses social aspects of conversion, for example Öyzürek (2015), Inge (2017), Amer (2020).

5) What are the differences in the identity processes and experiences of Polish female converts to Islam living in Poland and those who have settled in the more diverse and pluralistic United Kingdom?

This formulation of research questions allows for a novel approach to researching conversion to Islam, providing a framework for the first systematic application of Goffman's theoretical insights regarding spoiled identity and its management by converts. Furthermore, the oscillation between the Polish and the UK contexts sets stage for the first study where gender, conversion to Islam and an Eastern European migrant experience intersect, resulting in interwoven identities (and stigmas) that do not stack neatly on top of each other, but, rather, complicate each other in unexpected and paradoxical ways (Crenshaw, 1989).

The migration trajectories of participants were complex and dynamic. The women we interviewed had formed profoundly liminal identities (Piazza, 2019). They were formed by a variety of contexts – spatially, temporally, and through relationships. Therefore, we pivot away from the reified concept of culture and assume that engagement with certain cultural patterns does not require a specific physical location.

## Theoretical Background

The theoretical perspective we take in this research is based on symbolic interactionism (SI) and its focus on meanings attached to social events and their symbolic value that is then transmitted. Through this lens, female converts to Islam are active social actors who shape their experiences through their interactions and relationships with SOs. According to Blumer (1969), social interaction has four main principles:

1) Individuals act in reference to the subjective meaning objects have for them; as we show in this book, different objects are important to the converts, for example, variously families or the new religious communities may be of paramount importance which will dictate decisions that emphasise their importance, such as resisting or adopting the *hijab*.

2) Interactions happen in a social and cultural context where objects, people, and situations must be defined and characterised according to individuals' subjective meanings; consequently, after conversion, reasoning for a variety of everyday decisions may shift, for example respectful treatment of parents may be explained not as emotional bond or tradition, but, rather, religious obligation.

3) For individuals, meanings originate from interactions with other individuals and with society; here this principle of symbolic interactionism is clearly visible in the process of socialisation into the new religious culture. For example, positively evaluated interactions with "born" Muslims may result in a stronger commitment to participating in the global ummah; conversely, negatively evaluated interactions with "born" Muslims may encourage isolation within one's ethnic or cultural community. These meanings that an individual has developed are created and recreated through a process of interpretation that happens whenever that individual interacts with others. In this study, we observed in some cases a particular evolution of personal interpretations of religious requirements, from rigid, literalistic ones adopted early in the process to more flexible, context-based ones later on. This is particularly visible in Chapter 7 of this book where many participants narrate their shift away from Salafist ideals to more 'down to earth' Islam that allows freedom of interpretation.

We adopt a broader view of SI that integrates micro- and macrosociological perspectives. For example, features of SI such as role-taking, self-definition, and introspection allow for understanding communication as a ritual at the microlevel. As Carey argued that "communication is a symbolic process whereby reality is produced, maintained, repaired, and transformed" (1988, p. 23). This understanding of communication as a microsocial process in which individuals create symbolic forms underpins Carey's argument that macrosociological links bind communication and community. Interactionists have also been able to expand their definition and exploration of power by making the connection between microsociological communication processes and macrosociological community structures. These theorisations illuminate the emergence of particular communicative behaviours in converts' communities that involve adopting and hybridising Arabic loanwords, described in Chapter 5. This enables the creation of a specific religious language that also serves as a means of hierarchisation in the new community; mastery of this language affords individuals a higher status.

Our conceptualization of identity employs theories asserting that identity is constantly managed; negotiated in social interactions, continuously created and recreated, multivoiced, and embodied, (see Dialogical Self Theory (Hermans, 2001)). Interior self-making as well as meaning-making is predicated on assembling, negotiating, transforming, and materializing specific discourses in texts and artifacts (Gee, 1999).

We also draw on the theory of stigma and the management of spoiled identity developed by Erving Goffman (1963) and modified, in the context of research with Muslim women, by Nilüfer Göle (2003). From that point of view, we explore how Muslim women who voluntarily adopt Islamic symbols, and the stigma attached to them, turn them into assets. Goffman's now classic observations regarding spoiled identity have not been applied to the context of religious conversion before,[5] yet his perspective illuminates and explains vital aspects of converts' social realities, with their benefits, risks, challenges, and dilemmas. Key to our analysis is Goffman's dynamic understanding of stigma as a marker of spoiled identity: a deeply discrediting attribute that his best described through the language of relationships (1963); that is, what is discrediting in one network of relationships, for example the Islamic headscarf in a non-Muslim majority context, can be functioning in a positive way in a Muslim-majority context. Using that same example, Göle (2003, pp. 810–811) asserts that active appropriation of a stigma symbol is "a shift from a symbol of submissiveness to one of assertiveness. Second, the adoption of an Islamic symbol is not solely a personal choice but a collective one, in the sense that it follows a collective logic of a social protest movement". In our study, this social movement, organizing on the basis of the shared Muslim identity, can be approached as a particular form of "management of spoiled identity". Goffman, interestingly, notes in passing that agentic responses to stigmatization are often characteristic of religious and ethnic minority groups; he mentions Mennonites, the Roma, and "very orthodox Jews." He comments:

> it seems possible for an individual to fail to live up to what we effectively demand of him [sic], and yet be relatively untouched by this failure; insulated by his alienation, protected by identity beliefs of his own, he feels that he is a full-fledged normal human being … He bears a stigma but does not seem to be impressed or repentant about doing so. (Goffman, 1963, p. 16)

In line with Goffman's reasoning, we trace how Polish female converts respond to stigmatization in various psychosocial ways. Examples of resistance include refusing to be excluded from the sociopolitical collectivity of the Polish nation/society by claiming to be proudly Polish and Muslim (Krotofil et al.,

---

5  Greil (1977) considered conversion as a strategy to manage an identity spoiled pre-conversion. For example prisoners may decide to convert or be "born again" to atone for previous transgressions. For them, conversion demarcates the departure from the old life. In contrast, we are considering how conversion may spoil an identity that may have been previously "unspoiled" although, of course, many of our respondents had experienced stigmatization due to disability, divorce, or domestic violence.

INTRODUCTION                                                                                      7

forthcoming); organising with others on the basis of this shared identity; visibly communicating the signifiers of Muslimness such as the headscarf (Göle, 2003) or praying in public. Those who engage in these practices in the West (and associated areas such as Poland) are those who Goffman describes (1963, p. 13) as the "discredited" – those who can be immediately identified as bearing stigma by others. Göle notes (2003, p. 824) that "Islamic visibility (and not solely identity) creates such a disturbance because it is both inscribed in bodies and spaces, reminding a religious regime of self and of a gendered grammar for private and public frontiers."

Those who engage in avoidance of stigmatization – practising Islam in private or leaving Poland for the ostensibly more welcoming UK, keeping one's religious belonging secret (for example by giving health-related reasons for abstaining from alcohol and pork) and avoiding religiously-coded clothing would be classified as Goffman (1963, p. 13) as the "discreditable". They only manage to avoid stigmatization because they try, more or less consciously, to blend in with the majority. Notably, this group risks double stigmatization – by the mainstream society if "found out" to be Muslim, and by the Muslim community who might negatively judge what could be perceived as insufficient religious practice. Yet, as we demonstrate throughout the book, the respondents in our project tended to successfully integrate and, at times, embrace the idea of stigma as an unexpected asset.

### Literature on Conversion to Islam in the West, Eastern Europe, and Poland

Our study builds on two fields of inquiry and offers some new insights by putting them in conversation with each other. The first one comprises studies on conversion to Islam in the West. The second one, which is still forming, involves studies of Islam and Muslims in Poland.

Conversion to Islam existed in the West long before it caught the academic interest. The first comprehensive studies on contemporary conversion in the West emerged in the 90s (for example, Köse, 1996, Wohlrab-Sahr, 1999) and mid-00s (for example, Mansson McGinty, 2003; Roald, 2005; van Nieuwkerk, 2006; Zebiri, 2008). Most of the literature concerned women's conversion with a few exceptions of studies tackling conversion of men and women (for example, Köse & Loewenthal, 2000). These studies focused on three main topics: reasons for choosing Islam (for example, Maslim & Bjorck, 2009; Lakhdar, 2007), embracing new, pious identity (for example, Jeldtoft, 2011; Moosavi,

2012, Rao, 2015; Soutar, 2010; Winchester, 2008) and relations with Muslims and non-Muslims (for example, Roald, 2004; Zebiri, 2008). As the bulk of research on conversion to Islam in the West grew, new themes and approaches emerged including Islamic fashion (for example, Tarlo, 2020) with a focus on the issue of *hijab* (and *niqab*; for example, Piela, 2021), converts online and offline (for example, Piela, 2012 & 2015), or convert relationship to their cultures, countries and nations (for example, Inge, 2017; Midden, 2018; Özyürek, 2015 &; Younis & Hassan, 2017). These topics seem to broaden the field of inquiry and at the same time respond to the geopolitical situation of Muslim communities in the West, which has been profoundly changed by 9/11 and following events. That is why more and more studies tackled such topics as conversion and radicalisation (for example Wilkinson et al., 2021; Snook et al., 2021), or experiences of Islamophobia and racialisation of converts to Islam (for example Amer, 2020; Galonnier, 2015; Moosavi, 2015; Rogozen-Soltar, 2012).

These studies cover, almost exclusively, conversion in the West – Western Europe and North America. Experiences of converts to Islam who had been inhabiting Eastern peripheries and semi-peripheries of the West, i.e. from Central and Eastern Europe had remained unnoticed for many years (Račius, 2018). They have only emerged within the last decade as a field of academic inquiry. Interestingly, most of these (still few) studies had been published in English. Every emerging study was a pioneering one, usually the only one, or one of the few every conducted in Central and Eastern Europe such as Pirický (2018) in the Czech and Slovak Republics, Stoica (2011, 2013) in Romania, Shestopalets (2019) in the Ukraine, Shestopalets (2021) in Russia, or Račius (2011) in Lithuania. While some themes – notably, finding Islam as an alternative basis for one's identity following the collapse of the geopolitical order and the overwhelmingly secular Soviet bloc – often appear in this new literature about Eastern European Islam, Poland is the odd one out. While many of its neighbours, such as the former East Germany or Czech Republic, are characterised by the lowest levels of religiosity in Europe, Poland is intensely religious. It is a country where Catholicism was the main platform of resistance against the Soviet Union and is now a powerful political force. Thus, while many of the conversion arcs in Eastern Europe could be described as "from atheism to Islam", in Poland, the predominant arc is "from Catholicism (albeit often 'lapsed') to Islam". Özyürek (2015, p. 72) described how for her East German respondent, "the realisation of the existence of God" was the breakthrough moment in her religious journey. Among Polish converts, the most common narrative involves a conscious theological turn away from Christian and/or Catholic doctrine that involves the Trinity, divinity of Jesus, or veneration of Mary and saints. They tend to hold that they have always believed in the one

God (the *tawhid* principle) as formulated by the Qur'an, hence the conversion constituted an affirmation of an already-existing belief (Krotofil et al., 2021).

Özyürek (2015) in her discussion of East German converts to Islam addresses a problem that we identified in a sightly different format among the Polish converts to Islam living in the UK – that of a double stigmatization. She argues that for many East Germans, conversion to Islam was a coping strategy (or, as Goffman would say, a strategy to manage a "spoiled identity") that allowed them to come to terms with their second-class citizen status in the unified Germany after 1991. For Polish converts to Islam who emigrated to the United Kingdom, the stigma of being a Muslim intersected with the stigma of being an immigrant from Eastern Europe. Not all of these respondents converted after arriving in the UK, however; a considerable group converted prior to leaving Poland. Conversion, for them, was not a management strategy of a previous "spoiled identity" – rather, they managed their spoiled identities associated with conversion by emigrating to a country perceived as more welcoming to Muslims.

The extant literature on Islam and Muslims in Poland is dedicated mostly to one category of Muslims – the Polish Tatars. Just as other ethnic or national minorities in Poland, Tatars have witnessed a significantly increased interest especially after 1989. While most ethnic and national minorities are small in number, they attracted interest for their ability to survive in a homogenous Polish society and maintain their culture and tradition. The same applies to the Tatars, who are one of the least populous ethnic minorities in Poland. Their history, culture and religion have been studied extensively (Antonowicz-Bauer, 1984; Cieslik & Verkuyten, 2006; Danecki, 2011; Dziekan, 2011; Łyszczarz, 2011; Nalborczyk, 2016; Wiktor-Mach, 2008). Studies of migrant communities of Muslim background are less numerous as they require access to these communities, and, often, foreign language skills.

The literature on conversion to Islam in Polish is also scanty. Some studies tackle the notion of conversion to Islam in terms of radicalization within the security studies perspective. Some of these articles build its narrative around a vital "Islamic threat in Europe" (Guź, 2014, pp. 239–241). that is only strengthened by Europeans lured to convert to Islam by radical Islamist (Hinc, 2016). Such studies are based on secondary sources and only strengthen the negative stereotypes about a convert to Islam. Other studies refer to female converts to Islam and their identity. These are often small scale qualitative and quantitative studies – mostly BA dissertations (for example Rogowska, 2018; Pasierb, 2016; Skarżyńska, 2016; Pawlik, 2007; Stefańska, 2011). Most of these works focus on Polish female converts to Islam only, and some of them explicitly aim to challenge negative stereotypes around conversion to Islam in Poland.

Compared to the increasing number of student dissertations on the topic, the number of senior level scholarly studies on Polish conversion to Islam is much more modest and often in English. In fact, there are only two monographs in Polish on conversion to Islam – a study on Polish female convert identity (Ryszewska, 2018), and a book of case studies of selected Polish Muslim females written by a journalist (Dudek, 2016). Articles in English present the converts as an emerging category of Polish Muslims (Łojek-Magdziarz, 2007), religiosity or identity of Polish female converts to Islam (Krotofil, 2011; Krotofil et al. 2021), online activities (Górak-Sosnowska, 2013), or Polish converts to Islam abroad (Pędziwiatr, 2017).

The complexity of the subject calls for interdisciplinary research teams capable of combining Islamic studies knowledge with expertise in qualitative and quantitative research methods. The accessibility of data might pose some challenges for researchers interested in the subject; female converts to Islam form a closed and difficult to reach social category (the largest sample of Polish female converts ever recruited for participation in research (243) was for a dissertation of a student who was a female convert herself (Pawlik, 2007)). Many of these women are reluctant to become involved in research for the fear of being misunderstood or misrepresented. We hope to overcome these problems by employing the skills and knowledge of a multidisciplinary team and engaging the network of Polish female converts to Islam we established in previous small-scale studies of their online activities (Górak-Sosnowska, 2013) and identity (Krotofil, 2011).

## Methodology

This book is a collective endeavour of four researchers representing not only different academic disciplines, but also experiences of and positions within the Islamic community. While all of us focus in our research on Islam and Muslims in Europe, we approach it from different perspectives of social sciences and humanities including sociology, study of religions and Arabic and Islamic studies. Similarly, we all have various connections to the local Muslim community. One of us converted to Islam over 20 years before working on this project. She is not only an insider, but also one of the most experienced Polish converts to Islam who has vast knowledge of the Polish *ummah*. The other team members are not Muslim, but they have been actively engaged in the life of the Polish ummah. They are allies of the Polish Muslim community, attending meetings at the Islamic centre in Warsaw, and writing reports on hate speech and hate crimes against Muslims in Poland. Two team members spent over a dozen of years each working at British universities. Thus, they have first-hand experience in being a Polish migrant in the UK. This composition of the team afforded us a unique positionality in the process of the research.

We use the explanatory design model of mixed methods research whereby the results of quantitative research are used to design the qualitative component of the study (Creswell et al., 2003), in this case to explore in more depth the results of the questionnaire-based research.

Participants were recruited through online forums for Polish-speaking Muslims, and Muslim women in particular through a network of our personal contacts. This method of online recruitment has an additional advantage – the group members have well-established online social capital, they know each other from the real world and are relatively well-networked (Papacharissi, 2011). This gave us access to a larger group of potential participants through the snowball effect. Through the forum members' networks it was also possible to reach women from outside the forum.

We also used the snowball sampling method, with our existing contacts being starting points. This method has been confirmed as the most effective method for reaching the people surveyed in Poland and in the UK in the preliminary study. The recruitment was guided by the 'theoretical sampling' principles (Strauss & Corbin, 1996); we aimed to collect a research sample representative of a broad range of female converts' characteristics, circumstances and experiences. We also visited places where Polish Muslims meet, such as mosques and prayer halls. Reaching out to informal female Muslim associations was another point of reference.

Based on the results of preliminary research we chose a number of recruitment sites in Poland and in the UK – all locations with relatively large populations of female converts. For each potential participant we provided detailed information about the purpose of our study, data collection methods and dissemination plans. Researchers were available to answer any questions and our prospective participants were given appropriate time to consider their participation. Informed consent was obtained from those who decided to take part in the project. While arranging data collection sessions, we aimed to accommodate our respondents' schedules and use our resources efficiently by careful planning and grouping interviews in similar locations.

According to the principles of ethical research conduct set out by contemporary social science guidelines (Seidman, 2006) respondents' statements were treated as confidential and their anonymity has been preserved. Where possible, interviews were conducted at homes to ensure maximum privacy for the interviewees. Where face-to-face interviews were not possible or practical, we used videoconferencing software (Skype), increasingly popular in social science research due to minimising time and financial costs of research (Deakin & Wakefield, 2013; Piela, 2015b).

The main body of data in our study is gathered through in-depth interviews with female converts to Islam. The qualitative interviews focus on respondents' insights into their collective identity, self-representations (Brewer & Gardner, 1996), relationships with significant others and religious socialization. We conducted 56 interviews with Polish female converts, including 34 in Poland and 22 in the UK. Additionally, we interviewed eight key male Muslim stakeholders, including leader of three largest Islamic organisations in Poland, in order to ascertain how female Muslim converts to Islam were perceived by other Muslims. While we attempted to achieve diversity in terms of education, class background, age, marital/parental status, and Islamic affiliation, we recognize that some categories, for example rural women, are less represented in our sample. While most commonly the women did not identify with any particular school of Islam, some of our participants recognized their affinity with Salafi ideas and aspired to embody the traditional model of piety and devotion by relying on literal readings of Quranic texts and the Sunna. Another significant group of participants identified with more liberal and flexible interpretations of Islam, actively incorporating considerations of time and place in their perspective. Some women in this latter group self-identified as feminist, and/or leftist. Finally, a significant proportion of our participants highlighted the spiritual aspects of Islam, sometimes inspired by Sufi movement and characterized by a degree of religious individualization. As the sample is purposive, we do not make claims regarding the representativeness of our findings.

The semi-structured interview method enabled both qualitative and quantitative analysis of the material characterized by relatively high reliability and validity (Stemplewska-Żakowicz, 2005). The initial topic guide for the interviews was developed on the basis of existing literature and the questionnaire data. We aimed to use the guide flexibly, with researchers being open to respondents introducing themes important to them. We have chosen this method in an attempt to avoid reductionism, therefore the topic guides has been modified in the course of the data collection, in order to explore themes and elements introduced by respondents. The changes in the topic guide were informed by the results of preliminary analysis of early interviews, we approached data collection and analysis as interlinked, and parallel aspects of research work. Themes and categories emerging in the initial analysis were further explored in subsequent interviews (Braun & Clarke, 2006). Interviews were recorded where possible, and later transcribed by a professional transcriber.

## Reflexive Notes

The fundamental importance of the researcher's motivation, skills and positionality in the collection of research data and the development of new sociological and humanities thinking on any group renders reflexivity an integral part of qualitative research (Denzin, 1994; Silverman, 1985; Lincoln & Guba, 1985; Johnson & Rowlands, 2012; Temple, 2002). The "reflexive turn" in the social sciences broadened the understanding of situated knowledge, and the manifold factors shaping the processes of its construction (Haraway, 1988; Rose, 1997). Our contribution to the culturally, socially and historically embedded process of knowledge production presented in this book would not be complete without some thoughts about the context, complexity and unique character of the relationships we entered and developed in the course of the project. We present the following account not to centre ourselves, but, rather, to reflect on how our positionalities may have impacted the research process.

In this research project we engaged with a group that is at the centre of attention, often treated with hostility or at least deep suspicion. Such positioning of Muslims, of course, is not unique to the Polish socio-cultural context. Muslims in the West have been increasingly instrumentalized in politics, vilified by the media, right-wing populist parties and various individuals in positions of power who capitalise on othering of Islam and its adherents. The politicisation of Muslims has been reflected in academia by a surge of studies focusing on religious minorities, with Islam attracting disproportional scholarly attention (Buskens, 2016). The apparent intensification of the Western public gaze directed at Islam and Muslims is rooted in the political events emphasizing conflict and violence, such as the war in Afghanistan, Iranian revolution, the 9/11 attack and the military struggles in the Middle East and North Africa region. This genesis of the research interest contributes significantly to negative framings of this population which emphasize risks, violence, international security concerns and terrorism (Ogan et al., 2014; Mansouri, 2020). The hostile attitudes of different publics coupling the vociferous dislike of Muslims with feelings of threat and fear are also partially reproduced in academic discourses in Poland (Piela et al., forthcoming). As members of an intensively scrutinized group and sought-after research subjects, Muslims, including in Poland, respond to these processes emotionally and strategically, many of them avoiding any kind of engagement.

In this climate, researchers interested in Muslim experiences are embarking on research on vulnerable subjects – members of a minority group suffering great deal of deep-rooted prejudice, institutional discrimination and socio-cultural oppression (Piela, 2020; Pędziwiatr, 2011). This confronts us with a plethora of ethical and epistemological challenges when engaging in contemporary studies of Islam and Muslims in Poland (and in the West). The questions we need to ask ourselves first concern our constructions of research subjects. Therefore, we must critically analyze the sources and impact of our categorizations of Muslims and Islam and the type of research questions we are looking to answer. The way we delineated our group of interest was based on the assumption that converts share some experiences with other Muslims in Poland, but at the same time participate in unique socially determined interactions. Another category that in our view is central to understanding converts' experiences is that of gender. In the course of the project we attempted to problematize these boundaries and engage critically with intersectional positionings of our participants. Encounters with participants who did not fit neatly in our categories aided the process. For example, meeting women who belonged to indigenous Muslims in Poland, the Tatars, but at the same time self-identified as converts shed new light on our understanding of differences and similarities, connection and separateness of the two groups. It is, however, very likely that no matter how many times we interrogate ourselves about the extent to which our research framings may reinforce prejudice, some blind spots remain in our vision.

Another important question concerns the perceived useful outcomes of research engagement, including our non-empirical, often not fully formulated goals. The underlying reasons for the disproportionally high prevalence of Muslim-focused research framings have been noted by researchers and questioned by Muslim communities (Mansouri, 2020). When juxtaposing the size of the Muslim population in Poland with the number of research projects concerning this group, this problem gains even more gravity. As the bulk of the research projects is conducted by "outsiders" – Polish university students and scholars who do not share religious belonging with their target group – Muslims constitute a "hard to reach group" and often suffer from considerable research fatigue (Clark, 2008). Contemporary Islam in Poland is a crowded field, researchers compete for access to participants and struggle with a particular constellation of power relations and their implications, namely the dilemmas with regards to who can research whom, how the access and trust can be established, and what strategies need to be adopted to maintain rapport with local communities of interest. Underpinning these issues are the notions of insiders and outsiders, constructions of difference, potentially conflicting worldviews of researchers and those of their informants and expectations regarding positionality (Ryan & Golden, 2006; de Koning et al., 2011). These issues call for serious reflexive engagement with questions posed by Stuart Hall (1997), namely why is difference so fascinating and how do we represent people whom we believe to be significantly different from us? The answers to these questions will always be only partial and tentative. In this section we make the attempt to engage with them in an open and honest way. For this purpose, we lay bare our personal motivations, perceptions and goals which drove and shaped our engagement in this research.

As all social research is ideologically motivated to some extent, and so the insights to our personal motivations and agendas related to doing research on the experiences of Polish converts to Islam are necessary to achieving some transparency about how we collected and made sense of our data. In the research team, we all shared the experience of personal encounters with negative attitudes towards Muslims expressed by various social actors. Whether in university classes, on social media platforms, or in private casual conversations, we all have encountered a variety of remarks about our group of interest. These were rarely positive and typically ranged from naïve simplifications to intense hatred. We often reacted with disbelief, sadness, and a resolve to act. The hostile remarks were often "gendered" and directed specifically at women. The sense of gender solidary bolstered by our leanings towards liberal feminist progressive politics impacted the way we collected data. We conducted the interviews as women which most likely shaped our efforts to validate the views and experiences of the women who converted to Islam (Oakley, 1981) and, therefore, experienced gendered patterns of othering and hostility. In that we did not define the role of interviewees as subordinates or those who need to explain themselves and justify their "irregular" or "suspicious" choices.

> Katarzyna: Polish female converts to Islam are doubly stigmatized – for being Muslim and for "betraying" the Polish identity by embracing Islam. At the same time, they provoke a lot of interest – they are invited to talk shows, to give interviews, to participate in research carried out by BA or MA degree students. However, not much of this publicity translates into a meaningful participation of Polish female converts in Islam in Poland.

> Beata: The [Polish] *ummah* feels the need to develop its own story. A scholarly story about it could work. Without its own representation, the ummah wants to tell it at least this way, mediated by researchers. This story could be, in their view, a challenge of the ubiquitous slander. The converts want to show 'their' story that would help them resist the media-fuelled narrative that portrays them as traitors of the nation, and ostracises and exoticises them, or, at best patronises them. They argue that their subjectivity is removed, they are objectified and reimagined as the external 'Other'. In this situation, especially for people who do not

belong to or identify with Polish Muslim organisations, our team has been charged with the task of representation. We've been given a lot of trust, which for me personally may become a burden. Our work won't satisfy all of them, it may contradict the perspectives of many Polish Muslims and their outlook on the Polish ummah, it may disappoint and create resentment.

Joanna: On the personal level, I felt deep discomfort with the way converts to Islam are treated in mainstream discourses; especially as a feminist I object to framing female conversion to Islam in terms of "stupidity", "naivety" "brain washing", "sexual fascination with Arab men", etc. I was hoping that my work in this field will take a form of participatory action research.

Anna: I was surprised, as a Polish scholar of Islam living in the West, that the Western academic community was largely unaware of the existence of different Muslim groups in Poland. After all, Poland has its own indigenous Muslim population and a growing group of converts! I felt that this lack of knowledge contributed to the homogenisation and essentialization of Poland. Although Catholicism is the dominant religion, it is not the only one, and I wanted to counteract this symbolic erasure of this small Polish minority in Europe.

Because of this kind of personal emotional investment and the existing positionings of Muslim women placing them on the epistemic margins, we felt a sense of accountability. Moreover, we were acutely aware that for some participants the engagement in research procedure would be accompanied by some degree of psychological distress. In the conversion process, individuals strive to maintain their relationships and re-negotiate their positions in relation to significant others. Most of them are successful at achieving a new balance, where relationships flow smoothly in a non-reflexive, taken-for-granted way, and constitute shared positive identities. The smoothness might be disrupted by inquisitive probing. The probing is never devoid of uncertainty and apprehension founded on manifold, at times pre-reflexive assumptions. Finally, there are costs to us, as researchers. Are the risks involved in this particular field of production of knowledge not too high? Is the responsibility for the potential production and reproduction of negative framings and reification of reductionist categorizations, despite our good intentions, too much to bear? This question reverberated in our research diaries:

Katarzyna: While I could imagine getting access to some Polish female converts to Islam, I was worried about the outcome. As a team, we received a lot of trust and a great deal of responsibility. What if we go too far, too deep, or publish something that is misused by Islamophobic actors? The responsibility was even heavier as one of the team members is a Muslim herself – she had easier access to vulnerable information, access that we – non-Muslim researchers or allies – could never have.

The importance of social class, gender, age, and other social categorizations has been thoroughly discussed in methodological literature, with authors invariably pointing to the power relations impacting the way data is collected, analysed and represented (Abbas, 2010; Fawcett & Hearn, 2004). As variously positioned members of a research team with our unique professional and personal experiences we shared some "family resemblances" with "similarities overlapping and criss-crossing" (Wittgenstein [1953] 1986, p. 31). We had all worked in academia for a number of years, and brought to the project different perspectives and skills, as we represent different disciplines. Katarzyna graduated from business school and was trained in international relations and economics. She came to research on Islam through studies in intercultural psychology and, later, cross-cultural relations at the Faculty of Oriental Studies, University of Warsaw. Anna studied at the Department of Political Sciences and International Relations, and the Department of Communication and Cultural Studies at Jagiellonian University in Poland, and later specialised in Women's and Islamic Studies while doing her PhD at the University of York. Beata graduated from Arabic Studies at Jagiellonian University and works at the Faculty of Philology at another Polish university. Joanna studied psychology and religious studies in Poland, and clinical psychology in Great Britain. Although at the time of data collection, the members of the team lived in three different countries, we shared the experience of growing up in Poland in the 70s, 80s and 90s. This helped us to establish rapport with our respondents. We were able to communicate with the participants using different registers: the language of Islam with its Arabic phrases such as *ummah, Jannah, halal/haram*, but we were also able to mobilize memories of Communist Poland, provincial Poland, Polish bureaucracy, Polish education as things that we all had in common with the participants. Anna and Joanna lived in the UK 12 and 15 years, respectively. This further enhanced the rapport with the participants who lived in the UK at the time of the interview, through the shared identity as a Polish immigrant in the UK.

Joanna: My strategy for this project was to build good rapport with women who could be our research participants. I was very aware that despite me not being a Muslim, I shared other important experiences with them. At the time of the fieldwork, I was a settled migrant myself having spent nearly 15 years in the UK (albeit with plans of imminent return to Poland). I was also aware that the majority of our target group were women in roughly the same age group (late 20s–early 40s). Finally, as I discovered in other research projects, I was hoping that I would be able to relate to some of these women as a young mother. My daughter was only just born when I started my fieldwork, and so she accompanied me to a picnic organized by Polish converts in Regent's Park in London. I was invited to the picnic by one of the leaders of "Kobiety wiary" ("Women of Faith") who I approached about the project some months before. She was very positive about the research, and keenly noted that I was working at a university she graduated from a few years prior. She introduced me to her friends. At the picnic I spent most of the time chatting to another mother of a young baby. We shared some parenting tips, talked about everyday life as parents. Almost every woman I approached during the picnic agreed to meet with me some other time for the interview. They were interested in why I wanted to conduct this particular research and very welcoming. Some of them invited me to attend *halaqa* at their local mosque, others invited me to their homes.

These similarities notwithstanding, the intersectional perspective with its central assertion that there is not only one form of "otherness" and the existence of multiple forms of relations between researcher and researched (Fawcett & Hearn, 2004) draws attention to the complexity of the research paths which need to be navigated also in the situation when those coming to contact in the research context share some or many social and cultural positions. This is further complicated by the dynamic nature of the social world, which makes it impossible to assume a fixed, rigid standpoints of the social actors involved in research. The insights of Saba Mahmood were helpful in opening us and preparing for changes in preconceptions:

> Critique, I believe, is most powerful when it leaves open the possibility that we might also be remade in the process of engaging another's worldview, that we might come to learn things that we did not already know before we undertook the engagement. This requires that we occasionally turn the critical gaze upon ourselves, leaving open the possibility that we may be remade through an encounter (Mahmood, 2005, pp. 36–37).

INTRODUCTION

Reflecting back on our research journeys, we were indeed able to identify some of these changes:

> Katarzyna: Before the project I had very limited knowledge of Polish female converts to Islam. I could only see Slavic-looking women wearing headscarves. [...] I must admit that interactions "with the field" brought me a completely different understanding of Polish female converts to Islam. I am not sure, if I had known it all if I studied Arabic and Islamic studies – most probably not, as this understanding has to do with human dimension rather than knowledge one can get from a textbook.

> Beata: These conversations were an important spiritual experience for me. People I had known for a long time shared with me their reflections for the first time ever. I was honoured to be invited to listen to these confessions, to be given the trust and witness the richness of their experiences, their diversity and depth.

The key aspect of difference or similarity between the researcher and participants is the possession of the characteristic, role, and experiences under study, which defines the insider – outsider status. We were variously positioned on that continuum. While Katarzyna, Anna and Joanna did not identify as Muslims and remained to some extent conceptually and experientially detached from the everyday realities faced by converts, Beata was able to balance this perspective with her own lived experience of conversion.

> Beata: I've been a Muslim for 29 years. I've been active in the Polish ummah for 20 years, I've been going to conventions and meetings, official and unofficial ones. I also participated in the Muslim League structures. I have broad networks of converts, some of them are my close friends. Thanks to my contacts with Polish Muslims in the UK while I stayed there for a while, I also became familiar with the Polish Islam in the UK.

Beata had the opportunity to narrate her own experiences as a research participant during an in-depth interview conducted by another member of the team. In her other role, as a hands-on member of the research team Beata recruited participants and conducted the bulk of interviews. High level of indexicality (Agar, 1980) enabled her to adequately understand some of the more nuanced messages passed during the interviews and participant observation. Beata's longstanding membership in the Muslim community enhanced our recruitment of research participants.

> Beata: I was looking for participants among sisters who were close to me and those I had met during conventions and online groups. I was also given the names of the 'lone wolves' who don't engage with other converts which was a sign of trust. Trying to recruit random women after prayer in the mosque didn't work out at all, but strangers I met online were very helpful. The online groups were incredibly useful for our research. I and one other co-author interacted with the women on Facebook, we posted and they commented.

Beata's unique position brought undeniable advantages to the project, but also some limitations. The question of whether Muslims would conceivably be more likely to give consistent or more candid accounts, in situations where the ethnicity and religion of the researcher matches their own is not an uncomplicated one. In research exploring topics of a sensitive nature, shared ethno-religious characteristics between the researcher and the researched does not, by itself, circumvent the difficulties inherent in the process (Abbas, 2010). Data generated by a researcher who shares a common identity or experience with the research participants will not necessarily be richer or deeper based simply on that assumed commonality (Ryan & Golden, 2006). The sense of closeness and shared experiences might be helpful in establishing trusting relationships, but come with a heavy sense of responsibility.

> Beata: In the beginning, some of the converts, those I hadn't met in person, expressed hope that I, a convert myself, would maintain control over the team. Some worried I could be 'betrayed' and moved away from the publications, resulting in another sensationalised piece of academic work.

As Serrant (2002, p. 38) notes, "there appear to be as many arguments for insider research, as against". The other side of the coin are the concerns of participants about being judged by a peer, and despite assurances of confidentiality, worries about breaches of privacy and local gossip. Lundy and McGovern acknowledge that having researchers who were known to the participants and closely connected to the subject matter can lead to "guarded responses", "self-censorship" and in consequence only partial stories being told (2006, p. 58). Some participants are more encouraged by the opportunity to tell their stories to somebody from outside of their social circle. The researcher who appears to be part of the group can be placed by the studied group members at the outside at any time (Serrant, 2002). When this goes unnoticed, it is easy to ignore the communicative value of silences and omissions. Navigating this dynamic position of an insider and the inherent tensions can be at times a challenging task.

> Beata: My triple role – as a member of the studied group, a gatekeeper and a researcher caused me a lot of worry. Loyalty to the group I've long been a member of, with which I identify, and to the members of this group who are my friends, was one of my priorities. Representing this group fairly and accurately was a personal matter for me. My fears also related to my role in the [Polish] ummah where my views are known to many people; I have experiences conflict in the group, because I publicly criticise one of the Polish Muslim organisations; my loyalties obviously shaped the recruitment process.

For all of us the project was a process which constituted of establishing, renewing, maintaining, developing and in some cases ending relationships. Largely because of Beata's unique position in the convert community and the trust she enjoyed, Katarzyna and Joanna were able to significantly shorten the distance between themselves and research participants in the course of participant observation. Over time they acquired the status of peripheral member researchers, who do not participate in the core activities of group members but are considered members of the groups (Adler & Adler, 1987).

> Joanna: I developed a long-lasting relationship with the converts connected to one of the mosques in Warsaw, where I conducted participant observation of weekend gatherings for Polish converts. In order to enter the field and maintain the relationship I offered to actively participate in the workshops and lectures the women organized in the mosque and I gave a short talk and ran one workshop on two occasions. I chose subjects that were of interest to the women and ones I had some knowledge about as a psychotherapist and psychologist. I felt that the women welcomed my contribution and accepted my presence during their gatherings. I was invited to join them for an evening meal outside of the mosque and to come to a private gathering some months later.

> Katarzyna: We were kindly invited to the mosque in Warsaw and had a chance to interact with the local Muslim women's community. And we soon felt as if we were a part of this group. Our role inside the mosque was not easy – on the one hand, we were researchers, on the other, friends, and sometimes mentors. It seems that our project has influenced the way the women organize their meetings in the mosque. The first seminar we came to observe was organized with two male speakers from Saudi Arabia, whose speeches were translated from Arabic by another man. Backstage, we discussed the possibility to organizing a seminar for

women by women. And it happened. They organized it all by themselves. [...] Since then we participate as speakers in every seminars, even after we collected all our data.

This change of our position relative to the group supports the call of many qualitative researchers to abandon "constructed dichotomies and embrace and explore the complexity and richness of the space between entrenched perspectives" (Dwyer & Buckle, 2009, p. 62). Discussing the different terms our respondents used to address and introduce us, we reminded ourselves that the subjective proximity (reinforced by the label "sisters in society" which we were given by one of our gatekeepers) might be an illusion. We tried not to lose sight of the complexity of the research situation. It is possible to be simultaneously close and distant, the positioning changes, depending on the observer. The distance is seen differently by the researcher, the external reviewer, the participant, or the significant other. Finely, the position changes with time. When we compared our experiences of proximity, it became clear that every position on the insider-outsider continuum comes with its own specific advantages and challenges also in the context of exiting the field. Anna felt that she remained more firmly on the outside and reflected on the positive aspects of her position.

> Anna: As I live outside of Poland, I didn't get to interact with the participants face-to-face. It often felt like I was missing out on a vital aspect of the project, participant observation at mosque events, and at-home gatherings. This positioned me to a large extent as an outsider in the research team – I only met one other team member briefly face-to-face, and the other two I only ever met via Zoom or Teams. However, I tried to contribute to the project in other ways that I could do remotely. [...] The separation from the field – pre-research, and during research – had some other consequences for me too. I am less connected to the participants and so less impacted by negative outcomes of the process, such as conflict with participants, tensions, and professional image issues. Not being an academic in Poland and having less investment in cultivating particular relationships means that I have more agency over the decision if I exit the field or remain in it, and on what terms. This reflects a particular power dynamic between me-as researcher, the other researchers, and the participants. This does not mean that I do not care about these relationships – I am just differently limited/defined/structured professionally than the others on the team.

INTRODUCTION                                                                                         23

As the project comes to an end, we remain in our "in-between" positions with some of the participant, albeit it is now different "in-between" to that we occupied at the earlier stages of the project. Our relationships with some of the women who participated in the study ended, with others, we continue to interact with varying frequency and intensity, finding the ways to transform the relationships.

### Structure of the Book

As a collective of authors, we wrote individual chapters which we then extensively discussed and revised in several cycles. The result is that this is neither a traditional monograph or an edited collection; this structure reflects our complementary specialisms which remain interconnected by intellectual and ethical commitments. The structure of the book is as follows:

Chapter 1 presents the socio-historical context of Islam in Poland. It provides the vital sociopolitical context – in other words, the macro-level relationships posited by Goffman that situate the interactions between converts themselves and their social worlds. The case of Poland is unusual, as Islam has had a longstanding presence in this country in the form of Polish Tatars, the indigenous Muslim community. Muslims of migrant origin are sometimes pitted against the Tatars and portrayed as a foreign and threatening Muslim population. Converts to Islam tend to be positioned somewhere between these two groups – on the one hand, they are ethnically Polish, just like the Tatars, but on the other, they are considered to be culturally and religiously more consistent with the migrants. The chapter also presents the institutional landscape of Islam in Poland, dominated by the Tatars and the migrants.

Chapter 2 describes the profile of our survey sample. They are by no means a representative sample of Polish female converts, but rather a specific group of women – generally well educated, middle-aged, with a relatively long experience of being Muslim. They represent a group of converts who are likely to participate in studies like this one, or talk in public about their religion. In the chapter we address the process of embracing Islam, social activity and sources of Islamic knowledge. This chapter provides more information on micro-level relationships in which meanings and strategies are created, and identities managed.

In Chapter 3, the specific conditions framing the experiences of Polish converts to Islam who settled in the UK are explored. Polish women living in the UK who converted to Islam share a great deal with converts in Poland, but they also face cultural and structural conditions shaping their experiences in unique ways. The starting point for the discussion is the concept of multiculturalism. Critically approaching the relationship between territory, ethnicity, religion and belonging, we analyse the intersectional position of Polish converts in the UK in order to link the personal, social and political dimensions of conversion. The analysis focuses on manifold personal implications of acquiring the intersecting identities of a migrant from Poland *and* a Muslim convert living in the multicultural Britain. Although multiculturalism, tolerance, and diversity are frequently referenced and highly valued in the narratives of the study participants, the patterns of engagement with everyday multiculturalism are complex and indicative of some struggles. We bring to the fore the ambiguity of the experiences of Polish Muslims negotiating their positions in relation to different ethnic and religious groups in the UK, including other Muslims and other Polish migrants. The chapter is divided into four sections discussing: 1) the relationship between religion and migration; 2) the divergent contexts of everyday life in the UK and in Poland; 3) converts' diverse encounters with the lived Islam and 4) the reconstruction of the sense of belonging.

Chapter 4 focuses on Islamophobia in the Polish context as experienced by female converts to Islam. Here we focus on the process of stigmatization and how respondents develop their strategies in response to experiences shaped by stigma. Poland is a country to a great extent homogenous in ethnic, national and religious terms. Polish female converts to Islam stand out, especially if they are visibly Muslim. The lack of experience with cultural Others leads to exoticisation and racialisation of Muslims. The political shift in Poland that carried the Law and Justice Party to electoral victory has brought about authoritarian rule, and put Islamophobia into a different, more dangerous context. Suddenly, Muslims were transformed from exotic Others into enemies of the Polish nation and the Catholic religion. As the stigma of conversion has been amplified by a (negatively) changed context, it has made the experiences of Polish female converts much more painful. A comparison of experiences of Islamophobia in the Polish and British contexts makes this particularly clear.

Chapter 5 presents the issue of identity from the linguistic perspective, considering the language as a fundamental source of cultural production, and consequently, the production of identities. It showcases the strategy for managing spoiled identity that Goffman (1963) described as coming together of similarly stigmatised individuals to form "clubs", "associations", and "networks" that can eventually lead to the emergence of communities. The Polish ummah attempts to develop a specific 'insider' language, created from elements of the 'old' and 'new' languages of religion. This 'insider' speech can serve different purposes: it may function as a code that consolidates the group, or distinguish the new religious imaginary from the 'previous' catholic one. Revision of the old religious language related to the Catholic denomination gains particular significance. Such a revision is accompanied by, on the one hand, a need to excise the old and create a language of one's own and, on the other hand, a need to be included in the global English-speaking ummah. This language consists of unusually large number of loans occupying the semantic field related to Islam. The source of these borrowings is Arabic, with English serving as an intermediary. We discuss the role of the Arabic language in the religious life of Polish new Muslims and present a short review of issues related to the semantic borrowings. We also present other issues of spoiled identity by focusing on such linguistic behaviours as changes in the use of honorifics and linguistic attempts at defining the group's identity through the adoption of a religious language that involves a great deal of code-mixing. The language analysis becomes a basis for reflection on the community's identity and the conflicts about the shape of Polish Islam. Polonization of this language is connected with the feeling of nostalgia for the deeply rooted Polish religiosity.

Chapter 6 focuses on the ways in which Polish female converts approach Islam as an embodied religion, one that relies on spatial and material reconfigurations of the body as part of comprehensive religious practice. It situates the empirical data regarding these women's deployment of ritual Islamic practices that involve the body: the management of sexuality, in particular to maintaining ritual purity, the hijab (understood in the broader sense of modest behaviour, rather than just the headscarf), prayer, and food-related practices such as fasting and keeping halal. It demonstrates how symbolic stigma related to conversion in reinscribed on the body. The data related to incorporating the body in the process of conversion, or, rather, living conversion through the body, presented in this chapter resonates with both the ethical self and everyday religion discourses; here, striving for perfection is shown as often intertwined with embracing imperfection as emblematic of human action across different social contexts. Thus, the chapter shows how one's moral self cannot be divorced from the space in which it operates, or the ways in which the body of the believer is gendered, sexed, and racialized through the lens of religious practice. It concludes that learning, and associated ethical formation, involves disciplining the body, reconfiguring it into new positions, functions, and shapes; often, religious practices as discussed here involve discovering the body's new limits that are enabled by the pious intentionality inflected by everyday circumstances of living life as Polish Muslims.

In Chapter 7, we present different approaches to Islam among the female converts and discus possible factors that shape their religious trajectories that may also be conceived as a way of managing stigma of conversion. Most Polish converts to Islam start their journey to Islam from the position of (usually unconscious) interest in Salafism. This is followed by a questioning of these radical rules in the context of everyday life and often culminates in a crisis leading to mature, conscious rethinking of religious affiliation, or an ultimate rejection of Islam. There is a degree of difference between Polish Muslim living in Poland who have to negotiate their understanding of Islam within the society they live in and those living in the UK who do not seem to experience as much social pressure. More common among the converts residing in Poland is the attempt of constructing one's own version of Islam, which is often a mainstream theology, adjusted to the reality of life in Poland. We examine the way converts' political or social views (mostly left-wing-liberal and feminist) merge with understandings of Islam after conversion, as well as some Islamic affiliations such as progressive Islam, Sufism, and others.

## References

Abbas, T. (2010). Muslim-on-Muslim Social Research: Knowledge, Power and Religio-cultural Identities, *Social Epistemology*, 24 (2), 123–136.

Adams, G. & Markus, H. R. (2001). Culture as Patterns: An Alternative Approach to the Problem of Reification. *Culture Psychology*, 7 (3), 283–296.

Adler, P. & Adler, P. (1987). *Membership Roles in Field Research*. Sage Publications.

Agar, M. H. (1980). *The Professional Stranger: an Informal Introduction to Ethnography*. Academic Press.

Amer, A. (2020). Between Recognition and Mis/Nonrecognition: Strategies of Negotiating and Performing Identities Among White Muslims in the United Kingdom. *Political Psychology*, 41(30), 533–548.

Antonowicz-Bauer (1984). The Tatars in Poland. *Institute of Muslim Minority Affairs Journal*, 5(2), 345–359.

az-Zahra, A. & Kumpoh, A. (2016). The Relevance of Contextual Components in the Religious Conversion Process: The Case of Dusun Muslims in Brunei Darussalam. In V. King, Z. Ibrahim & N. Hassan (Eds.) *Borneo Studies in History, Society and Culture. Asia in Transition*, 4, 493–510.

Blumer, H. (1969). *Symbolic Interactionism*. University of California Press.

Bonnett, A. (2017). *The Idea of the West: Culture, Politics and History*. Palgrave Macmillan.

Braun, V. and Clarke, V. (2006). Using thematic analysis in psychology, *Qualitative Research in Psychology*, 3(2), 77–101.

Buskens, L. (2016). Introduction Dichotomies, Transformations, and Continuities in the Study of Islam. In: L, Buskens and A. van SandwijkIslamic (eds.), *Studies in the Twenty-First Century*, pp. 11–27. Amsterdam University Press.

Brewer, M. & Garnder, W. (1996). Who is this "we"? Levels of collective identity and self-representations. *Journal of Personality and Social Psychology*, 71(1), 83–93.

Carey, J. (1988). *Communication as Culture: Essays on Media and Society*. Unwin Hyman.

Cieslik, A. & Verkuyten, M. (2006). National, Ethnic and Religious Identities: Hybridity and the case of the Polish Tatars. *National Identities*, 8(2): 77–93.

Clark, T. (2008). 'We're Over-Researched Here!' Exploring Accounts of Research Fatigue within Qualitative Research Engagements. *Sociology*, 42(5), 953–970.

Crenshaw, K. (1989). Demarginalizing the Intersection of Race and Sex: A Black Feminist Critique of Antidiscrimination Doctrine, Feminist Theory and Antiracist Politics. *University of Chicago Legal Forum*, 1: 139–167.

Creswell, J. W., Plano Clark, V. L., Gutmann, M., & Hanson, W. (2003). Advanced mixed methods research designs. In A. Tashakkori & C. Teddlie (Eds.), *Handbook of mixed methods in social & behavioral research* (pp. 209–240). Sage.

de Koning, M. J. M., Bartels, E. A. C. and Koning, D. (2011). Claiming the researcher's identity: anthropological research and political religion. *Social and Cultural Anthropology*, 6(2), 168–186.

Danecki, J. (2011). Literature of the Polish Tatars. In K. Górak-Sosnowska (Ed.), *Muslims in Poland and Eastern Europe. Widening the European Discourse on Islam* (pp. 40–52). University of Warsaw.

Dwyer, S. C., & Buckle, J. L. (2009). The Space Between: On Being an Insider-Outsider in Qualitative Research. *International Journal of Qualitative Methods*, 8(1), 54–63.

Dziekan, M. M. (2011). History and culture of Polish Tatars. In K. Górak-Sosnowska (Ed.), *Muslims in Poland and Eastern Europe. Widening the European Discourse on Islam* (pp. 27–39). University of Warsaw.

Deakin, H. & Wakefield, K. (2013). SKYPE interviewing: reflections of two PhD researchers. *Qualitative Research*, 14(5), 603–616.

Denzin, N. (1994). The art and politics of interpretation. In N. Denzin & Y. Lincoln (Eds.), *Handbook of qualitative research* (pp. 500–515). Sage.

Dudek, A. (2016). *Poddaję się. Życie muzułmanek w Polsce*. PWN.

Fawcett, B. and J. Hearn.(2004). Researching others: epistemology, experience, standpoints and participation, *International Journal of Social Research Methodology*. 7(3), 201–218.

Goffman, E. (1963). *Stigma – Notes on the Management of Spoiled Identity*. Simon and Schuster.

Gallonier, J. (2015). The racialization of Muslims in France and the United States: Some insights from white converts to Islam. *Social Compass*, 62(4), 570–583.

Gee, J. P. (1999.) *An Introduction to Discourse Analysis: Theory and Method*, Routledge.

Gooren, H. (2007). Reassessing Conventional Approaches to Conversion: Toward a New Synthesis. *Journal for the Scientific Study of Religion*, 46(3), 337–353.

Göle, N. (2003). The Voluntary Adoption of Islamic Stigma Symbols. *Social Research*, 70(3), 809–828.

Górak-Sosnowska (2013). Między fitną a idyllą. Wirtualne społeczności polskich konwertytek na islam. In K. Górak-Sosnowska & A. Kozłowska (Eds.). *Tożsamość na przełomie wieków. Nowe możliwości, nowe wyzwania* (pp. 53–70). SGH.

Guź, J. (2014). Muzułmanie i neofici muzułmańscy – zagrożenie dla Europy Zachodniej czy szansa na pokojowe współżycie? Wprowadzenie do zagadnienia. *Acta Erasmiana*, 6, 235–266.

Hall, S. (2007). Living with difference: Stuart Hall in conversation with Bill Schwarz. *Soundings*, 37, 148–158.

Haraway, D. (1988). Situated knowledges: The science question in feminism and the privilege of partial perspective. *Feminist Studies*, 14(3), 575–599.

Heatherton, T., Kleck, R., Hebl, M., Hull, J. (2007). *Społeczna psychologia piętna*. PWN & Collegium Civitas.

Hermans, H. (2001). The Construction of a Personal Position Repertoire: Method and Practice. *Culture and Psychology*, 7(3), 323–366.

Hinc, M. (2016). Motywacja udziału neofitów islamskich w aktach terrorystycznych – analiza psychspołeczna. *Securo*, 3, 54–63.

Inge, A. (2017). *Making of a Salafi Muslim Woman: Paths to Conversion*. Oxford University Press.

Jeldtoft, N. (2011). Lived Islam: Religious Identity with 'Non-organized' Muslim Minorities. *Ethnic and Racial Studies*, 34(7): 1134–1151.

Johnson, J. M. and Rowlands, T. (2012). The interpersonal dynamics of in-depth interviewing. In J. F. Gubrium, et al. (Eds.), *The Sage Handbook of Interview Research: The Complexity of the Craft* (2nd ed., pp. 99–115). Sage.

Köse, A. (1996). *Conversion to Islam. A Study of Native British Converts*. Kegan Paul International.

Köse, A. & Loewenthal, K. (2000). Conversion Motifs Among British Converts to Islam. *The International Journal for the Psychology of Religion*, 10(2), 101–110.

Krotofil, J. (2011). "'If I am to be a Muslim, I have to be a good one' – Polish migrant women embracing Islam and reconstructing identity in dialogue with self and others". In K. Górak-Sosnowska (Ed.), *Muslims in Poland and Eastern Europe. Widening the European Discourse on Islam* (pp. 154–168). University of Warsaw.

Krotofil, J., Piela, A., Górak-Sosnowska, K., & B. Abdallah-Krzepkowska, Theorizing the Religious Habitus in the Context of Conversion to Islam among Polish Women of Catholic Background. *Sociology of Religion*, 82(3), 257–280.

Lakhdar, M., Vinsonneau, G., Apter, M. & E. Mullet (2007). Conversion to Islam Among French Adolescents and Adults: A Systematic Inventory of Motives. *The International Journal for the Psychology of Religion*, 17(1), 1–15.

Lincoln, Y. S. and Guba, E. G. (1985). *Naturalistic Inquiry*. Sage Publications.

Lundy, P., & McGovern, M. (2006). Participation, Truth and Partiality: Participatory Action Research, Community-based Truth-telling and Post-conflict Transition in Northern Ireland. *Sociology*, 40(1), 71–88.

Łojek-Magdziarz, A. (2007). New Islam in Poland – Polish Converts. *ORMA. Revistă de studii etnologice şi istorico-religioase*, 6, 55–62.

Łyszczarz, M. (2011). Generational change among young Polish Tatars. In K. Górak-Sosnowska (Ed.), *Muslims in Poland and Eastern Europe. Widening the European Discourse on Islam* (pp. 53–68). University of Warsaw.

Mahmood, S. (2005). *Politics of Piety: The Islamic Revival and the Feminist Subject*. Princeton University Press.

Mansouri, F. (2020). On the Discursive and Methodological Categorisation of Islam and Muslims in the West: Ontological and Epistemological Considerations. *Religions*, 11(10), 501.

Maslim, A. A., & Bjorck, J. P. (2009). Reasons for conversion to Islam among women in the United States. *Psychology of Religion and Spirituality*, 1(2), 97–111.

McGinty, Mansson (2003). *Becoming Muslim: Western women's conversions to Islam*. Palgrave Macmillan.

Midden, E. (2018). Rethinking 'Dutchness': Learning from the intersections between religion, gender and national identity after conversion to Islam. *Social Compass*, 65(5), 684–700.

Moosavi, L. (2012). British Muslim Converts Performing 'Authentic Muslimness'. *Performing Islam*, 1(1), 103–128.

Moosavi, L. (2015). The Racialization of Muslim Converts in Britain and Their Experiences of Islamophobia. *Critical Sociology*, 4(1), 41–56.

Nalborczyk, A. (2016). Polish Tatar Women as Official Leaders of Muslim Religious Communities and the Sources of their Authority. *Comparative Islamic Studies*, 12(1–2), 37–54.

Oakley, A. (1981). Interviewing Women: a Contradiction in Terms. In: H. Roberts, (Ed.), *Doing Feminist Research* (pp. 30–61). Routledge and Kegan Paul.

Ogan, C., Willnat, L., Pennington, R., Bashir, M. et al., (2014). The rise of anti-Muslim prejudice: Media and Islamophobia in Europe and the United States. *The International Communication Gazette*, 76(1), 27–46.

Özyürek, E. (2015). *Being German, Becoming Muslim. Race, Religion, and Conversion in the New Europe*. Princeton University Press.

Pappacharissi, Z. (2011). *A networked self: identity, community and culture on social network sites*. Routledge.

Pasierb, A. (2016). *Tożsamość religijna polskich konwertytek na islam. Przykład społeczności krakowskiej*. Unpublished Master Degree paper. Uniwersytet Jagielloński, https://ruj.uj.edu.pl/xmlui/handle/item/209676.

Patel, S. (2009). The Anti-terrorism Act and National Security: Safeguarding the Nation against Uncivilized Muslims. In: J. Zine (Ed.), *Islam in the Hinterlands: Muslim Cultural Politics in Canada* (pp. 272–292). UBC Press.

Pawlik, K. (2007). *Kobieta w rodzinie muzułmańskiej na przykładzie małżeństw Polek z wyznawcami islamu.* Unpublished Master dissertation. Uniwersytet Łódzki.

Pędziwiatr, K. (2011). "The Established and Newcomers" in Islam in Poland or the Intergroup Relations within the Polish Muslim Community. In K. Górak-Sosnowska (Ed.), *Muslims in Poland and Eastern Europe* (pp. 169–182). University of Warsaw.

Pędziwiatr, K. (2017). Conversions to Islam and identity reconfigurations among Poles in Great Britain. *Studia Religiologica*, 50(3), 221–239.

Piazza, R. (ed). (2011). *Discourses of Identity in Liminal Places and Spaces*. Routledge.

Piela, A. (2021). *Wearing the Niqab. Muslim Women in the UK and the US*. Bloomsbury.

Piela, A. (2011). *Muslim Women Online: Faith and Identity in Virtual Space*. Routledge.

Piela, A. (2013). "I Am Just Doing My Bit to Promote Modesty": Niqabis' Self-Portraits on Photo-Sharing Website. *Feminist Media Studies*, 13, 781–790.

Piela, A. (2015a). Muslim Women Speak Online. Religion, Conversion, Activism, and Art. *Hawwa: Journal of Women of the Middle East and the Islamic World*, 13, 271–278.

Piela, A. (2015b). Videoconferencing as a tool facilitating feminist interviews with Muslim women who wear the niqab. In S. Cheruvallil-Contractor & S. Shakkour (Eds.) *Digital Methodologies in the Study of Religion*. Bloomsbury.

Piela, A., Górak-Sosnowska, K., Abdallah-Krzepkowska, B. (forthcoming). Teaching Against Islamophobia. In Nielsen, J. (Ed) *Navigating the Non/confessional in University Islamic Studies*. Edinburgh University Press.

Piricky, G. (2018). Merging Culture with Religion. Trajectories of Slovak and Czech Muslim Converts since 1989. In K. van Nieuwkerk (Ed.) *Moving in and out of Islam*, (pp. 107–129). Texas University Press.

Popay, J., Roberts, H., Sowden, A., Petticrew, M., Arai, L., Rodgers, M., Britten, N. (2006). *Guidance on the Conduct of Narrative Synthesis in Systematic Reviews*. Lanchester University.

Račius, E. (2011). Revival at the expense of survival? In K. Górak-Sosnowska (Ed.), *Muslims in Poland and Eastern Europe. Widening the European Discourse on Islam* (pp. 207–221). University of Warsaw.

Račius, E. (2018). *Muslims in Eastern Europe*. Edinburgh University Press.

Račius, E. (2013). A 'virtual club' of Lithuanian converts to Islam. In G. Larsson & T. Hoffman (Eds.). *Muslims and the New Information and Communication Technologies: Theoretical, Methodological and Empirical Perspectives* (pp. 31–47). Springer Verlag.

Rao, A. H. (2015). Gender and Cultivating the Moral Self in Islam: Muslim Converts in an American Mosque. *Sociology of Religion*, 76(4), 413–435.

Rambo, L. (1993). *Understanding Religious Conversion*. Yale University Press.

Roald, S. (2004). *New Muslims in the European Context. The Experience of Scandinavian Converts*. Brill.

Roald, S. (2006). The shaping of a Scandinavian "Islam": converts and gender equal opportunity. In K. van Nieuwkerk (Ed.) *Women Embracing Islam. Gender and Conversion in the West* (pp. 48–70). University of Texas Press.

Rogowska, B. (2018). *Wpływ Polaków nawróconych na islam na społeczności lokalne w Polsce*. Unpublished Doctoral dissertation. Uniwersytet Łódzki, https://dspace.uni.lodz.pl/handle/11089/25290.

Rogozen-Soltar, M. (2012). Managing Muslim Visibility: Conversion, Immigration, and Spanish Imaginaries of Islam. *American Anthropologist*, 114(4), 611–623.

Rose, G. (1997). Situating knowledges: positionality, reflexivities and other tactics. *Progress in Human Geography*, 21(3), 305–320.

Ryan, L. and Golden, A. (2006). 'Tick the Box Please': A Reflexive Approach to Doing Quantitative Social Research. *Sociology*, 40(6), 1191–1200.

Ryszewska, M. (2018). *Polskie muzułmanki. W poszukiwaniu tożsamości*. Uniwersytet Mikołaja Kopernika.

Said, E. (1978). *Orientalism*. Pantheon Books.

Serrant, L. (2002). Black on black: methodological issues for black researchers working in minority ethnic communities. *Nurse Researcher*, 9(4): 30–44.

Shestopalets, D. (2019). Conversion to Islam in Ukraine: Preliminary observations. *Східний світ*, 2019, 4, 130–139.

Shestopalets, D. (2021). Between faith and ethnicity: motifs of conversion and attitudes to ethnic Muslims in the discourses of Russian converts to Islam. *Contemporary Islam*, 15(3), 357–380.

Silverman, D. (1985). *Qualitative Methodology and Sociology: Describing the Social World*. Gower Publishing Company.

Skarżyńska, O. (2016). *Islam, kobieta, wspólnota. Analiza narracji polskich konwertytek*. Unpublished Master dissertation. Uniwersytet Warszawski, https://depot.ceon.pl/handle/123456789/9439.

Snook, D., Fodeman, A., Kleinmann, S., & Horgan, J. (2021). Crisis as Catalyst: Crisis in Conversion to Islam Related to Radicalism Intentions, Terrorism and Political Violence, https://doi.org/10.1080/09546553.2021.1938003.

Soutar, L. (2010). British female converts to Islam: choosing Islam as a rejection of individualism. *Language and Intercultural Communication*, 10(1), 3–16.

Stefańska, O. (2011). *Drogi do islamu: polskie konwertytki*. Unpublished Master's dissertation. Szkoła Wyższa Psychologii Społecznej w Warszawie.

Stemplewska-Żakowicz, K. (2006). O różnorodności form wywiadu oraz prób jej uporządkowania. In K. Krejtz & K. Stemplewska-Żakowicz (Eds.). *Wywiad psychologiczny. Wywiad jako postępowanie badawcze*. Pracownia Testów Psychologicznych PTP.

Stoica, D. (2011). New Romanian Muslimas. Converted women sharing knowledge in online and offline communities. In K. Górak-Sosnowska (Ed.), *Muslims in Poland and Eastern Europe. Widening the European Discourse on Islam* (pp. 266–287). University of Warsaw.

Stoica, D. (2013). *Women Converts. Transformations, Knowledge Perspectives, and Narratives*. Lampert Academic Publishing.

Suleiman, Y. (2013). *Narratives of Conversion to Islam in Britain Female Perspectives*. University of Cambridge.

Temple, B. (2002). Crossed Wires: Interpreters, Translators, and Bilingual Workers in Cross-Language Research. *Qualitative Health Research*, 12(6), 844–854.

van Nieuwkerk, K. (2006). *Women embracing Islam: gender and conversion in the West*. University of Texas Press.

Wiktor-Mach, D. (2008). European Islam: The Case of Polish Tatars. *Hemispheres*, 23, 145–157.

Wilkinson, M., Irfan, L., Quraishi, M., & Purdie, M. (2021). Prison as a Site of Intense Religious Change: The Example of Conversion to Islam. *Religions*, 12(3), 162.

Winchester, (2008). Embodying the Faith: Religious Practice and the Making of a Muslim Moral Habitus. *Social Forces*, 86(4), 1753–1780.

Wittgenstein, L. ([1953] 1986). *Philosophical Investigations*. Basil Blackwell.

Wohlrab-Sahr, M. (1999). Conversion to Islam: Between Syncretism and Symbolic Battle. *Social Compass*, 46(3), 351–362.

Young, R. (1990). *White Mythologies and the West*. Routledge.

Younis, T., & Hassan, G. (2017). Changing Identities: A Case Study of Western Muslim Converts Whose Conversion Revised Their Relationship to Their National Identity. *Journal of Muslim Minority Affairs*, 37(10), 30–40.

Zebiri, K. (2008). *British Muslim Converts. Choosing Alternative Lives*. Oneworld Publishing.

CHAPTER 1

# Setting the Scene: Islam in Poland

*Katarzyna Górak-Sosnowska* | ORCID: 0000-0002-1121-6240
SGH Warsaw School of Economics

**Introduction**

Conversion to Islam in Poland, on the scale seen in the last two decades, is unprecedented in Poland. The history of Islam in Poland is much longer, as the first Tatar settlements can be dated back to the late 14th century. This chapter introduces the topic of Islam in Poland by giving an overview of indigenous and immigrant Muslim histories in this country.

The chapter starts with a discussion of available data about Muslims in Poland, with a proviso that numbers provided here are estimates. Next, two Polish Muslim populations are described – the "established" Tatar Muslim community and the newcomers – Muslims of immigrant origin. We touch upon the institutional landscape of Islamic organisations in Poland. The next section covers a short history of conversion to Islam by Poles. The last part of the chapter addresses the under researched topic of Polish Muslim diaspora with a focus on Polish Muslims in the UK – most probably the largest diaspora of Polish Muslims. We provide the background on Polish conversion to Islam, situating the experiences of Polish female converts to Islam in a wider perspective.

In regard to the history, size and interactions with local Muslim communities, Poland differs from most other EU countries. On the one hand it is home to one of the oldest Muslim communities in Europe and was one of the first countries to formally recognize Islam. On the other hand, it has not experienced noticeable immigration from Muslim majority countries. Thus, regardless of the data source, Muslims constitute only around 0,1% of the Polish population. Despite joining the EU in 2004, Poland is a less attractive destination for third country nationals than Western European countries. Moreover, Poland itself is a labour-exporting country with over 2.5 million Poles living in other EU countries. It is quite often abroad that Poles have their first direct interaction with a person of Muslim faith.

While it is easy to conceptualize a typology of Muslims in Poland as based on the division between the indigenous and immigrant Muslim populations, it is much harder to estimate their sizes. The longstanding historical presence of Polish Muslims combined with their ethnic and national diversity makes any estimations tenuous. According to the 2011 Census, around 5100 individuals in Poland declared to be Muslim (GUS, 2015), which is a significantly smaller number than estimates suggested by Islamic organisations at approximately 42000 Muslims (GUS, 2019a, p. 23). The eightfold difference is striking but given the low number of Muslims in Poland it is easy to over- or underestimate the size of a particular Muslim branch or group.

The Muslim Religious Union declared 523 members in 2018 (most of them are Tatars; GUS 2019a: 251), while different estimates point at between three and six thousand of Tatars in Poland (and closer to three thousand – see Łyszczarz, 2011, pp. 53–54). These estimations result, to some extent, in the connection between Tatar ethnicity and belonging to the Polish nation. Fewer than five hundred individuals declared Tatar ethnicity according to the 2002 Polish Census[1] (GUS, 2002, p. 40). The number of Muslims of immigrant origin is even harder to estimate. Muslim organisations in Poland estimate their members at thirty-five thousand Sunnis, six thousand and seventy-six Shias, and forty-five Ahmadis (GUS, 2019b). If we assume that the majority of these members are Muslims of immigrant origin, this suggests the number of over forty thousand Muslims living in Poland. These numbers, however, do not correspond with the number of nationals from Muslim-majority countries living in Poland, which in 2018 was at around 16700 (Andrejuk, 2019b, p. 211). While there are many Muslims who come from non-Muslim majority countries (for example India and Russia) and some of them are granted the Polish citizenship, and there are some Polish converts to Islam, the discrepancy of twenty-four thousand is significant.

Estimating the number of Polish converts to Islam is challenging, as there is only limited data (Kościelniak, 2016, p. 26), and only a handful of researchers provide an estimate. For instance, Egdūnas Račius (2020) suggested that there may be five thousand Polish converts residing in Poland and abroad (p. 158). Our opinion leaders estimated their number from several dozen to several thousand. As Račius (2020) noted, a lot of East European converts to Islam live abroad – mostly in the UK, but also in Ireland, the Netherlands and Spain. Therefore, they are not only hard to count, but also to identify, unless they get locally organised. In addition, many Polish converts to Islam are still formally Catholic (Rogowska, 2017), so they can be doubly counted, which further blurs the picture. In similar manner, embracing Islam is not always formally

---

1 The respondent could only select one ethnicity – selecting the Tatar ethnicity meant that one could not simultaneously identify as Polish.

reported or registered with the local Muslim community. Finally, conversion to Islam is a two-directional process with some people embracing and others leaving Islam.

With the total number of over 50 thousand Muslims in Poland and of Polish origin, we estimate the number of Tatars up to four thousand (Łyszczarz, 2011), Muslims of immigrant origin – at around 40 thousand (according to Polish Muslim organisations – it is true that they may overestimate the number of Muslims, but we also take into account the 'silent majority' of unaffiliated Muslims and Chechen refugees – some of whom have no access to Muslim organisations) and the five thousand of converts to Islam (Račius, 2020) – both in Poland and abroad.

## Tatars – The Indigenous Muslim Population of Poland

Poland is one of the few EU countries that have their own indigenous Muslim population. The Polish-Lithuanian Tatars are one of the smallest ethnic minorities in Poland, estimated at around three to four thousand people. They have lived in Poland for over 600 years and have remained a distinctive community of Poles of the Muslim faith; they fought in Polish wars and uprising and faced resettlements after the Second World War (Miśkiewicz, 1990). Until the 80s, the position of the Tatars as *the* Muslims of Poland was unchallenged. It was indicated by the Polish ethnonym pertaining to the Tatars, "Muślimowie" ('the Muslims').

The Tatar identity is built around three intersecting components – ethnicity, nationality and religion (Warmińska, 1999). Tatars consider themselves to be Polish, since they have lived in Poland for centuries, and always been loyal to Polish authorities. The collective memory of Tatars fighting side by side with other Poles for the sake of Poland has been cultivated not only by Tatars themselves, but also by the Polish state (Łyszczarz, 2011). Ethnicity is at the core of the Tatar identity and involves the Tatar history, culture, and tradition (Górak-Sosnowska and Łyszczarz, 2018). Moreover, ethnicity provides a framework for the last element of Tatar identity – their religion, Sunni Islam. This combination of ethnicity and religion makes the Tatar Islam unique – just as many other local lived types of Islam.

Three distinct factors underlie the uniqueness of the Tatar Islam. One, the Islam that they practised was enriched by Turkic and pre-Islamic traditions. The Turkic elements are visible in the names of the prayers, while the pre-Islamic ones are mostly visible in magical and healing practices. The second factor was life within the Polish Catholic society. In the beginning of their settlement the

Tatars engaged in exogenous marriages, spoke Polish and settled down. All these activities were very pragmatic. Tatars who came to Poland were mostly males, so it would have been difficult to find Tatar wives locally. The Tatars also spoke different languages, so Polish was not only a means to assimilation but also to communicate with each other. Moreover, they Slavicised their names by adding the Polish suffix *-icz* (for example, Józef > Józefowicz; Dziekan, 2000, p. 41). They incorporated some Christian elements into their traditions, such as celebrating Christmas (as the birth of the Prophet Isa), or the All Saints' Day (Kamocki, 2000, p. 140). The third factor was Tatars' peripherality in the Islamic world. They historically interacted with the Ottomans and the Crimean Khanate (Bohdanowicz et al., 1997, p. 17). This means that their Islam has been only marginally influenced by other Muslims and their ideas of how to believe and practice Islam.

The ethnic character of the Tatar Islam sets the Tatars apart from Polish converts. The Tatar Islam is embedded into a particular set of traditions which have sometimes been labelled as "folk Islam" (Benussi, 2020). The peculiar perception of the Tatar Islam in the eyes of Polish converts has been elaborated by one of Polish convert community leaders:

> Most converts look at the Tatar Islam in Poland and see something that I call 'a beautiful heritage museum' – a respected tradition, but because of only faint religiosity among most contemporary Tatars, this tradition does not have a lot to offer to [other Polish] Muslims in terms of their religious needs. (Janusz)

For Polish converts, this embeddedness of the Tatar Islam in the Tatar ethnicity is a difference marker. Asked if the Polish converts are closer to the Tatars or the Muslims of immigrant origin, all of our opinion leaders unanimously chose the latter option. According to two Muslim leaders of migrant origin:

> [The Polish converts] are closer to Muslims of immigrant origin, because both identify as Muslims and then there is the cultural context. In the case of the Tatars (not all) it goes the other way round – they stress their heritage and culture and later comes the faith. (Fatima)

> Tatars in Poland are not only Muslims, but also an ethnic minority that has its customs and practices. (Mustafa)

It seems that the Tatar ethnicity has kept them apart from Polish converts to Islam, even if some of the first converts actually collaborated with the Tatar community (Berger, 2015). For these, as well as spatial reasons (Tatars live in enclaves in the east of Poland), it is unlikely that a Polish convert to Islam and a Tatar would meet. As one of the leaders we interviewed said: "most converts have never seen a Tatar in their life" (Paweł). While this might be true mostly for those converts who settled abroad, it still indicates that being Muslim and Polish is not enough to bring both groups together.

One other factor keeps these two groups apart – that is, the way they are perceived by the mainstream Polish society. Muslims are often categorized in Western societies as 'good' and 'bad' ones (Mondon and Winter, 2019, p. 63), and in Poland, the Tatars are perceived as the good, legacy, 'our' Muslims, converts and immigrant Muslims are seen as alien, fundamentalist and 'Oriental'. Paradoxically, despite both groups being Polish, the Tatars and the converts are ascribed opposite identities (Górak-Sosnowska, 2014, p. 103). For the Tatars, their patriotic commitment to the Polish cause and privatised religiosity work to their advantage. The converts' commitment to the Polish cause is questioned as their religious identity makes them 'spoiled' and discounted or discredited.

Since the end of the 20th century, the Tatars have been focused on rebuilding their culture and tradition. For example, they have established a youth dance and song group called 'Buńczuk' [Tatar for "panache"] to cultivate Tatar songs and traditional dances, built a Tatar Yurt – an inn to cultivate Tatar cuisine, and organised a variety of Tatar festivals including Sabantuj [Tatar for "feast of the plough"] – the festival has been relaunched in 2007 after a century. These efforts are significantly challenged by the aging demographic profile of the Tatar community. There is a generational shift; younger Tatars are less involved in maintaining the traditions which they perceive as folklore (Łyszczarz, 2011). Still, ethnic mobilisation seems to be the main way in which the Tatars can distinguish themselves from other Muslims in Poland. In fact, they are now one of many ethnic minorities that make up the Muslim population of Poland. Their central position started to change as Muslims form Middle East, Sub-Saharan Africa and Central Asia began emigrating to Poland.

### Polish Muslims of Migrant Origin

Just as Western Europe, Poland has experienced an influx of migrants from Muslim majority countries, but on a much smaller scale. Poland was a country of the Soviet bloc, and so only citizens of fellow communist countries were allowed to enter Poland. The main thrust of migration to Poland resulted from bilateral agreements between Soviet bloc countries that promoted scientific and technical collaboration. Inviting students from Asia and Africa to Polish universities and polytechnics was a part of such agreements. First students from Syria, Iraq, and Sudan came to Poland in the late 50s (Swiat, 2017, p. 208). Estimates of foreign student numbers in communist Poland vary from a few thousand up to a hundred thousand. In the 80s and early 90s, Iraq sent the most students to Poland (Gomółka, 2016, p. 6). Even if their numbers were not significant, they established a Muslim (mostly Arab) diaspora in Poland. Its members were educated, spoke Polish language and were willing to settle down in their new country – they had substantial cultural and social capital. Prior to commencing their studies, they were required to learn Polish language which would facilitate their settlement in Poland. Most foreign students in Poland began their educational journeys at a handful of Polish language centres located by major universities. While most of these students decided to return to their home countries, some of them settled in Poland and married Polish women. Kościelniak (2016, p. 47) estimates that approximately 10–20% of foreign students remained in Poland.

This emerging Muslim diaspora largely integrated into the Polish society. This integration was enabled by their education (usually technical or medical) and perfect Polish language skills. Some of them attempted to engage with local Muslim communities which comprised, almost exclusively, the Tatars. There was a potential for such collaboration as Arab migrants knew Arabic and were closer to the Islamic orthodoxy, while the Tatars had a vast experience of living in the Catholic Poland. However, mutual relations between these two communities were marked by episodes of competitiveness, culminating at the beginning of the 2000s, when Muslims of migrant origin founded their own religious association (Pędziwiatr, 2011).

The new Muslim diaspora in Poland has brought much more diversity to the small local Muslim community. Since the late 90s, it was possible to travel to Poland as the communist regime had collapsed and the political transformation had begun. The new Poland – not communist, but not yet fully capitalist – was a new territory for business endeavours. This is when Turkish economic migrants started to arrive in Poland and start their business (Andrejuk, 2019a). Soon they were followed by economic migrants from the Middle East, North Africa and South Asia who found jobs in the hospitality (Nowaczek-Walczak, 2011), and transport sectors.

In 2004 Poland became a member of the European Union. This somewhat improved the appeal of Poland as a destination for potential migrants from Muslim majority countries. Due to the slow but steady economic convergence, Poland became more attractive as a country to settle down in. In addition, the Polish membership in the EU eased the way to the "old" EU member states for residents of Poland. However, overall, the inflow of migrants from

Muslim-majority countries was still rather limited: in 2005 only 110 nationals of Muslim-majority countries received a permanent residence permit; in 2010 and 2019 these numbers were 279 and 423, respectively. Temporary stay permits were issued to more nationals of Muslim-majority countries: 1166 in 2005, rising to 4461 in 2018[2] (GUS 2019b, pp. 339–440). A significant number of Muslims in Poland are mostly Chechen refugees. Their number is estimated at several thousand. Many of them consider Poland to be a transit country on their way to the West, and many had their applications for international protection refused by Polish authorities. The Chechens who decided to stay in Poland have very limited opportunities to interact with the Polish mainstream society, not only due to the fact that many of them are placed in refugee detention centres, but also due to hostility that they experience (Grzymała-Moszczyńska and Trojanek, 2011).

The development of an established Muslim diaspora did not result in many conversions to Islam among Poles. Even if married to a Muslim man of migrant origin, many Polish women decided to keep their faith, while children from these mixed marriages were often unfamiliar or superficially familiar with the religion and language of their father. Later in life, some of them took up the study of the Arabic language and Islam at one of Polish universities. Few Polish women who decided to settle with their Muslim husbands in their origin countries embraced Islam. In the context of the new diaspora, conversion to Islam was facilitated by the existing Muslim infrastructure[3] (mosques, prayer rooms, but also virtual Islamic environments) – different from the Tatar (ethnicity-based) one, and interactions with more Muslims of migrant origin.

According to the opinion leaders – regardless of their ethnicity and denomination – it is the Islam of the migrants that appeals to the Polish converts:

> People who embrace a new religion usually want not only to practice Islam, but to do it in an environment that guarantees some sort of orthodoxy, so naturally Polish converts come closer to the migrant Muslim communities, which – regardless of their political or cultural aspects – are, in the strictly religious sense, just ordinary, mainstream Sunni. (Paweł)

---

2 These numbers are based on the author's own estimation, based on the total permits issued to nationals of Afghanistan, Albania, Algeria, Azerbaijan, Bangladesh, Egypt, Iraq, Kyrgyzstan, Libya, Morocco, Nigeria, Pakistan, Syria, Tunisia and Uzbekistan.
3 For more about mosques in Poland, see Nalborczyk (2011).

Our interlocutor clearly assumes that the political or cultural aspects limit the scope of strictly religious engagement. The discussion about the ethnic-national orientation vs. the universalist orientation of local Muslim organisations (Dialmy, 2007) is reflected in the two following statements of opinion leaders:

> Converts seek Islam without cultural or customary accretions of cultures or ethnic groups. They search for an organisation where multiculturalism prevails, and the [Muslim] League is one such organisation. Its members come from different countries and there is no place for mixing religion and traditions. (Mustafa)

> Only newcomers from Arab countries are recognized as "real" Muslims and experts in all knowledge related to Islam. It is not necessarily true, but the "magic" works. (Ahmad)

Symptomatically the above opinions were expressed by an Arab living in Poland and a Tatar. It is true that the above-mentioned Muslim League is much more diverse than the Tatar-led Muslim Religious Union in terms of ethnic and national background of its members. This diversity may support establishing a religious platform beyond any ethnical or cultural divisions. Polish converts to Islam could have their place there together with other ethnic or national Muslim communities. At the same time, the League has been dominated by the Arabs (Kościelniak, 2016; Pędziwiatr, 2011), which may influence at least some of its activities. The second interlocutor quoted above is irritated by the assumptions that Tatars are not "real" Muslims. This conflict defines the relationship between the Tatars and the migrant Muslims.

### The Polish Muslim Organisational Landscape

Poland was one of the first European countries to institutionalize its relations with its indigenous Muslim community represented by the Tatar-led MRU in 1936. There was no other Muslims organisation in Poland and "Tatar" has been a synonymous with "Muslim". A Polish convert to Islam we interviewed anecdotally encountered a Tatar in the early 70s who told him that he had just met a "Sudanese Tatar". Our interlocutor was surprised to hear that were Tatars in Sudan. After further questioning, he realized the story concerned a Sudanese Muslim. This misnomer indicates that the Tatars had no "competition" in Poland at the time. There were only Polish Tatars and a handful of converts and migrants. Islam in Poland was essentially the Islam of Polish Tatars (Dziekan, 2011).

The MRU was established in 1925 to unite Polish Muslims. In 1936 it became the sole Muslim representative body in Poland according to legislation from the 21 April 1936 "On the Relations of the State to the Muslim Religious Union".[4] Today, the MRU is headed by Tomasz Miśkiewicz, a Polish Tatar educated in Saudi Arabia, who is also the Mufti of Poland. There are currently five Muslim communities affiliated with the MRU: one each in Warsaw, Gdańsk, Białystok and two small Tatar villages – Bohoniki and Kruszyniany. Members of MRU have to be Muslim and may not belong to any other religious associations. Only Polish citizen members have the right to vote or to be elected for roles in the Union. One of the aims of the MRU is "to protect the identity, culture and heritage of Tatars – Polish Muslims" (paragraph 3 1.14 of the MRU Statue).

After over half a decade, four other Muslim religious associations were registered by the Polish Ministry of Internal Affairs, yet none has been elevated to the rank of MRU as far as the relations with the State of Poland are concerned. These associations are:

- Association of Islamic Unity (Stowarzyszenie Jedności Muzułmańskiej; AIU) registered on 31 January 1990 and headed by Rafał Berger – the head Imam
- Islamic Association Ahmadiyya (Stowarzyszenie Muzułmańskie Ahmadiyya; IA Ahmadiyya) registered on 23 December 1990 and headed by Zafar Mashhood Ahmad – head of the association[5]
- Islamic Assembly Ahl ul-Bayt (Islamskie Zgromadzenie Ahl-ul-Bayt; IA Ahl ul-Bayt) registered on 17 December 1990 and headed by Ryszard Ahmed Rusnak – the head Imam
- Muslim League in the Republic of Poland (Liga Muzułmańska w Rzeczypospolitej Polskiej; ML) registered on 6 January 2004 and headed by Youssef Chadid (head of the main board), while Nedal Abu Tabaq (deceased in 2020) was the Mufti of Poland at the Muslim League.

Additionally, there are several Islamic organisations[6] which are registered as associations or foundations without being recognised as religious organisations by the Polish state. Therefore, there are five Islamic religious associations

---

4 (Dz. U. [*Journal of Laws*] from 1936, No 30, Item 240.)
5 Zafar Mashhood Ahmad is listed as the head of the association on their website, however the information seems not to have been updated in the last years. Moreover, it seems that he has taken the post of the imam at a German Ahmadi mosque in Lübeck (Ahmadiyya.de, 2021).
6 Association of Muslim Students in Poland; Nemezis; The Ayatollah Chomeini Association of Muslim Youth Integration in Organisation of Alimentation, Science and Sport; Association Institute of Islamic Studies.

in Poland: two Sunni (MRU and ML), two Shia (AIU and IA Ahl ul-Bayt) and one Ahmadi (IA Ahmadiyya). Interestingly, the first two associations that were registered in the early 90s were non-Sunni. It may have been the result of religious preferences, but from the formal point of view it seems that no one was able to challenge the dominant role of MRU among Sunni Muslims in Poland. This changed after the establishment of the Muslim League.

The ML commenced its activities around 2001 and three years later became an officially registered Sunni religious association. It has been established by Muslims of migrant origin and converts – two groups that felt that there was not enough space for them in the Tatar-led MRU. Remarkably, the first head of the ML was a Polish female convert to Islam, Iwona Alkhalayla. According to the Statute, members of ML are Polish Muslims, as well as Muslims in possession of the temporary or the permanent residence permit in Poland. Two of ML's statutory aims are to "integrate with Polish society by maintaining an Islamic identity", and "defending human rights, combating all manifestations of racism and intolerance".

A comparison of statutory aims of these two key Polish Sunni organisations clearly indicates their focus. While MRU strives to maintain the Tatar identity, the ML is keen to integrate into the Polish mainstream society. Having lived in Poland for over 600 years, the Tatars have become a part of Polish society, and the recent rise of anti-Muslim discourse has affected them, but to a lesser degree than other Muslims in Poland. The ML is composed predominantly of Muslims of migrant origin, and some converts to Islam. It aims to showcase that Islam and its believers fit into the Polish and the wider European societies. Furthermore, until 2012, only Polish nationals were allowed to become members of MRU which significantly limited the opportunities for Muslims of migrant origin to join this organisation. The Shia organisations were not involved in that conflict. As the leader of one of Polish Shia organisations says:

> … we never had any problems with that. We have always approached Tatar merits with respect, we acknowledge that their tradition is also our tradition, of course without any appropriation – it comes from the significance of identity, Polishness, fondness for history. At the same time, as Shias, sensitive to Shiite history, we were not involved in the tensions arising between the migrants and the Tatars. (Adam)

The position of converts within these organisations varies. There are hardly any converts at the MRU, and only a few among active members, while all top management positions are occupied by the Tatars. It seems that the Tatars do not need the converts for pursuing MRU's goals, while the MRU itself is still perceived as a Tatar association. There are many more convert members at the ML – some of them are wives of Muslims of migrant origin, others have joined the ML on their own. Two out of five top management positions are occupied by converts, although theirs are the less significant roles (treasurer and a board member), other are taken by Arab migrants. In the beginning, the converts were useful for setting up the organisation and now they seem to be used – just as in Western Europe (Moosavi, 2015, p. 1919) – as the public relations team, "the friendly face of Islam" – to appeal to both the converts and to the Polish mainstream public. The spokesperson of the ML is also a Polish convert.

Interestingly, the heads of the two Shia organisations are Polish converts to Islam. Both Shia organisations were established by their respective leaders just at the beginning of the political transition of Poland and right after the borders were opened. Their Polish founders were the only individuals capable of establishing a religious association in Poland. Thus, both Polish Shia organisations seem to follow the pattern observed in other Central and East European countries (in Czech Republic (Bureš, 2010, p. 26), Hungary (Csicsmann and Vékony, 2010, p. 60), or Romania (Stoica, 2011, p. 269), where first Islamic religious associations were established by converts to Islam who knew the language and had sufficient social and cultural capital). The Ahmadiyya organisation was established approximately at the same time as the Shia organisations, and its founder was an Ahmadi missionary. However, the first Ahmadi missionary came to Poland in the late 30s, so the idea to have a registered organisation had a much longer history and was supported from abroad by the global Ahmadi movement (Stawiński, 1994).

## Converts to Islam from a Historical Perspective

While the Poles have been familiar with Islam through the Tatars, they never converted in large numbers. Most historical conversions to Islam were instrumental, for political reasons. The history of conversion to Islam in Poland could be fascinating for the biographies of selected famous Poles who turned to Islam, yet it does not bear much relevance for the contemporary phenomenon of conversion to Islam due to a completely different historical and political setting. Thus, it is presented only briefly.

Most probably, the first Polish conversions to Islam were involuntary and linked to the trade of Slavic slaves which began approximately mid-8th century AD. By that time, *Bilad as-Saqalibah* ('the land of Slavs', that is, Central Europe) was one of the biggest slave supply markets for the Muslim lands, with the major castration centre in Prague (Heck, 2006, p. 316). As a unified territory, Poland came into existence only in mid-10th century AD, so it is hard to determine, whether and how many of these slaves originated from the territory of the future Poland. Moreover, by embracing Christianity, Slavs became less attractive as candidates for slaves, since they now also believed in one God and belonged to the People of the Book (*ahl al-kitab*). Thus, the slave trade became limited and stopped two centuries after Poland adopted Christianity in 966 AD. Some of these early Slavic slaves may have converted to Islam – as it was feared by the Iberian Christian clergy (Wexler, 1996, p. 46).

The 15th century brought back slave trade to the Slavic lands. Prisoners of war captured by the Ottoman army were frequently enslaved. Some managed to achieve a higher social status. One of the most successful slaves was Hurrem Sultan known as Roxelana, a female from Ruthenia (which belonged to the Kingdom of Poland at the time) who was kidnapped by the Crimean Tatars, put into a harem, and later became a legal wife of Suleiman the Magnificent and one of the most powerful women of her era. For male slaves, becoming Muslim was also a strategy for upward mobility in the Turkish army. This way, some of the Polish converts made a career in the highest ranks of the Ottoman army, while some others advanced as local craftsmen.

The first Polish converts to Islam who were known by their names lived in the 15th century. One of the first known Polish converts was Jan Winko, a knight from the city of Cracow, who made a pilgrimage to the Holy Land in 1446 in order to repent for his sins. As he arrived in Jerusalem, he decided to stay and embrace Islam (Podolska, 1996, p. 217). Another one was Jan Kierdej, who was captured by the Ottomans and converted to Islam. He was subsequently assigned by the Sublime Porte, the central Ottoman Empire government, to diplomatic missions to Poland. Quite a few Poles converted to Islam and decided to stay in the Ottoman Empire – some of them had better career opportunities, while some others feared returning to Poland (Kroll, 2013).

By the end of the 17th century, Poles began feeling the pull of the Orient in their own kind of way that was different from the romantic, colonially inspired West European Orientalism. The key cultural concept of that time in Poland was Sarmatism – an idea that Polish nobility were descended from the Sarmatians, the ancient Indo-European warriors (Sulimirski, 1970). The many advocates of this idea believed that Poland had a historical mission to play in Europe as the bulwark of Christianity. However, they had a penchant for "Oriental" fashion, arms, and crafts, to such an extent that Polish and Turkish fashions became almost undistinguishable. Only later did Poles become attracted to the Orient in the manner popularised in the West (Krzywy, 2012). However, this attraction was more oriented to science and culture than religion. Wacław Rzewuski

(1706–1779), a Polish orientalist, traveller and poet famously adapted "Oriental" dress and lifestyle, but it is rather unclear whether he actually converted to Islam (Kopanski, 2009, p. 99).

In 1795, Poland lost its independence and its territory had been divided between Prussia, Austria, and Russia. During the time of the partition of Poland, the Ottoman Empire was an unexpected ally of Poland, and it never recognized the partition. Some Poles went as far as converting to Islam for political reasons. This way, they were able to join the Turkish army to fight against the enemies of Poland. Michał Czajowski and Józef Bem were the two most notable high ranking Polish army officials active in Turkish army. Czajkowski managed to assemble a regiment and fought in the Crimean war. However, after over 30 years of political and military struggle he had finally conceded a defeat – he decided to return to Eastern Europe and converted to Greek Orthodox Christianity (Bracka, 2020, p. 36). By the end of his life, the Polish general Józef Bem arrived in Turkey and continued his fight against Russia as a Muslim citizen of the Ottoman Empire. He did so for political reasons, but "maintained Christianity in his heart", as he admitted in one of his letters (as quoted in Harbut, 1929, p. 26). Conversions were exceedingly rare until the 1990s.

### Polish Muslims Abroad

It is estimated that as many as 20 million Poles live abroad (MFiPR, 2019). They are known as the Polish diaspora, Polish emigrants, or simply "Polonia" (Lesińska, 2018). Regardless of the scope of these terms (which can encompass people who may have Polish roots, but not necessarily be citizens of Poland), some of them are Muslim. The Polish Muslim diaspora includes members of all the main Polish Muslim groups.

The oldest Polish Muslim diaspora are the Tatars. Some of them decided to stay in the newly formed Soviet Union, despite the forced resettlements after the Second World War that resulted from the border shifts (Poland lost a significant part of its territory which today is Lithuania, Belarus and Ukraine). Some others decided to move to Crimea to join Tatar communities there. Finally, some Tatars decided to emigrate to the UK to assist the Polish government in exile. Their offspring, often from mixed Tatar-Polish-British marriages still live in the UK (Miśkiewicz, 2017).

A relatively small and recent section of Polish Muslim diaspora includes Muslims of migrant origin who were granted the Polish nationality, but subsequently decided to emigrate either to back their home countries, or to the West. Quite often, the reasons for emigration were pragmatic and were related to the rising Islamophobia in Poland. Our interview data indicates that many children from mixed marriages were bullied at schools, which was an additional motivation for emigration. Emigration of Muslims of migrant origin from Poland is a recent phenomenon that started around the 2014–2015 in the wake of the so-called European refugee crisis which coincided with the sharp rise of right-wing sentiment in Poland.

The bulk of Polish Muslims abroad are Polish converts to Islam. They live in other EU countries with larger local Muslim communities. In England and Wales, the home to one of the biggest Muslim communities in Europe *and* many Polish migrants, over 2000 Poles who arrived in the UK between 2001 and 2011 identified themselves as Muslim (UK Office of National Statistics, 2014). The Polish Muslim diaspora likely constitutes a significant segment of Polish Muslims. We will present this community further in Chapter 3.

Polish Muslims are a diverse community with a long history of living in mainstream Polish society. Out of these communities Polish converts to Islam have a particularly vulnerable position. As we will elaborate in the following chapters Polish mainstream society is a particularly stigmatising environment in which they manage their religious and national identities. So far the concept of 'spoiled identity' has been implemented to study groups and communities that are considered as stigmatised due to their health (Fraser and Treloar 2006, Camlin et al., 2017), delinquent behaviour (Hepburn, 1977, Harris, 1976), sexuality (Grossman, 1997), or habits (Wigginton and Lafrance, 2016). Only in one case the concept has been applied to studying a religious group – anabaptist Christians (Schuurman, 2020). Due to the peculiar position of Polish female converts to Islam in Polish society we decided to bring this concept to study this group.

### References

Ahmadiyya.de (2021). *Bait-ul-Afiyat Moschee in Lübeck*, Ahmadiyya. Retrieved August 8, 2021, from https://ahmadiyya.de/gebetsstaette/moscheen/luebeck/browse/1.

Andrejuk, K. (2019a). Strategizing Integration in the Labor Market. Turkish Immigrants in Poland and the New Dimensions of South-to-North Migration. *Polish Sociological Review*, 206(2), 157–176.

Andrejuk, K. (2019b). Politicizing Muslim immigration in Poland – discursive and regulatory dimensions. In K. Górak-Sosnowska, M. Pachocka, & J. Misiuna (Eds.),

*Muslim minorities and the refugee crisis in Europe* (pp. 207–224). SGH Warsaw School of Economics.

Benussi, M. (2020). "Sovereign" Islam and Tatar "Aqīdah": normative religious narratives and grassroots criticism amongst Tatarstan's Muslims. *Contemporary Islam*, 14, 111–134. https://doi.org/10.1007/s11562-018-0428-8.

Berger, R. (2015). Szyici w Polsce na tle tatarskiej tradycji i polskich organizacji muzułmańskich. *Nurt SVD*, 2, 134–153.

Bohdanowicz, L., Chazbijewicz, S., & Tyszkiewicz, J. (1997). *Tatarzy muzułmanie w Polsce*. Niezależne Wydawnictwo Rocznik Tatarów Polskich.

Bracka, M. (2020). Myth and Politics in the Historical Novels of Michał Czajkowski. In G. Borkowska & L. Wiśniewska (Eds.), *Another Canon. Polish Nineteenth-Century Novel in World Context* (pp. 35–52). Lit Verlag.

Bureš, J. (2010). Muslims In The Czech Republic: Integration Into The Closed Society, In J. Hunterová & H. Suchardová, *Muslims in Visegrad* (pp. 25–38). Institute of International Relations, Prague.

Camlin, C., Charlebois, E., Gerg, E., Semitala, F., Getahun, M., Kampiire, L., Buksi, E., Sang, N., Kwarisiima, D., Clark, T., Petersen, M., Kamya, M., and Havlir, D. (2017). Redemption of the "spoiled identity": the role of HIV-positive individuals in HIV care cascade interventions. *Journal of the International AIDS Society*, 20:e25023.

Csicsmann, L. and Vékony, D. (2010). Muslims In Hungary: A Bridge Between East and West? In J. Hunterová & H. Suchardová, *Muslims in Visegrad* (pp. 57–71). Institute of International Relations, Prague.

Dialmy, A. (2007). Belonging and Institution in Islam. *Social Compass*, 54(1), 63–75.

Dziekan, M. (2000). *Tatarzy – polscy muzułmanie*. Jednota, 8–9, 41–44.

Dziekan, M. (2011). History and culture of Polish Tatars. In K. Górak-Sosnowska (Ed.), *Muslims in Poland and Eastern Europe. Widening the European Discourse on Islam* (pp. 27–39). University of Warsaw.

Fraser, S., and C. Treloar (2006). 'Spoiled identity' in hepatitis C infection: The binary logic of despair. *Critical Public Health*, 16(2), 99–110.

Gomółka, K. (2016). *Polityka Polski wobec studentów, doktorantów i stażystów z państw poradzieckich*. Wydawnictwo Adam Marszałek.

Górak-Sosnowska, K. (2014). *Deconstructing Islamophobia in Poland. Story of an Internet Group*. University of Warsaw.

Górak-Sosnowska, K. & Łyszczarz, M. (2018). Can a Tatar move out of Islam?, In K. van Nieuwkerk (Ed.), *Moving in and out of Islam* (pp. 162–175). Texas University Press.

Grossman, A. (1997). Growing Up with a "Spoiled Identity". *Journal of Gay & Lesbian Social Services*, 6(3), 45–56.

Grzymała-Moszczynska, H. & Trojanek, M. (2011). Image of the world and themselves built by young Chechens living in Polish refugee centers. Intercultural conflict.

In K. Górak-Sosnowska (Ed.), *Muslims in Poland and Eastern Europe. Widening the European Discourse on Islam* (pp. 69–88). University of Warsaw.

GUS (2002). *Raport z wyników Narodowego Spisu Powszechnego Ludności i Mieszkań 2002*. Główny Urząd Statystyczny. https://stat.gov.pl/spisy-powszechne/narodowe-spisy-powszechne/narodowy-spis-powszechny-2002/raport-z-wynikow-narodowego-spisu-powszechnego-ludnosci-i-mieszkan-2002,3,1.html.

GUS (2015). *Struktura narodowo-etniczna, językowa i wyznaniowa ludności Polski. Narodowy Spis Powszechny Ludności i Mieszkań 2011*. Główny Urząd Statystyczny. https://stat.gov.pl/spisy-powszechne/nsp-2011/nsp-2011-wyniki/struktura-narodowo-etniczna-jezykowa-i-wyznaniowa-ludnosci-polski-nsp-2011,22,1.html.

GUS (2019). *Wyznania religijne w Polsce w latach 2015–2018*. Główny Urząd Statystyczny. https://stat.gov.pl/obszary-tematyczne/inne-opracowania/wyznania-religijne/wyznania-religijne-w-polsce-20152018,5,2.html.

GUS (2019b). *Rocznik demograficzny 2019*. Główny Urząd Statystyczny. https://stat.gov.pl/obszary-tematyczne/roczniki-statystyczne/roczniki-statystyczne/rocznik-demograficzny-2019,3,13.html.

Harbut, J. (1929). *Generał Bem w Turcji*. Książnica-Atlas.

Harris, A. (1976). Race, Commitment to Deviance, and Spoiled Identity. *American Sociological Review*, 41(3), 432–442.

Hepburn, J. (1977). Official Deviance and Spoiled Identity: Delinquents and Their Significant Others. The Pacific Sociological Review, 20(2), 163–179.

Heck, G. (2006). *Charlemagne, Muhammad, and the Arab Roots of Capitalism*. Walter de Gruyer.

Kamocki, J. (2000). Zderzenie obyczajów i zwyczajów muzułmańskich Tatarów ze zwyczajami ludowymi chrześcijańskiej ludności polskiej. In *Orient w kulturze polskiej. Materiały z sesji jubileuszowej z okazji 25-lecia Muzeum Azji i Pacyfiku w Warszawie. 15–16 października 1998*. (pp. 139–144). Wydawnictwo Akademickie Dialog.

Kopanski, A. (2009). Muslim Communities of the European North-Eastern Frontiers: Islam in the Former Polish-Lithuanian Commonwealth. In C. Marcinkowski (Ed.), *The Islamic World and the West. Managing Religious and Cultural Identities in the Age of Globalisation* (pp. 85–108). Lit Verlag & University of Malaya.

Kościelniak, K. (2016). *Muzułmanie Polscy. Religia i kultura*. Wydawnictwo M.

Kroll, P. (2013, October 25). *Polish Converts to Islam in the Service of the Sultan*. Pałac Wilanów. https://www.wilanow-palac.pl/polish_converts_to_islam_in_the_service_of_the_sultan.html.

Krzywy, R. (2012, March 12). *Paradoksy szlacheckiego orientalizmu*. https://www.wilanow-palac.pl/paradoksy_szlacheckiego_orientalizmu.html.

Lesińska, M. (2018). Polska diaspora, polonia, emigracja. Spory pojęciowe wokół skupisk polskich za granicą. *Polski Przegląd Migracyjny*, 1(3), 9–23.
Łyszczarz, M. (2011). Generational changes among young Tatars. In K. Górak-Sosnowska (Ed.), *Muslims in Poland and Eastern Europe. Widening the European Discourse on Islam* (pp. 53–68). University of Warsaw.
Miśkiewicz, A. (1990). *Tatarzy polscy 1918–1939. Życie społeczno-kulturalne i religia*. Państwowe Wydawnictwo Naukowe.
Miśkiewicz, A. et al. (2017). *Słownik biograficzny Tatarów polskich XX wieku*. Muzułmański Związek Religijny w RP.
Mondon, A. & Winter, A. (2019). Mapping and mainstreaming Islamophobia: between the illiberal and liberal. In I. Zempi & I. Awan (Eds.), *The Routledge International Handbook of Islamophiobia* (pp. 58–70). Routledge.
Moosavi, L. (2015). White privilege in the lives of Muslim converts in Britain. *Ethnic and Racial Studies*, 38(11), 1918–1933. https://doi.org/10.1080/01419870.2014.952751.
Nalborczyk, A. (2011). Mosques in Poland. Past and present. In K. Górak-Sosnowska (Ed.), *Muslims in Poland and Eastern Europe. Widening the European Discourse on Islam* (pp. 183–193). University of Warsaw.
Nowaczek-Walczak, M. (2011). The world of kebab. Arabs and gastronomy in Warsaw. In K. Górak-Sosnowska (Ed.), *Muslims in Poland and Eastern Europe. Widening the European Discourse on Islam* (pp. 108–125). University of Warsaw.
MFiPR (2019, August 30). *Kongres 60 milionów łączy Polaków i Polonię z całego świata*. Ministry of Development Funds and Regional Policy. https://www.gov.pl/web/fundusze-regiony/kongres-60-milionow-laczy-polakow-i-polonie-z-calego-swiata.
Pędziwiatr, K. (2011). "The Established and Newcomers" in Islam in Poland or the inter-group relations within the Polish Muslim community. In K. Górak-Sosnowska (Ed.), *Muslims in Poland and Eastern Europe. Widening the European Discourse on Islam* (pp. 169–182). University of Warsaw.
Podolska, J. (1996). Pielgrzymi polscy w Ziemi Świętej 1350–1450. *Peregrinus cracoviensis*, 4, 213–223.
Račius, E. (2020). *Muslims in Eastern Europe*. Edinburgh University Press.
Rogowska, B. (2017). *Wpływ Polaków nawróconych na islam na społeczności lokalne w Polsce* [Unpublished doctoral dissertation]. University of Łódź.
Schuurman, P. (2020). Redeeming a Spoiled Identity: Purge Sunday at the Anabaptist Megachurch. *Liturgy*, 35(2), 3–10.
Stawiński, P. (1994). *Ahmadijja – islam zreforomowany*. Wyższa Szkoła Pedagogiczna w Częstochowie.
Stoica, D. (2011). New Romanian Muslimas. Converted women sharing knowledge in online and offline communities. In K. Górak-Sosnowska (Ed.), *Muslims in Poland*

and Eastern Europe. Widening the European Discourse on Islam (pp. 266–287). University of Warsaw.

Sulimirski, T. (1970). *The Sarmatians*. Praeger.

Switat, M. (2017). *Społeczność arabska w Polsce. Stara i nowa diaspora*. Wydawnictwo Akademickie Dialog.

UK Office for National Statistics (2014, November 25). *Census – Country of birth by year of arrival by religion – England and Wales*. https://webarchive.national archives.gov.uk/ukgwa/20160110200016mp_/http://www.ons.gov.uk/ons/about-ons /business-transparency/freedom-of-information/what-can-i-request/published-ad -hoc-data/census/ethnicity/ct0265-2011-census.xls.

Warmińska, K. (1999). *Tatarzy polscy. Tożsamość religijna i etniczna*. Universitas.

Wexler, P. (1996). *The Non-Jewish Origins of the Sephardic Jews*. State University of New York Press.

Wigginton, B., and M. Lafrance (2016). How do women manage the spoiled identity of a 'pregnant smoker'? An analysis of discursive silencing in women's accounts. *Feminism & Psychology*, 26(1), 30–51.

CHAPTER 2

# The Socio-Demographic Profile of Survey Respondents

*Katarzyna Górak-Sosnowska* | ORCID: 0000-0002-1121-6240
SGH Warsaw School of Economics

## Introduction

The estimates of the number of converts to Islam in Poland vary significantly, indicating between several hundreds and several thousands. So far there have been only a few quantitative surveys of Polish female converts to Islam – mostly student dissertations. For instance, Pawlik, (2007) conducted a study among Polish females who married Muslim men. Out of the 243 respondents, 39% were Muslim. Górak-Sosnowska's (2015) sample in a study on Polish female convert Internet activity totalled 47 individuals. The largest quantitative study of Polish female converts to Islam with 171 respondents was conducted by Rogowska (2017) as a part of her PhD thesis on convert involvement in local communities; 124 of her respondents were women. Several qualitative studies were published as articles (Łojek-Magdziarz, 2007; Pędziwiatr, 2017), chapters (Rzepecka, 2001; Krotofil, 2011), and two monographs (Dudek, 2016; Ryszewska, 2018). This brief overview of existing studies on Polish female converts to Islam indicates that reaching more than a hundred of respondents presents a challenge. Moreover, due to the lack of sampling framework, it is impossible to draw a representative sample of Polish female converts to Islam.

It is likely that some of the respondents have participated in more than one research study. We personally know most of the authors mentioned above and share social networks with them. Moreover, based on their published methodologies, it is likely that many researchers have used similar places of participant recruitment – especially in Poland. Examples of such places include the local mosques and Islamic centres located in the largest cities, as well as events in which Muslims participate – such as the Muslim Reunion, an annual event organised by the Muslim League, attended by both Muslims of migrant origin and converts to Islam. As regards the questionnaires distributed online, there are also some prominent groups and forums that are frequently mined by researchers. The Muslim community in Poland is so small that if an extensive qualitative study about Polish female converts to Islam is published, often the participants are able to guess who was interviewed – even if the data was anonymised.

In our survey we asked the respondents whether they had participated in another study; and over half of them had, at least once. As the number of studies on Polish converts to Islam is relatively small and fairly easy to keep track of, this brings two methodological issues; one, we risked relying on the same respondents as other researchers. Thus, it was of significance to ensure that the questions we asked were different from those asked in previous studies with this population. The second one is that a significant proportion of our sample could be labelled as 'duty Muslims' or 'everyday explainers' (Harris and Hussein, 2018), that is, people who are often recruited to participate in research. Here, we are not going to present a representative picture of all Polish female converts to Islam, but rather, some insights about our qualitative and quantitative study participants. (Some of our interviewees declared that they had also completed the questionnaire.)

There were 127 respondents in our study. Seventy-five completed the whole survey questionnaire, and fifty-two left some questions unanswered. The questionnaire, designed with the use of online software, was placed on the project website. The questionnaire we developed was lengthy – the maximum number of entries was 259. We decided to use such a wide brushstroke approach, because we knew that the female converts population was very diverse. In this chapter, we focus on the basic descriptive data to draw up a social and religious profile of our respondents.

## Demographic Profile

Our respondents are Polish women who converted to Islam. Most of them are between twenty and fifty years old, including fifty-three respondents in their 30s, thirty-two in their 40s, and thirty-one in their 20s. Ten respondents are over fifty years old and only one is younger than twenty. The average age of our respondents is thirty-six. Most of them embraced Islam in their twenties (sixty-four respondents), or thirties (twenty-seven respondents). Twenty respondents converted to Islam at an age younger than twenty, and twelve were over forty years old, as illustrated below.

In most cases, conversion occurred after reaching legal adulthood (which in Poland is marked by reaching the age of eighteen), and the average age at conversion was twenty-seven. Overall, conversion is not, therefore, an adolescent phenomenon, dovetailing with findings of other studies on conversion to Islam in Europe (Köse, 1997).

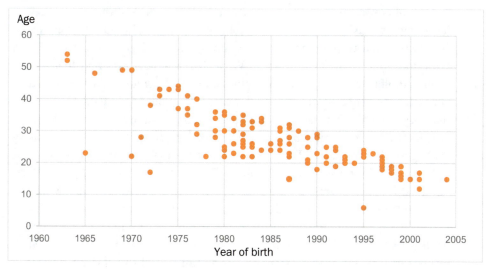

FIGURE 1   Age at conversion by year of birth
SOURCE: PROJECT SURVEY DATA

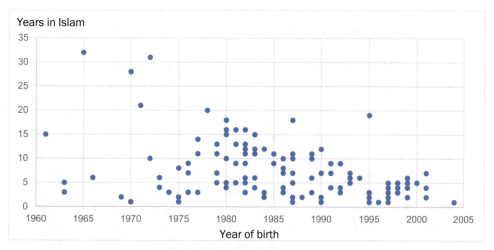

FIGURE 2   Years in Islam by year of birth
SOURCE: PROJECT SURVEY DATA

At the time of the data collection, most of our respondents had been Muslims up to ten years, with forty-four respondents – between five and ten years, and thirty-five respondents – less than five years. Thirty-six respondents had been Muslims for over ten years, including six who embraced Islam over twenty years earlier, as the chart below illustrates.

Most of our respondents are converts in the literal sense of the word – they have converted to Islam from another religion, most often Roman Catholicism (109 cases). Ten respondents indicated no previous religion, two had been Protestant, one Orthodox, and one Wicca. Three others indicated that had been Catholic, but later became areligious and, finally, embraced Islam. Asked about their current religious self-identification, 110 of our respondents declared that they were Muslim, eleven as Sunni, one as Shia, while three chose different identities – European, Polish and "a believer". We further explore the paths leading to Islam and the different types of religious identities in Chapter 7.

Polish female converts to Islam who participated in our study are predominantly well-educated, middle class and live in large cities. Approximately half have a university degree (59) and the other half completed secondary-level education (56). 9 have completed vocational education programmes. Our respondents work full-time (53), are university students (22), and some run their own businesses (15). Twenty-four respondents do not work in paid employment. Most of those who do, are employed in professional positions (46), and many are executives (23). Thirteen are blue-collar workers. Our respondents work mostly in services, education, healthcare, commerce and administration. The sample corresponds with the profile of converts to Islam offered by several studies conducted among female converts to Islam in the West (Roald, 2006, p. 48; Badran, 2006, p. 197; van Nieuwkerk, 2006, p. 95).

Fifty-seven of our respondents live in a city of over 0.5 million inhabitants. One should take into account the urban landscape of Poland. The biggest city is Warsaw with 1.7 million inhabitants and there are only five more cities with over 500,000 inhabitants. Only six respondents live in small towns or villages of less than twenty thousand inhabitants. Others live in cities below 100,000 inhabitants (23) and villages up to 500 inhabitants (37). Interestingly, a significant proportion of our respondents (54) live outside of Poland. They live mostly in other European countries – the UK (34), but also in Germany (10). Other countries of residence include Belgium, France, Italy, the Netherlands, Spain and Sweden. A few live in Muslim-majority countries – Lebanon, Pakistan, Morocco, Qatar and United Arab Emirates. The large number of converts living abroad indicates clearly that one cannot speak about this group only in the Polish setting. This way we could exclude a significant number of Polish female converts who are Polish or consider themselves Polish, yet they live abroad. In order to complement our Polish-centric picture we decided to introduce a sample of Polish converts who live in the UK – the second biggest country in terms of the size of the Polish female converts community, according to our study.

The high number of Polish female converts to Islam who live outside of Poland seems to be explained by two reasons. The first one is the marginal number of Muslims in Poland – this makes potential encounters with Islam unlikely. The second one is that Poles are mobile. It is estimated that Poles were the second largest group of EU mobile citizens, with over 1 million living in other EU countries (Eurostat, 2021). Studies on Polish female converts to Islam generally focus on the women who live in Poland. While it is hard to estimate the number of Polish converts to Islam, many of them live in other European countries, mostly in Western Europe. This can definitely change the religious landscape of Polish Islam, as Polish converts communicate in Polish and maintain transnational social networks, regardless of the physical place of residence (Górak-Sosnowska, 2015). It is by no mean exceptional; the same pattern has been observed by Račius (2011) among Lithuanian converts to Islam, and across Central and Eastern Europe, in countries with marginal Muslim populations (Račius, 2020).

Most of our respondents are married (76), eighteen have a partner. Twenty-three respondents are single. The most frequent countries of origin of the husbands or partners are: Algeria (14), Egypt (11), and Poland (11). Other countries of husbands' origin include: Morocco (8), Pakistan (6), India (4), Jordan (4), Libya (3), Palestine (3), Bangladesh (2), Lebanon (2), Saudi Arabia (2), and Turkey (2). Kenya, Iran, Iraq, Macedonia, Somalia, Syria, and Tunisia each were countries of origin of one husband. There are also two British and one Belgian-Moroccan husband. Women who live in Poland often have Polish (10) or Egyptian (9) husbands or partners. Over half of the participants have taken the last name of their husband.

Most of those who are married, were married in both civil (state) and Islamic marriage ceremonies. Marital patterns of Polish female converts to Islam differ based on the country of residence. Out of the twenty-three single participants, eighteen live in Poland and five in other EU countries. Participants who live in Poland are more likely to cohabitate (fifteen, compared to three respondents in other EU countries). Outside of Poland, the option of entering Islamic marriage only (no civil ceremony) is more popular (10) among the respondents than in Poland (3). The vast majority of our respondents' husbands or partners are Muslim (81), and only nine are non-Muslim. Only those respondents who live in Poland have non-Muslim husbands or partners.

The much higher proportion of single female converts in Poland may be caused by limited possibilities of finding a Muslim spouse in Poland. Additionally, the conversion pattern in Poland is usually not related to a relationship or interactions with Muslims. Poland is culturally a largely homogenous country, and the dominant desire regarding cultural "Others" is their assimilation rather than integration (Zick et al., 2011). In West European countries, Muslim minorities may exert stronger pressure on their members to get married.

Polish is the dominant language in which respondents' families communicate. It was selected by eighty respondents. At the same time, sixty-six respondents also use foreign languages to communicate with their family members, including their husband and his family, and sometimes also with their children. Among these, English is the most prevalent language of communication (39), followed by German (8). Other European languages include French, Dutch, Spanish and Italian. A handful of respondents communicate in Arabic (6); other languages used in Muslim-majority countries include Turkish, Urdu and Kurdish. Sometimes, respondents communicate in several different languages – Polish, a European language and a language used in a Muslim-majority country. In the case of respondents who live in Poland, most of them use Polish only (52), but a significant minority communicate in English (14) and two in Arabic. In the case of respondents who live in European countries the linguistic diversity is much broader, twenty-five communicate in Polish, and twenty in English. Among the respondents who live in a Muslim-majority country, four use English, two – Polish, two – Arabic and one a mix of Arabic, Polish and Spanish.

The political profile of our respondents is intriguing, compared to the mainstream Polish society. We asked them about their political views and voting preferences. Our respondents were free to choose all political options that fit to their views, and so they could have selected more than one. Around half of our respondents consider themselves to be liberals, a third identify as feminist and another third identify as leftist. There are also small but visible groups of respondents who declare being centrist, conservative, and right-wing.

It appears that our respondents declare mostly liberal/leftist/feminist views,[1] which are on the one hand less visible among Polish mainstream population and on the other, not attributed to them in the mainstream Polish discourse about Muslims. Since 2015, the Polish political scene has been dominated by the right-wing conservative Law and Justice (Prawo i Sprawiedliwość) party, which has now won the majority in the Polish Parliament twice and secured

---

1 Certainly, the political labels used here, and the attempt to align political parties with political views have to be both viewed with caution. The concepts of right- or left-wing are hard to define in Western context, but in Central and Eastern Europe it is even more challenging due to the regions' post-communist past. Given this context, the division between the right and the left becomes a matrix of three layers: the economic (the role of the state in the economy), the cultural (the attitude to "traditional" Polish values) and the historical (approach to the communist legacy; Pająk-Patkowska, 2010) ones.

the position of the president. The largest opposition party is the centrist-liberal Civic Coalition (Koalicja Obywatelska). Other political options are represented by small, yet significant minorities in Polish parliament. Asked which political party they would vote for in the upcoming elections, almost half of our respondents declared that they had not chosen any political party. Out of those who had picked a political party, the two most popular were Civic Coalition and the Left (Lewica). The political and ideological profile of our respondents differs significantly from the Polish mainstream. Moreover, their views seem to contradict the stereotypical image of Islam and Muslims. They self-identify as liberal (whereas Islam is often deemed as inherently conservative), feminist (challenging the perceptions of the status of women in Islam) and leftist.

### Embracing Islam

Becoming Muslim is an individual decision but has significant social consequences for the individual in question. Converts to Islam have to negotiate their new religion with themselves and their social circles (Duderija & Rune, 2019). In the following parts of the questionnaire, we have asked them about issues that are linked to their formal religious status as Muslims, religious practices, and how their religion is perceived by their significant others and wider society.

Most of our respondents have not formally left the Catholic Church by declaring apostasy.[2] Only six of them admitted to having become apostates. Thus, the. majority are still formally members of Catholic Church. Most state that they do not consider it important. They do not feel any connection to the Catholic faith, and do not care if they are considered members of the Catholic Church. Some of our respondents have not formally abandoned the Catholic Church for family reasons. Leaving the Church in Poland is a burdensome procedure as one must declare apostasy in writing, provide the original certification of baptism, and attend a meeting with the parish priest. Such a meeting is sometimes unpleasant, even for non-Muslims. Two of our respondents indicated that they attempted to leave Church but were treated by the priest who saw them in an offensive manner and gave up mid-process.

---

2  The phenomenon of apostasy is becoming more pronounced in Poland, but detailed data is unavailable, because the Church does not make its records public regularly. According to the Polish Institute of Statistics of the Catholic Church (ISKK, n.d.), in 2010 there were 459 Poles who formally left the Catholic Church. An online "apostasy counter" indicated 2713 apostasies between December 2020 and November 2022 – see: https://mapaapostazji.pl.

Changing religion significantly impacts respondents' dress, diet and daily practices, as well as religiosity style. Before conversion, around half were not religious. After conversion, all but one respondents declare they are religious. Most engage in Islamic practices – the five *arkan al-din* – the basic acts of faith considered obligatory in Islam. They give *zakat* (most of them, as much as is prescribed in Islam), they fast in the holy month of Ramadan (and again, most of them as much as it is prescribed), and they perform the five daily prayers (sometimes fewer times than five). Compared to these three pillars, relatively few of our respondents have gone on *hajj*, the pilgrimage to Mecca: 12 have performed *hajj*, and 44 are planning to travel to Mecca one day. There are only a few respondents who declare that they are not pracitising.

Almost all of our respondents celebrate the two most important Islamic holidays – *'Eid al-Fitr* and *'Eid al-Adha*. Several celebrate *Ashura* (the Shia holiday commemorating the death of Al-Husayn) and *Mawlid* (the birthday of Prophet Muhammad). Some celebrate non-Islamic holidays, both religious and secular. Four out of ten celebrate Christmas, three out of ten – Easter, and two out of ten – the All Souls' Day. In these cases, celebrating means active celebration and participation. Christmas in Poland is perceived not only as a religious holiday, but most of all (and despite its religious character) – a family holiday (CBOS, 2019). Easter plays a similar role. Celebrating these holidays gives the respondents an opportunity to meet their close family, as a matter of upholding Polish tradition. Moreover, the respondents celebrate secular holidays. The Independence Day is celebrated by four out of ten our participants and the Women's Day – by three out of ten. Christmas and Easter are celebrated more often by the respondents who live in Poland. On the other hand, the Independence Day is celebrated more by those who live abroad.

Embracing Islam transforms value systems. Some norms or values accepted in secular environments can be considered morally wrong in Islam. Therefore, we asked our respondents whether certain actions are morally permissible. We selected issues fiercely debated in Poland, as well as those which are opposed based on traditional Islamic jurisprudence. Most respondents find the following acceptable: using contraceptives, in vitro reproduction, donating organs for transplantation, and male circumcision. Our respondents differ on the issues of: abortion, polygamy and death penalty. Same-sex marriage, euthanasia, cohabitation and vaccine refusal are believed to be immoral by most of our respondents. Social issues such as abortion, in vitro are currently hotly debated in Poland (Desperak, 2003; Mishtal, 2015; 2019; Kozub-Karkut, 2017), some of them – like same-sex marriage – do not even reach the level of public debate (Libura, 2009).

The respondents are selective in communicating their new faith. In all but four cases, the closest family know about their conversion. Some distant relatives and acquaintances may be informed. People with whom they live in the same building or work usually know about their conversion. two out of three respondents believe that their non-Muslim family accept their decision to embrace Islam. After coming out as Muslims, converts might become 'intimate strangers' to their closest family and friends, resulting in a painful experience of alienation (Ramahi & Suleiman, 2017).

Over two thirds have changed their diet and dress style. Over half of them have changed their lifestyle and relationship with unrelated males, and around a half – their friends. Changing diet or style of dress might mean different things in different context. In Poland, halal food is much harder to obtain and wearing the hijab is makes one more conspicuous than in culturally diverse societies of Western Europe. Some respondents eat only halal food, several exclude pork and/or alcohol, and some are vegetarians. Clothing-wise, respondents use a wide range of styles to abide by their new religion. Over half wear long trousers with a tunic or long skirts, another half wear loose clothing. Less than half wear the hijab. Other styles and accessories are far less popular with a handful of respondents wearing abayas, turbans, and just three – the niqab. The hijab is much more popular among those who live abroad, compared to those who live in Poland. We elaborate more on these embodied religious practices of Polish female converts to Islam in Chapter 6.

While there can be many reasons for wearing or not wearing the hijab, one is definitely to do with the sense of security. The respondents who live in Poland feel significantly less secure wearing the hijab or other Islamic attire at school, at work or generally in public. Many respondents who live outside of Poland declared that they do not wear the hijab in Poland but do so abroad. Some of them switch to a turban or other, less conspicuous head coverings, while others do not wear hijab at all in order to avoid negative reactions. While we are aware that veiled women in West European countries attract unwanted social and political attention, and often face Islamophobic prejudice (Almila, 2019; Bowen, 2007; Piela, 2021), being veiled may be even more challenging in Poland. Living in Poland appears to make the experience of being Muslim less comfortable. Poland-based respondents experience alienation due to being the only Muslim in their social networks. At the same time, respondents are exposed to a great deal of Islamophobic narratives in the media, regardless of their location. Respondents who live outside of Poland are accused more often of "betraying Poland" by embracing Islam than those living in Poland. The charge of "betraying the Catholic faith" is levelled at respondents in both subsets equally frequently. Chapter 4 reflects further on Polish Islamophobia and how does it impact identity management strategies of Polish female converts to Islam.

## Social Activity of Polish Female Converts to Islam

Polish female converts to Islam constitute a minority within a minority (van Bommel, 2006), both in Poland and abroad. They are a minority among Polish Muslims who also comprise the indigenous Polish Muslims, the Tatars, as well as Polish Muslims of migrant origin. They are also underrepresented in Polish Muslim religious associations. Abroad, they are additionally immigrants. This positions them as outsiders in relation to majority Muslims. They share the same religion, interact regularly and learn together.

Before we analyse their interactions within the Islamic community, let us begin with those within the mainstream society. Most of our respondents socialize with both Muslims and non-Muslims. Most have non-Muslim acquaintances and even close friends.[3] There is a visible gender pattern. Only three out of 127 respondents have no female non-Muslim acquaintances (compared to 104 who have some or many) and only seven have no non-Muslim close friend (unlike 98 others who do). As far as socializing with non-Muslim males is concerned, these interactions are less frequent – 25 respondents have no male, non-Muslim acquaintances whereas 53 have no male, non-Muslim close friends. At the same time, 33 respondents have several close non-Muslim male friends and 17 have many.

The same gendered pattern organizes interactions with Muslim close friends and acquaintances, with women being selected as friends more often than men. Muslim male friends are only slightly more popular than non-Muslim male friends with 14 out of 127 respondents who have no Muslim male acquaintances and 41 respondents who have no Muslim male friends. Only 5 respondents indicated they had no female Muslim acquaintances and 22 – no female Muslim friends.

Respondents tend to have more non-Muslim female friends and acquaintances than Muslim ones. Almost all of our respondents have at least some non-Muslim female acquaintances, and non-Muslims are close friends more frequently than Muslims. This is not surprising, as that Polish converts to Islam

---

3   We are using Polish word *przyjaciel* the equivalent of a 'close friend' in English, rather than just *a* friend, the equivalent of *znajomy* in Polish (yet we are using acquaintance to differentiate between these two types of relationship) – see Wierzbicka (1997).

live in a non-Muslim-majority society and they naturally interact more with non-Muslims than Muslims. It is possible that Polish female converts to Islam do not consider shared faith to be the ultimate factor when investing in friendships. We do not know whether friendships with non-Muslims are from the time before the conversion (as pre-conversion friends may find it challenging to accept the new faith; Duderija & Rune, 2019, p. 152). The collected data does shed some light on social lives of Polish female converts to Islam.

Polish female converts to Islam have relatively limited opportunities for meeting other Muslims. They mostly meet them in informal settings and through their own efforts. The two most important social venues are Muslim local communities and the Internet. The latter is especially important for female converts who live in Poland (28 indicated that they often meet other Muslims this way, compared to only two respondents living in other European countries). While the online space also plays a significant role in enabling identity performance and socializing for non-Polish Muslims, (Piela, 2010; 2015), it seems that in Poland it is even more important. Many Polish female converts lack the access to other Muslims, as there are no local Muslim communities where they live. Only a handful of respondents indicated that they met new Muslim friends at meetings and events hosted by Muslim organisations.

Our respondents feel largely accepted by born Muslims. Only a few complain that they are not perceived as "real Muslims" and report discrimination by born Muslims. At the same time, most of our respondents socialize more with born Muslims than with other converts. It might be due to the minority status of the convert community, but also internal divisions within the convert section of the Polish ummah (Górak-Sosnowska, 2015). The warm relations between Polish converts to Islam and born Muslims can be also attributed to the background of immigrant Muslims living in Poland. Many of them graduated from Polish universities and secured employment, subsequently integrating, or even assimilating with the mainstream Polish society. While there are cultural differences between born Muslims (and their diverse backgrounds) and the Polish converts, born Muslims of migrant are perceived as well educated and integrated.[4]

According to our survey, most respondents participate in activities organised by the local ummah. Some of them are offered by local Muslim organisations, but often they are grassroots activities. These include mostly *Jumu'ah* prayers and meetings after these prayers, *taraweeh* prayers (during Ramadan),

---

4   This perception is in strong contrast to German converts' views about born Muslims living in Germany. The former believe that the latter should be better educated, integrated, and "theologically reformed" (Özyürek 2010: 174).

and *iftars*. Other activities include *halaqa* (studying Qur'an), *I'tikaf* (night prayers at mosque), *mawlid* (Prophet's birthday) and *dhikr* (reciting the name of God). Some of our respondents indicate that they have very limited opportunities to participate in such events as the closest mosque may be located hundreds of miles away.

Relatively few respondents (8) formally belong to a Muslim organisation. Three belong to the Muslim League, and one to each of the following: the Centre for Islamic Culture in Warsaw, the Association of Polish Muslims, Halaqa, the Association of Muslim Students in Duisburg and the UK-based Women of Faith. Except the Muslim League, none of the other organisations have a legal status of a religious association as defined by the Polish law. This means that legally, most of these organisations are just regular associations – as thousands of other associations in Poland. As such, they do not enjoy financial privileges granted to religious organisations in Poland, including significant tax exemptions and state subsidies[5] (Skorek, 2017). Only the Muslim League can be represent Polish female converts to Islam as religious believers. All but the Association of Muslim Students in Duisburg are Polish organisations (run by Poles or residents of Poland; all of them are based in Poland except Women of Faith in the UK).

The marginal engagement of Polish female converts with formal Muslim religious associations is not unusual. In fact, the majority of European Muslims are not members of such organisations and, as a consequence, are underrepresented in the public discourse (Akbarzadeh and Roose, 2011). However, a lack of commitment to Muslim organisations may be related to the fact that they are negatively perceived by Muslims themselves. Most of our respondents believe that the interests of Muslims in Poland are not represented well enough (43 out of 127). Twelve believe that the interests are represented well only by individual Muslim activists. Only nine respondents believe that Muslim organisations represent well the interests of Polish Muslims.

Strikingly, a significant minority are members of an organisation (24 respondents, compared to 51 who are not), but only nine of them are members of a Muslim organisation. Over half were engaged in voluntary work in the year prior to completing the survey. It means that Polish female converts to Islam have the potential to contribute to the umma as they do for their local communities. Moreover, our respondents are active ambassadors of Islam. They actively engage with non-Muslims to explain Islam. Almost all are occasionally asked by strangers about Islam. A third published content related to Islam on the Internet. A fifth gave an interview about Islam to a journalist, and – as

---

5   See also the *Polish Official Gazette*, 2005, no. 231, item 1965.

mentioned in the introduction – over half participated in another study related to Islam. Polish female converts often organise events – over half of respondents stated that they had organised events for Muslims and non-Muslims.

### Sources of Islamic Knowledge

The concept of knowledge in Islam transcends the academic understanding of acquiring, processing and producing information. Learning is an Islamic duty and Arabic term *'ilm* is often contrasted with *jahl* – ignorance, referring to the pre-Islamic Arabia (Solihu, 2014: 25). In our study the sources of Islamic knowledge are important for one more reason, namely the small number of Muslims living in Poland and a lack of Islamic knowledge infrastructure. There are only a few purpose-built mosques across the country (two in Tatar villages located in the east of Poland, two in Warsaw and one in Gdansk). In some cities, Muslims congregate in Islamic cultural centres (that intentionally aim to provide more services than a mosque, such as outreach) for example the Kraków one. There are approximately 8 locations in Poland where formal religious instruction for Muslim students is organised and delivered. In order to participate in a collective prayer, or a program of study, many Polish Muslims would have to travel hundreds of miles. One could easily be the only Muslim in their town or village.

Most of our respondents first came into contact with Islam by meeting a Muslim outside a Muslim-majority country (36). Only 7 respondents indicated that they had first encountered Islam while travelling to an Islamic country. Other 32 respondents first encountered Islam without any interactions with a Muslim. 15 respondents in that subgroup first learnt about Islam from the Internet, 14 from literature (mostly academic) and 3 in classes (at school or at university).

In Western Europe we observe two forms of Islamic knowledge production and dissemination: the classical one – top-down, where knowledge is delivered at a local Islamic centre, a mosque, or a dedicated educational institution and production and exchange with active involvement of all stakeholders (van Bruinessen, 2010). In Poland, the former has limited scope due to the scant Islamic infrastructure. Thus the converts have to rely on their own study and interpretation of Islamic sources. The individually accessed textual source of knowledge about Islam that is used most frequently is the Qur'an (in a Polish or an English translation). Other sources of Islamic knowledge are used by just over a half of our respondents. These include information gleaned from the Internet, (groups/forums for Muslims and websites about Islam), other

Muslims such as one's husband or friends, and literature (both academic and published by religious organisations). The majority of converts in our sample (49) use sources of information in a language different than Polish, mostly English. Only 28 respondents indicated that they used Polish textual sources to learn about Islam.

In her study on Romanian converts, Stoica (2011) indicates that online Islamic environments serve as an important repository of Islamic knowledge for Eastern European converts due to limited contact with other Muslims and no access to Islamic infrastructure. For Polish converts, online environments are an important space for acquiring Islamic knowledge, but also a space for meeting fellow Muslims. While there are sometimes ideological clashes between Polish Muslims who have different perspectives, the online environment offers Polish converts a sense of belonging (Górak-Sosnowska, 2015). There are dozens of personal blogs on Facebook, private groups for Muslims, as well as some podcasts and YouTube channels founded by Polish female converts to Islam.

Polish female converts to Islam use resources in Polish and English. The Polish resources include established websites such as Planeta Islam (n.d.) or a blog 'Islam bez tajemnic' (n.d.) ('Islam without secrets') that reaches out to people of all faiths and educates them about Islam. Some of our respondents mentioned the Salafi-oriented website IslamQA (n.d.). Interestingly, there has been no reference of official websites of the Polish Islamic religious associations. All the mentioned Polish websites are grassroots initiatives, some authored anonymously, and some by named Muslim (such as Arkadiusz Miernik, a Polish Shia Imam living in the UK) and non-Muslim authors (the 'Islamista' (n.d.) blog) known in the local or online Polish Muslim community.

The literature used by Polish female converts to Islam is academic and confessional, and variously in Polish or English. Often it is distributed free of charge at mosques, or brochures published by Islamic organisations (often in English or translated into Polish from English or Arabic). These are publications related to certain topics (for example, the status of women in Islam, prayer in Islam), Hadith collections or the theology of Islam more widely. Some of our respondents have also indicated that they study academic literature written by both Muslim and non-Muslim authors. The former include Tariq Ramadan, Tahar Ben Yelloun or Reza Aslan. The latter include the two founders of modern Arabic and Islamic studies in Poland – Janusz Danecki[6] and Marek

---

6   Janusz Danecki is a professor of Arabic and Islamic Studies at the University of Warsaw, and author of pioneering works in Polish on the Arabic grammar, an Arabic-Polish dictionary or the book *Introduction to Islamic studies*. Since 9/11 he has often appeared as an expert on

Dziekan.[7] Asked about the scholars of Islam they consider authoritative, the respondents name mostly English-speaking, internationally known scholars who are Muslim (e.g. Mufti Menk, Zakir Naik, Nouman Ali Khan). Interestingly again, there is no mention of any Polish Muslim scholar in these responses. We expand on the significance of these scholarly influences in Chapter 7.

## Conclusions

By using an online questionnaire, we have been able to draft a socio-religious profile of our research sample. Our respondents are mostly middle-class and live in larger cities. Unlike in Western Europe, many Polish female converts live outside of their home country. There seem to be significant differences in the marital status between converts based on their place of residence. Those who live in Poland are more likely to have a Polish husband, and a spouse more generally than those who live abroad.

Embracing Islam often does not result in formally leaving the Catholic Church. The majority of our respondents are still included in the official statistics as Catholics. This reflects the pattern of religiosity in Poland, where many more people declare anti-clericalism (a stance that is not necessarily correlated with atheism) than there are apostates, and a steadily growing number of Poles turn away from the Church and its teachings (Radzikowska, 2017; Zawadka, 2021). Politically, Polish female converts to Islam are on the left-centrist end of the political spectrum and many of them declare to be liberal or feminist. This alignment significantly deviates from the current majority Polish society and can be explained by a stronger relationship between leftist/liberal views and the critical views of the Roman Catholic Church in Poland (Bąk, 2021). While in the Polish context leftist views are often associated with atheism and rejection of spirituality, our study evidences the existence of a subset of the Polish population that embraces "leftist"/liberal values, such as social justice, women's rights, and separation of religion from the state that is keen to frame these values religiously using a different faith tradition, such as Islam.

Polish female converts to Islam are inclusive in the process of building and maintaining their social networks – both with non-Muslims and Muslims.

---

Islam in the Polish media. He is considered to be one of the most renowned Polish scholars of Islam.
7  Marek Dziekan studied under Danecki and is a professor of Arabic and Islamic Studies at the University of Łódź and the University of Warsaw. He writes about Arab culture, politics and literature. He strongly criticised the invasion of Iraq in the Polish media.

In fact, they have more non-Muslim female friends and acquaintances than Muslim female friends. This might result from the small size of the Muslim community in Poland. However, it can be observed also in the other EU countries where Polish female converts to Islam live. It seems therefore that religion is not the main dimension in network-building. Polish female converts to Islam actively participate in mostly grassroots activities and events led by the local ummah.

Most respondents practice the pillars of Islam. They also celebrate the two most important Islamic holidays – ʿEid al-Fitr and ʿEid al-Adha. Many also participate in Catholic and secular holidays in Poland, especially Christmas (which is considered by many to be a family gathering) and the Day of Independence. Polish female converts to Islam come out as Muslims to their closest family and in those social circles where they interact on a daily basis. Converting to Islam influences the diet, social life, and dress of many Polish female converts. Their dress style is significantly influenced by the place of residence – those who live in Poland tend to report more challenges related to wearing Muslim clothing in public.

Polish female converts to Islam tend to discover Islam in two different ways – through interactions with a Muslim, or through texts. While the sources of knowledge are diverse and include academic literature, online content, and interactions with other Muslims, most of them are in English, not Polish This suggests scarcity of Polish language resources about Islam. The existing ones are either brochures translated from English or Arabic into Polish, or blogs and websites developed by grassroots Muslims. In a similar manner, Polish female converts to Islam tend to follow English-speaking scholars in their search for religious authority.

While our sample does not allow us to draw conclusions that could be generalised onto the whole population of Polish female converts to Islam, our respondents' answers help us elaborate on some unique features of this community. First, Polish female converts to Islam are likely more cosmopolitan the mainstream Polish population. A significant proportion of our respondents live outside of Poland, mostly in the UK. Out of those who are not single, most have partners or husbands who are not ethnically Polish. Many Polish female converts to Islam learn about their religion in English.

Second, our respondents, by virtue of being a small minority, are bound to interact with each other in person, or more often, virtually. This is regardless of the differences in their lifestyles, political views, or perception of religion and religiosity. Moreover, the anti-Muslim attitudes prevalent in the mainstream society strengthen their group solidarity and a sense of belonging in the otherwise troubled and internally divided Polish ummah (Pędziwiatr, 2011).

Third, despite the anti-Muslim sentiments, our respondents remain rooted in Polish society. They maintain family bonds, they have non-Muslim friends – often more numerous than Muslim ones. They want to feel at home in Poland. Being neither Tatar not immigrant Muslim, many of them see themselves as the representatives of Polish Islam.

## References

Akbarzadeh, S. & Roose, J. (2011). Muslims, Multiculturalism and the Question of the Silent Majority. *Journal of Muslim Minority Affairs*, 31(3), 309–325.

Almila, A. (Ed.) (2019). *Veiling in Fashion. Space and the Hijab in Minority Communities*. Bloomsbury.

Badran, M. (2006). Feminism and Conversion. Comparing British, Dutch, and South African Life Stories. In K. van Nieuwker (Ed.). *Women embracing Islam. Gender and conversion in the West*. University of Texas Press.

Bąk, M. (2021, February 8). *Jak PiS wychował „lewaków". W ciągu roku aż dwukrotnie wzrosła liczba młodych Polaków o lewicowych poglądach*. Bezprawnik.pl. https://bezprawnik.pl/lewicowe-poglady-mlodych-polakow/.

van Bommel, A. (2006). Muslim in the Netherlands or Dutch Muslim: a Minority within a Minority. In E. van der Borght (Ed.). *Affirming and Living with Differences* (pp. 101–107). Brill.

Bowen, J. (2007). *Why the French don't like headscarves. Islam, the State, and Public Space*. Princeton University Press.

van Bruinessen, M. (2010). Producing Islamic Knowledge in Western Europe: Discipline, Authority, and Personal Quest. In M. van Bruinessen & S. Allievi (Eds.). *Producing Islamic knowledge: transmission and dissemination in Western Europe* (pp. 1–27). Routledge.

CBOS (2019, December). *Boże Narodzenie 2019. Komunikat z badań. nr 164/2019*. Centrum Badań Opinii Społecznej. http://www.cbos.pl/SPISKOM.POL/2019/K_164_19.PDF.

Desperak, I. (2003). Antykoncepcja, aborcja i ... eutanazja. O upolitycznieniu praw reprodukcyjnych w Polsce. *Acta Universitatis Lodziensis. Folia Sociologica*, 30, 193–207.

Dudek, A. (2016). *Poddaję się. Życie muzułmanek w Polsce*. PWN.

Duderija, A. & Rune, H. (2019). *Islam and Muslims in the West. Major issues and debates*. Palgrave Macmillan.

Eurostat (2021, August). EU citizens living in another Member State – statistical overview, June, https://ec.europa.eu/eurostat/statistics-explained/index.php?title=EU_citizens_living_in_another_Member_State_-_statistical_overview.

Górak-Sosnowska, K. (2015). Between Fitna and the Idyll, Internet forums of Polish female converts to Islam. *HAWWA. Journal of Women of the Middle East and the Islamic World*, 13(3), 344–362.

Harris, A. & Hussein, S. (2018). Conscripts or volunteers? Young Muslims as everyday explainers, *Journal of Ethnic and Migration Studies*, 46(19), 3974–3991. https://doi.org/10.1080/1369183X.2018.1516547.

ISKK (n.d.). Statystyki na temat apostazji w Polsce. Instytut Statystyki Kościoła Katolickiego. Retrieved August 8, 2021, from http://www.iskk.pl/badania/religijnosc/303-statystyki-nt-apostazji-w-polsce.

Islam bez tajemnic (n.d.). Retrieved August, 8, 2021, from http://islambeztajemnic.wordpress.com.

Islam QA (n.d.). Retrieved August, 8, 2021, from http://islamqa.info.

Islamista (n.d.). Retrieved August, 8, 2021, from http://islamistablog.pl.

Köse, A. (1997). Religious Conversion: Is it an adolescent phenomenon? The case of native British converts to Islam. *The International Journal for the Psychology of Religion*, 6(4), 253–262.

Kozub-Karkut, M. (2017). Religia w dyskursie polityki – polski spór o aborcję. *Annales UMCS*, 24(2), 237–255.

Krotofil, J. (2011). 'If I am to be a Muslim, I have to be a good one'. Polish migrant women embracing Islam and reconstructing identity in dialogue with self and others. In K. Górak-Sosnowska (Ed.), *Muslims in Poland and Eastern Europe. Widening the European Discourse on Islam* (pp. 154–168). University of Warsaw.

Libura, A. (2009). Metamorfoza pojęć ważnych społecznie. O próbach zmiany pojęcia małżeństwa w dyskursie na temat homoseksualizmu. *Oblicza komunikacji*, 2, 285–292.

Łojek-Magdziarz, A. (2007). New Islam in Poland – Polish Converts. *ORMA. Revistă destudii etnologice și historicoreligioase*, 6, 55–62.

Mishtal, J. (2015). *The politics of morality: the church, the state, and reproductive rights in postsocialist Poland*. Ohio University Press.

Mishtal, J. (2019). Reproductive Governance and the (Re)definition of Human Rights in Poland. *Medical Anthropology*, 38(2), 182–194.

van Nieuwkerk, K. (2006). Gender, Conversion, and Islam. Online and Offline Conversion Narratives. In K. van Nieuwkerk (Ed.), *Women embracing Islam. Gender and conversion in the West* (pp. 93–119). University of Texas Press. https://doi.org/10.7560/712737-007.

Özyürek, E. (2010). German Converts to Islam and their ambivalent relations with immigrant Muslims. In A. Shyrock (Ed.), *Islamophobia/Islamophilia. Beyond the Politics of Enemy and Friend* (pp. 172–194). Indiana University Press.

Pająk-Patkowska, B. (2010). Wymiar lewica – prawica w Polsce – podziały ideologiczne w polskim społeczeństwie. *Środkowoeuropejskie Studia Polityczne*, 1, 79–96.

Pawlik, K. (2007). Kobieta w rodzinie muzułmańskiej na przykładzie małżeństw Polek z wyznawcami islamu [Unpublished master's thesis]. University of Łódź.

Peppiatt, R. (2011). Women & Islam: The Rise and Rise of the Convert. *The Independent*, 6 November. https://www.independent.co.uk/news/uk/home-news/women-islam-the-rise-and-rise-of-the-convert-6258015.html.

Pędziwiatr, K. (2011). "The Established and Newcomers" in Islam in Poland or the inter-group relations within the Polish Muslim community. In K. Górak-Sosnowska (Ed.), *Muslims in Poland and Eastern Europe. Widening the European Discourse on Islam* (pp. 169–182). University of Warsaw.

Pędziwiatr, K. (2017). Conversions to Islam and Identity Reconfigurations among Poles in Great Britain. *Studia Religiologica*, 50(2), 221–239.

Piela, A. (2010). Muslim Women's Online Discussions of Gender Relations in Islam. *Journal of Muslim Minority Affairs*, 30(3), 425–435. https://doi.org/10.1080/13602004.2010.515827.

Piela, A. (2015). Online Islamic Spaces as Communities of Practice for Female Muslim Converts who Wear the Niqab. *Hawwa. Journal of Women of the Middle East and the Islamic World*, 13(3), 363–382.

Piela, A. (2021). *Wearing the Niqab. Muslim Women in the UK and the US*. Bloomsbury.

Planeta Islam (n.d.). Retrieved August, 8, 2021, from http://planetaislam.com.

Račius, E. (2011). Revival at the expense of survival?. In K. Górak-Sosnowska (Ed.), *Muslims in Poland and Eastern Europe. Widening the European Discourse on Islam* (pp. 207–221). University of Warsaw.

Račius, E. (2020). *Muslims in Eastern Europe*. Edinburgh University Press.

Radzikowska, J. (2017, April 16). *Czy Polska to nadal katolicki kraj?*. Polityka. https://www.polityka.pl/tygodnikpolityka/spoleczenstwo/1611795,1,czy-polska-to-nadal-katolicki-kraj.read.

Ramahi, D. & Suleiman, Y. (2017). Intimate strangers: perspectives on female converts to Islam in Britain. Contemporary Islam, 11, 21–39.

Roald, A. (2006). The Shaping of a Scandinavian "Islam". Converts and Gender Equal Opportunity. In K. van Nieuwkerk (Ed.), *Women embracing Islam. Gender and conversion in the West* (pp. 48–70). University of Texas Press. https://doi.org/10.7560/712737-005.

Rogowska, B. (2017). *Wpływ Polaków nawróconych na islam na społeczności lokalne w Polsce* [Unpublished doctoral dissertation]. University of Łódź.

Ryszewska, M. (2018). *Polskie muzułmanki. W poszukiwaniu tożsamości*. Wydawnictwo Uniwersytetu Mikołaja Kopernika.

Rzepecka, E. (2001). Małżeństwa Polek z wyznawcami islamu. Analiza czynników wpływających dezintegrująco na związki heterogeniczne. In D. Chmielowska, D. Grabowska & E. Machut-Mendecka (Eds.), *Być kobietą w Oriencie.* (pp. 176–201). Wydawnictwo Akademickie Dialog.

Skorek, A. (2017). Finansowanie Kościołów i związków wyznaniowych ze środków publicznych. *Politeja*, 46, 167–190.

Solihu, A. (2014). An Axiological Dimension of Qur'ānic Epistempology. *Ilorin Journal of Religious Studies*, 4(1), 21–38.

Stefańska, O. (2011). *Drogi do islamu. Polskie konwertytki* [Unpublished master's theses]. Warsaw School of Social Sciences and Humanities.

Stoica, D. (2011). New Romanian Muslimas. Converted women sharing knowledge in online and offline communities. In K. Górak-Sosnowska (Ed.), *Muslims in Poland and Eastern Europe. Widening the European Discourse on Islam* (pp. 266–287). University of Warsaw.

Wierzbicka, A. (1997). *Understanding Cultures through their key words: English, Russian, Polish, German, and Japanese.* Oxford University Press.

Zawadka, G. (2021, March 16). *Sondaż: Co młodzi Polacy sądzą o Kościele?* Rzeczpospolita.pl. https://www.rp.pl/Kosciol/303169900-Sondaz-Co-mlodzi-Polacy-sadza-o-Kosciele.html.

Zick, A. et al. (2011). *Intolerance, Prejudice and Discrimination. A European Report.* Friedrich Ebert Stiftung.

CHAPTER 3

# Old and New Connections: Religious and Cultural Belonging Post-conversion among Polish Female Converts to Islam in the UK

*Joanna Krotofil* | ORCID: 0000-0003-2308-5329
Jagiellonian University

## Introduction

In this chapter I explore the specific conditions framing the experiences of Polish converts to Islam who settled in the UK. In the discussion that follows I problematize the relationship between territory, ethnicity, religion and belonging and engage with the concept of multiculturalism in order to link the personal, social and political dimensions of conversion with the concept of spoiled identity and its management. Polish women living in the UK who converted to Islam share a lot with converts in Poland but they also face specific cultural and structural conditions shaping their experiences in unique ways.

The focus on the UK was inspired by the estimates of Muslim leaders and observations of our "insider" experts that the country is home to the largest community of Polish converts to Islam outside of Poland. With the growing network of grass root initiatives and organisations attracting Polish converts, as well as a greater level of "lived multiculturalism" born out of the strong presence of born Muslims with diverse ethnic and cultural backgrounds, the UK can be seen as a different "stage" on which the spoiled identity is formed and managed. By including this location to our data collection we were hoping to identify some contextual factors which might be especially relevant to the development and management of converts' identities, however, it is important to note that the cultural contexts of Poland and the UK could not simply be classified as "home" and "away" in the narratives of our participants. The understanding of culture as a dynamic notion of "a multiplicity of positions among which dialogical relationships can develop" (Hermans, 2001: 243) (as opposed to culture as a static, internally homogeneous entity bounded by nation-state boundaries) means that it would not be productive to frame the experiences of converts in the two countries, as resulting from "cultural differences". While the notion of entity-like cultures is useful in accounting for the formation of explicit cultural identity, it is inadequate when applied to the problem of the embeddedness of the self in the implicit, largely pre-reflexive cultural patterns (Adams and Markus, 2001).

The women whose experiences are the main focus in this chapter, are "not all about Islam" (Jeldtoft, 2011, p. 1135); their lived religious beliefs, practices and identities are at times marked by ambivalence, or overshadowed by other concerns and identities (Schielke, 2009 and 2010). As Yuval-Davis argues, "specific positionings and (not necessarily corresponding) identities and political values are constructed and interrelate and affect each other in particular locations and contexts" (Yuval-Davis, 2006, p. 200). In the analysis presented here I explore personal implications of acquiring the intersecting identities of a migrant from Poland and a Muslim convert, living in the multicultural Britain. I argue that although multiculturalism, tolerance and diversity are frequently referenced and highly valued in the narratives of the study participants, the patterns of engagement with everyday multiculturalism are complex and indicative of some struggles. The experiences of Polish Muslims negotiating their positions in relation to different ethnic and religious groups in the UK, including other Muslims and other Polish migrants, are marked by a high level of ambiguity. The chapter is divided into five sections discussing: 1) the relationship between religion and migration; 2) the differing contexts of everyday life in the UK and in Poland; 3) encounters of the converts in the study with the lived Islam and 4) the reconstruction of the sense of belonging. The discussion presented here focuses on a section of the collected data that encompasses the 23 interviews conducted with Polish converts to Islam who settled in the UK in the last two decades. As discussed in chapter two, the women we spoke with constitute a diverse group with regards to how long ago they migrated to the UK; how long they have been Muslim, their paths to Islam and different takes on Islamic belief and practice. Most women in this sub-sample embraced Islam after they moved to the UK, a smaller group converted before settling in the UK (some in Poland, one in a Muslim majority country, and some in other Western Europe countries).

## Religion and Migration

Great Britain became the most popular destination for migrants from Poland following the Polish accession to the European Union in 2004.[1] The exact

---

1 According to the Central Statistical Office nearly 800 thousands of Poles were living in Great Britain at the end of 2017. Retrieved June 20, 2020 from https://stat.gov.pl/obszary

number of Polish migrants in the UK is difficult to establish, even more problematic is the assessment of the number of Polish converts to Islam living in the UK. Based on the latest available Census data, Pędziwiatr (2017) estimates that in 2011 there were over 2000 Polish Muslims in the UK.

Migration has many different faces, but invariably it places individuals at the intersection of social, economic and political forces driving the globalized mobility of people. Although the vast majority of Poles who migrated to the UK in the last two decades did that as a matter of their choice and migrated mainly to improve their economic situation, many became subjected to the demand of "a new brand of competitive individualism, whereby people [...] must develop individual strategies and take personal responsibility for their success, happiness, and livelihood by making the right choices in an uncertain and changeable environment" (Harris, 2004, p. 4). These demands often put individuals under pressure and evoke disorientation. In the process of settlement in a new country, some migrants experience a lack of ontological security (Kinvall, 2004), go through "an adjustment" process (Goffman, 1972) and invest considerable amount of energy in a quest for normality. As Ryan (2010, p. 361) notes, "this process of 'adjustment' involves not only adaptation to a new situation but also elements of 'continuity' with former frames of reference". At this point of the story about migration, religion usually enters the picture. The maintenance of continuity can be mediated through religion (see, e.g. Barth, 1996; Mol, 1971; Mitchell, 2006), as has been also demonstrated in relation to Polish migrants in the UK (Ryan, 2010; Grzymała-Moszczyńska et al., 2011; Krotofil, 2013; Trzebiatowska, 2010). Continuity achieved through religion in the context of Polish migrants is usually explored with reference to Catholicism, whereas conversion to Islam evokes the ideas of crossing religious, ethnic and cultural boundaries. Although the continuity seems to be especially compromised when migration is accompanied by religious conversion, I argue that, paradoxically, the latter can facilitate integration of an individual's biography. The new religion might become the means by which discordant identities are "brought into consonance", as fragmented life stories came increasingly under the rubric of a single, overarching narrative of "coming home" (Collins, 2002, p. 147).

-tematyczne/ludnosc/migracje-zagraniczne-ludnosci/informacja-o-rozmiarach-i-kierunkach-czasowej-emigracji-z-polski-w-latach-2004-2017,2,11.html.

## Diversity as a Context of Everyday Life: Dominant Discourses on Multiculturalism

Converts' experiences and identity development are inseparably linked to the nationally framed models of engagement with cultural and religious diversity in which they are situated. To shed more light on this relationship, as part of our study we set out to include both Poland and the UK, which differ significantly when it comes to the understanding and the lived experiences of multiculturalism. The term 'multiculturalism' is not only of a descriptive value, it has strong normative connotations, as it has been linked with a positive attitude towards the presence in a society of diverse ethnic and religious groups (Farrar, 2012) and is often associated with the "celebration of diversity" (Parekh, 2000). Modood (2013, p. 64), for example, argues that multiculturalism goes beyond tolerance, as it "involves active support for cultural difference, active discouragement against hostility and disapproval and the remaking of the public sphere in order to fully include marginalized identities", and as such, it is much more concerned with commonalities than difference.

The relative positioning of Great Britain and Poland in relation to multiculturalism is made more complex by the dominant and persistent epistemological categories locating the respective countries historically and geographically in "postcolonialism" and "permanent post communism" (Kulpa, 2014). While Great Britain seen from this perspective is still grippling with "the logic of colonialism", Poland, is perceived as in many ways subordinate to the West and on "a never ending journey of catching up with the always more developed West" (Narkowicz and Pędziwiatr, 2017, p. 4; see also Kulpa, 2014). Taking the critical stance towards these categories in our analysis we juxtapose the popular discourses on multiculturalism and diversity in the respective countries with subjective, lived experiences described by our respondents.

### *Multicultural Britain vs Monocultural Poland*

The current strengthening of right-wing populist and extreme right-wing positions in many European countries affects both Poland and Britain, however the power relations and specific discourses positioning Muslims in relation to the countries' history and socio-cultural heritage in the two settings are radically different. In this section I sketch out the main differences in regard to this matter between the two countries.

The emergence of multiculturalist discourse in Britain dates back to the 1960s. It developed alongside the introduction of practical policies for the elimination of racial discrimination and promotion of the social integration of ethnic minorities. In this process, multiculturalism became a widespread "aspirational" concept in the 1980s (Farrar, 2012). As a political ethos, in the post-colonial Britain it has come to be seen as, for example, advocacy for sympathetic recognition by members of the majority ethnic group of the various "other" cultures that comprise the society. In contemporary Poland, on the other hand, the problem of integration policies remains abstract and has not yet sparked major public debates (Staiger, 2014), however with the growing popularity of populist discourses, multiculturalism is increasingly presented as an emerging threat (Cap, 2017) and a sign of moral decline. Positive narratives of multiculturalism in the mainstream discourses are based on historical memory of the Commonwealth of Poland and Lithuania in 16th–17th century. These positive historical examples are cherry-picked in a quest to protect Polish exceptionalism, based on the discourses on Polish non-participation in colonialism and multiculturalization of the country's past. Their primary function is to refute any accusations of racism (Pasieka, 2014).[2]

Some authors question whether multiculturalism remains a valid idea and continues to shape policies and practices. The narrative of a linear, simple "movement from the monoculture to multiculture that decentres the old, nineteenth-century European nationalisms" (Birt, 2009, p. 216) is challenged by the unexpected shifts in the multicultural project. The number of high-profile events that occurred in Britain and other Western countries in the last two decades, including the 7/7 bombings in London and 9/11 attacks in the USA, placed Muslims at the centre of debates on terrorism, migration, community cohesion and human rights. The questions regarding Muslim integration and Muslim loyalty following those tragic events seem to be driving an assimilationist turn in Britain (McGhee, 2008). In this social climate, Muslims in Britain regularly make headlines as targets of moral panics. They are presented by large sections of the media as a troublesome minority, a dangerous and unpatriotic fifth column (Petley and Richardson, 2011; Birt, 2009). Increasingly, British social and political problems are blamed on Muslims and the perceived failure of multiculturalism (Sealy, 2017). The growing number of British converts to Islam seem to be represented even less favourably than born Muslims in popular media (Brice, 2010; Sealy, 2017). As a result of these competing narratives on multiculturalism, "Muslim assertiveness emerged as a domestic political phenomenon" (Modood, 2003, p. 105) and Muslims in Britain became a "protected group" (McGhee, 2008). This results in foregrounding of reified, discrete identities and antagonisms arising in the competition for scarce

---

2 Recently these discourses have been increasingly challenged in academia. For example, Balogun (2020) explores the mechanisms of exclusion operating as the racial contours of Polish self-conception.

resources whereby "Muslimness" is treated differently to other modalities of "difference" (Modood, 2013, p. 65). The instrumentalization and essentialization of Muslim identity in the multiculturalist project seem to be the costs in the process of the creation of institutional space for "religion" in the public sphere which makes room for Islam (Lewis, 2015).

One of the key differences is the level of secularism and the related position of Muslims in the political discourses of respective countries (see Modood, 2013). While the multicultural accommodation of Muslims goes well with moderate secularism (Modood, 2013), such as the British one, some commentators note that public display of religious identity in Britain is at times met with hostility (Cheeseman and Khanum, 2009). In Poland, on the other hand, public expression of religious identity is widely accepted, albeit limited to culturally and politically sanctioned "appropriate" religion(s).[3] As Renata Włoch (2009) argues, the Catholic Church in Poland might be considered as "an opportunity structure", an agent that paved the way to the presence of religion in public sphere in contemporary Poland. Many commentators observe, however, that the potential problem with harnessing this opportunity are the claims of Catholic Church in Poland to representing the whole nation (Hann, 2000) and the ambivalent attitude of the Church in Poland towards Islam (see, e.g., Piela, 2020; Krotofil and Motak, 2018; Narkowicz and Pędziwiatr, 2017). Paradoxically, the combined strong political position of the Catholic Church and the small size of the Muslim population in Poland underwrite the absence of prohibitive legislation regarding the expression of religious identities in public sphere, giving Muslims in Poland a degree of freedom.[4]

In Poland, however, the position of Muslims as political actors is much weaker than in the UK. In the recent years, the discourses of ethnic nationalism and religious homogeneity, in particular, the national mythology positioning Poland as a last bastion of Christianity in Europe, have been steadily gaining popularity. In these narratives, Muslims are portrayed as a threat to the imagined Polish nation that is ethnically, religiously and culturally homogenous. These ideas dominated political debates on the large-scale influx of Muslim refugees to Europe, the so called 'migration crisis' (Goździak and Márton, 2018; Krotofil and Motak, 2018). During this period, expressions of public contempt towards Muslims became more acceptable in the mainstream discourses and

---

3  Islam is accepted only in its "folk" form represented by the Tatars, Polish autochthonous Muslims (see, e. g. Dziekan [2005]; Pędziwiatr [2011]).
4  Examples of such unregulated area include the right to veil and the issue of praying in the street that have been a subject of legislative procedures in some Western countries, but so far have not been addressed by legislators in Poland.

very quickly reached the threshold of moral panic related to the imagined imminent, rapid increase of numbers of Muslims living in Poland (Lipiński, 2020; Krotofil and Motak, 2018). State-controlled media continue to portray Muslims as 'the Other' *par excellence*; backward, violent and barbaric (Piela, 2020) and place them in "discredited person" position, to use Goffman's (1963) term. In the last decade, the populist, conservative Law and Justice (PiS), currently holding the majority of mandates in the Polish Parliament, has absorbed a big portion of the radical nationalist ideology and cadres (Pankowski, 2012), unanimously rejecting the multiculturalist ideology.

Based on this development, Rogowska (2017) questions whether Poland is a good place for Muslims to be, not only in terms of national politics, but also the prevalent attitudes of the Polish mainstream society. As Narkowicz and Pędziwiatr (2017) demonstrate, hostility towards Muslims is not limited to the right end of the political spectrum. Similar to France (Scott, 2007), feminist discourses are deployed by both secular liberals and Catholic conservatives in Poland to legitimise opposition against Muslims in Poland, evoking anti-Muslim sentiments on the grounds of "liberal values". The history of the small group of indigenous Muslims in Poland – the Tatars – illustrates "the way in which the acceptance of an ethnic and/or religious minority can be attained; it is based on partial assimilation and modesty in declarations or practices, as well as 'refraining from radical otherness' in the public sphere" (Buchowski and Chlewińska, 2012: 5). As Buchowski and Chlewińska (2012, p. 4) note, the dominant understanding of multiculturalism in Poland is "folkloristic" and based on historical memory rather that everyday experience of cultural diversity and pluralism. Implementation of multiculturalism focused on "celebration of *exotic* cultural attractions" obliterates the more serious debate on the existing marginalisation of ethnic and religious minorities in the public sphere.

Islamophobia is present in Great Britain as well as in Poland, however, the key difference is the degree to which multiculturalism has been embraced in these countries. In the UK, the multiculturalism influences the views and practices at the local level and results in its greater prevalence of the community-level, subaltern public spheres operating outside of the hegemonic public sphere in the UK (McGhee, 2008; Birt, 2009). It translates to a subjective experience of greater diversity and its acceptance. People who self-identify as Muslims in the UK are a diverse group with regards to ethnic makeup, the intensity of religious practice, and adherence to a particular branch of Islam. It is a growing and dynamically changing population. Important for understanding the position of Polish converts to Islam is the fact that in the UK, Muslims have an established status as a group participating in the power struggles played out in the framework of multiculturalism, they are "recognized", to use Taylor's term (1994). As the largest religious minority in the UK, Muslims are much more visible than they are in Poland. In the UK, Islam is "part of the scene" (Sealy, 2018), much less exposed to "invasions of privacy" (Goffman, 1963: 26). Muslim identity movements are recognised as actors on the UK multicultural scene, and have much more political capital than Muslims in Poland. There is, however, no straightforward answer to the question whether migrant converts, such as the Polish converts engaged in this study, are able to tap into that capital. In the following section, I focus on the subjective and intersectional experiences of multiculturalism and diversity of Polish Muslim women living in the UK. I demonstrate that intersectional positionality is key to understanding the process of managing spoiled identities. While the stigma of being the religious "Other" is more easily managed in the UK, through the embracement of the "multiculturalism" narrative and due to a greater presence of Islam in this country, the more intensive interactions with born Muslims of various ethnic backgrounds at times lead to further stigmatization through questioning of converts' authenticity. In similar way, the management of stigma attached to being a racialized "Eastern European" migrant through the foregrounding of Muslim identity, in some cases, comes with spoiling of converts' identity in the eyes of the members of Polish migrant community who start perceiving them through Islamophobic lenses.

### *Diversity and Multiculturalism in Subjective Experiences of Polish Converts*

In the Polish converts' narratives, the strong visibility of diversity and its relative acceptance in everyday life seem to be prioritized over the more political formulations of multiculturalism. The sizes of the Muslim populations in Poland and in the UK is one of the key elements shaping different experiences of converts in the respective countries. With the proportion of Muslims in the UK estimated at between 4–5% of the general population and set to reach about 50% in the largest British cities such as London, or Birmingham, Muslims are much more visible in the public in the UK, compared to Poland. In line with previous research (Pędziwiatr, 2017), the British society is perceived by the Polish converts in a better light then Poland when it comes to diversity and its acceptance, as the following quotes illustrate:

> Here, we have the multiculturalism, let's say. And this is remarkable. Children who go to school here – for them it is completely normal that everyone if different. They truly teach them just that. Some time ago we had this phrase in Poland 'everybody is different, all are equal', everybody

was wearing that t-shirt, nobody lived by its message [...] Great Britain is an open country, despite some incidents. Generally, multiculturalism is a normal thing here, especially in London and other big cities. For sure it is easier. You can work, go to school, have a normal life without any fear for yourself, or your family.[5] (Loubna)

It seems to me that England is a really open country. There are groups that are capable of "showing you" that you are inferior, but there are also groups that would say to you: "if you want to contribute, you are most welcome. This is because we are trying to build something better for our children, for our offspring and for ourselves". (Sadeeqa)

You know, I live in Birmingham. Here, you know, everyone is wearing the headscarf, half of the city. But when you go to Poland, suddenly, I don't know ... this distance. (Angelika)

The diversity of the multicultural landscape of Britain for some converts is embodied in the visibility of different religions peacefully sharing public space:

The Ummah in Poland does not want to show itself in public. Here, in England we see each other. We pass each other on the streets and we know who is a Muslim by their clothes. [...] What I like here, is the display, the open stands, where the follower of Bhagavad Gita is standing and singing "Hare Krishna" right next to a pastor, I am not sure from which church. The pastor is Black. And a few streets away there is a stand where Muslims give copies of the Qu'ran away and encourage people to read it. (Barbara)

In many respondents' view, the visibility of Muslims in the UK is the outcome of strong grass root mobilization of the Muslim community. The perceived lack of initiative and engagement with the mainstream society of Muslim communities in Poland was aptly summarised by one of the women who lives in a big city in Poland:

In Poland nothing was happening before and still nothing is being done for people to learn about other nationalities, cultures or religions. [...] Some meetings are organized, such as 'Why Muslims love Jesus', so it is

---

5 As Daria's quote on page 11 indicates, this acceptance of diversity in British schools is not as universal as Loubna suggests.

known that for us, Jesus, Moses, or Muhammad are almost equally important. But this is too little. Nobody talks about this in everyday life, these are events happening once a year and really it is not like the audience hall is full. Perhaps three-quarters [of seats are taken] and those are usually the same faces, people I know, because I saw them here or there before. So in my opinion, this [engagement] does not reach broader audiences [...] (Angelika)

The predominantly positive view of the British society with regard to ostensible acceptance of diversity was, however, contested by some of the converts, as this quote regarding personal experiences of wearing the headscarf illustrates:

It [the headscarf] is in my way. Even at a [British] shop, when they see the headscarf, they treat me as the Other, because I am a Muslim. And on the top of that, they think that I have to be stupid, uneducated, and that I sit at home. The headscarf is a stigma. It does not protect a woman. [...] It does not make me untouchable, and sometimes it creates a wall. (Daria)

In this fragment, Daria talks about stigma that is immediately visible to other people and places her in the position of a "discredited" person (Goffman, 1969, p. 13). In explaining her feelings, she evokes the gendered othering of Muslims, whereby Muslim women are constructed as oppressed subjects.

The disregard for diversity as a value is seen by some converts as mutual – coming from both sides – the non-Muslim majority and the Muslim minority. As such, it is not only personally hurtful, but also seen as being in direct opposition to Islamic values, as illustrated in the following fragments:

In Islam, you are not a true Muslim as long as you don't want for your brother whatever you want for yourself. You cannot discriminate against anybody or judge anybody, because in truth, God knows what you are like in this, or another situation. He knows what intentions somebody has. (Arleta)

First of all, what is in the Qu'ran? Respect for the neighbour. And this is not mentioned only in relations to Muslims, this is about the whole of humanity, we need to respect one another. We are all created by God. God created us all and this is what I like in Islam, that you cannot hurt anyone without a reason. (Eleonora)

[...] there is some kind of non-Muslim phobia among Muslims. At least the local ones, they grew up as Muslims and they feel more legitimate and generally better than the rest of the world, right? They do not see their own behaviour, they don't see their shortcomings. The very fact that someone is not a Muslim puts them in inferior position and [Muslims] look down at him. How can we expect to be treated well if we do not treat [others] well. (Czesława)

In these narratives, our respondents seem to question the idea that the UK is a place where the Islamic values can be implemented, but mostly they agree that in the UK, Polish converts have a greater chance for recognition as Muslims. They feel more comfortable expressing their religious identity in the public sphere and are able to "blend in" to some extent. This is reflected, for example, by a larger proportion of converts in the UK wearing the hijab, compared to converts who live in Poland. The statement by Barbara illustrates a common sentiment:

> I don't have any resistance here, I feel free, more free. For me, it is this kind of freedom, where I simply feel free, whether I have the hijab, or I am without hijab, with an Arab-Muslim husband, or Black [...] Nobody will offend me, or make a comment. This is the freedom that is still non-existent in Poland.

Some of the women who wear hijab in the UK, take it off when visiting Poland. Agata, for example, admitted: "when I go [to Poland], I go mainly to stay with my family, to visit my family, not for any other purposes. And because we live in a village, and it is a really small village, I do not put the headscarf on. Instead I wear a hat, or I use a hood to cover my head." Similarly, Ola said: "I didn't go to Poland straight away. I went there after 3 years [since conversion]. When I was in Poland, I was wearing a hat, not a headscarf".

In our interviews we find many instances of converts comparing Poland and the UK, however, these narratives reflect privatized understanding of multiculturalism and support the observation that despite Muslims being singled out in British multiculturalist identity politics, identity is not "constructed by its outside" (Birt, 2009). Our respondents do not define themselves through the dominant categories based on popular binaries, but instead embrace their complex, intersectional positioning.

### The Lived Islam in the UK

Despite the UK becoming a popular migrant destination for Poles after the enlargement of the EU in 2004, the focus on the assumed temporal and liquid character of the migratory movements within the EU meant that initially, relatively little academic attention was paid to how Polish migrants negotiated attachments, belonging and how they engaged with multicultural social environment in the destination countries (Ryan, 2018; Collett, 2013; Erdal and Oeppen, 2013). Although the results of early research on the post-accession migration suggested that many saw themselves returning to Poland in the future (Eade, Drinkwater and Garapich, 2007), gradually, it became apparent that a significant proportion of that group settled more permanently. The attachments formation process in the migration context is dynamic and multidimensional. Multicultural Britain, in particular the superdiverse British cities, offer place-specific opportunities for building ethnically diverse social networks (Vertovec, 2007). However, the existing literature on the post-accession Polish migrants settling in the UK, and strategies they use to acquire social capital, offers a complex picture. While some authors suggest that the majority of Polish migrants develop new social relationships following the re-settlement, form diverse relationships across ethnic boundaries and thus, have a first- hand experience of British multiculturalism (Milewski and Ruszczak-Żbikowska, 2008),[6] others are less optimistic. Grzymała-Kazłowska (2018), for example, notes that most Poles in the UK maintain social networks composed almost exclusively of their close family members, or other migrants from Poland. In the context of this study, Polish converts' experiences speak to the former view. Muslim converts are most likely among the migrants who form very close relationships with born Muslims living in the UK.

Some converts in our sample embraced Islam before moving to the UK, but most of the women converted after settling in the country. Some researchers argue that the support, guidance and acceptance of the receiving religious community is key to staying converted (Rambo, 1995), however, there is also evidence demonstrating that even the converts who become disillusioned with the Muslim community, maintain their commitment to Islam. As Zebiri (2008) notes, it is difficult to capture the complexity of this relationship with very limited access to those who became disenfranchised and whose views and experiences could be compared with the converts who remained in their religious community. With this limitation in mind, we can attempt to explore what it means to Polish female converts to Islam to be able to access Muslim communities and interact with born Muslims. In the UK, compared to Poland, converts to Islam have many more opportunities to come into contact with the

---

6  The authors state that only about a quarter of Poles in the UK limit their social contacts to their own national group (Milewski and Ruszczak-Żbikowska, 2008).

lived Islam and therefore function in stronger plausibility structures (Berger, 1990; Zebiri, 2008).

### Encounters with Born Muslims

Many commentators observe that the identity politics inherent in the political multiculturalism marginalize the interplay between personal and political agency and overstate the "pre-packaged", essentialized identities (Birt, 2009: 210; see also, e.g. McGhee, 2008). This is true also in relation to the Muslim community. The imagined Muslim community is a complex and dynamic entity constituted by three intertwined cultural worlds: moral community, aesthetic community and political community. The first is based on the sense of responsibility for others, it is a community of co-responsibility. The second is sustained by multiple voluntary organisations that share cultural knowledge, and creative passion. Finally, the political community is "a community of suffering" that demands recognition by the state and protection against discrimination (Werbner, 2002: 70). This complexity is rarely recognised in mainstream discourses; however, it is experienced by converts to Islam who strive to become members of Muslim communities usually dominated by born Muslims.

The level of different Polish converts' engagement with the multicultural environment and with born Muslims varies considerably. It is to some degree spatially differentiated, as Polish migrants settle in areas that differ in terms of physical presence of other Muslims. It has been argued that British cities provide ample opportunities for low-level sociability across ethnic and religious boundaries in everyday urban public encounters. The effects of these, however, do not necessarily translate into meaningful engagement, exchange or connection (Amin, 2002; Valentine, 2008). Our respondents engage in diverse encounters with born Muslims which take different forms, from casual interactions to intimate relationships. Many women experience a sense of belonging and being an appreciated member of the religious community when encountering born Muslims, as illustrated in the following excerpts:

> When I became a Muslim I went to the mosque in the evening, for the first time. There was only one sister in the mosque on Wembley. She cried. She was there with a little girl, with her daughter, they came to pray and she was meant to go home quickly. She stayed with me until one AM, with this poor child, because she was so happy for me. She recited the Qur'an for me and taught me how to tie the hijab. (Paulina)

> Many Muslims, when they see you are a convert, they think you are a better person, because they were born in this religion and did not have much

choice and even tried to rebel and tried everything else. And when they see a person who totally changes everything, it's: "wow, you are better, more holy". (Ola)

Some of our respondents were met with admiration, as their decision to convert was seen as a sacrifice by born Muslims.[7] The sacrificial dimension of conversion to Islam is not bounded to the demands placed on converts by the proscriptions of the new religion (Rao, 2015), it relates also to the palpable change in convert's position in their social structure. As Moosavi observes, white converts to Islam "experience a re-racialization whereby they are no longer able to access white privilege in a way they once were" (2015, p. 42; see also Galonnier, 2015 for similar observations in the US and French contexts).

Alongside the sense of belonging and being appreciated, the Muslim community also provides guidance for converts navigating the diversity inherent in Islam. Meeting zealous, practising Muslims creates an opportunity to observe and learn lived Islam:

> After I met her, she showed me this Islam, like, like … this life, life style. [She showed me] that Islam can be our life style. Because some…, it is more by the book, step by step, imitation. But they showed me the whole thing just by being themselves. (Lidia)

> I had a good friend, a Turkish woman. She didn't even realize it, but by being a good Muslim, she was a role model for me. She did not talk to me about Islam, nothing about religion, zero. But her identity, the way she acted, the way she talked to her parents, and how acted towards her, this was like wow to me. They respected each other; it was mutual! The way she was towards her parent, the same way they treated her. And it was all very sensible, it was a good home. She was a good role model for me and it started with her, my return to Islam. (Paulina)

The encounters with born Muslims are, however, very often shaped by complex patterns of identification and power relations. Religion as a basis of defining identity and difference cannot be considered as a discrete category in isolation from other identities, such as gender, ethnic and cultural ones (Yuval-Davis, 2011; Sealy, 2018). Polish converts in the UK interact with born Muslims from many racial and ethnic groups and make attempts at deconstructing the

---

7  This form of gratification is much less frequently experienced by converts in Poland, due to lack of established receiving community of born-Muslims.

conflation between religion, culture and ethnicity. Some women in our sample highlighted the limits of interactions across ethnic boundaries and alluded to the sectarian segmentation among British Muslims (Baumann, 1999; Farrar, 2002):

> I see that [Muslims] from North Africa are very open to other cultures and other languages. They are very open; Morocco, Algeria, Tunisia. They have no problem with talking to you whether you are Christian, Muslim. The bigger problem is with Asians, because they came with their families, with their own food, and they sit in that culture. I don't know why they were not able to integrate more. I think this is their choice, this is not something you can force anyone to do. (Ola)

Similarly, Daria spoke about the divisions of Muslim community along ethnic and national lines:

> There is lots of hypocrisy among Muslims. They are prejudiced towards each other and they do not mix across different nationalities. It does not matter that you are a Muslim; if you are from another country, you are a stranger. Arabs, for example, see themselves as being above everyone else. (Daria)

Further on in the interview, she reflected on the personal experiences related to cultural diversity in Britain and expressed disappointment, and a sense of isolation and rejection. Her account demonstrates that these interactions can be challenging even at a very private, intimate level:

> I concluded that people from different cultures should not mix. This is difficult. It is much easier to develop relationships with somebody from your own culture, or nation. [...] I never expected that I would be married to someone of a different nationality, and even less so to someone of a different religion. He is Asian, I am European, this requires lots of sacrifices. [Once you are in a mixed marriage], you are accepted by neither ethnic community. Muslims think that I am not a true Muslim, and Poles imagine that I betrayed my nation, because I embraced an alien religion and culture. (Daria)

Relying on the revivalist dichotomy "Islam vs culture" (Bolognani and Mellor, 2012, p. 213) converts ascribe the views and behaviours they find difficult to accept to "culture" and separate it from the religion – Islam. While they are keen to accommodate their everyday life choices within tenets of Islam, they tend to be more apprehensive and selective about the cultural practices of different ethnic groups, particularly with regards to practices reproducing gender inequality (see also Krotofil, 2011). One of our respondents' description of her marriage provides a good illustration:

> Sometimes I would ask him to do something and he would reply: "[but] you know, because my mother this, or my sister that" [...] So men are brought up in these cultures in such a way that a Muslim woman does everything. Most of them also..., some understand, some know Islamic law and help their wives. [...] So I do not mix the culture with Islam. But not all [born Muslims] follow Islam, they follow the culture more. And then we have a problem, because if they follow Islam, they are great husbands, they respect their wives, they respect their rights and help them with the housework and children, with everything. (Anita)

Although many Polish converts develop close relationships with Muslim families of a different ethnic origin by marriage,[8] this is by no means a rule. The intensity of interactions with their spouse's family varies, depending on individual circumstances. While some women in our sample lived with the extended family of their Muslim husband, others had no relationship at all with their in-laws or other family members. In the latter group, some of the women we spoke with rejected the tradition of living under one roof with the husband's parents as a cultural custom that had nothing to do with religion; others had spouses whose families did not live in the UK.

Some women reported that they received practical help from other Muslims, but many point to the limitations of the "moral community" at the micro-level, lived multiculturalism, as exemplified by this statement by one of the women who was very active in the community of Polish female converts in the UK:

> I don't know how they [Polish sisters] are treated. For sure, with respect, and generally "it is cool that you converted to our faith, you are unique". But later on, they are forgotten, they have no support. And it is much more difficult for them to find a job, most of all to find a job. And the born Muslims will not help them find a job. Or, if they have any problems, very

---

8  With time, many single post-accession migrants married and, what is important for our discussion, among those who entered marriage, there was a significant rate of mixed marriages (Milewski & Ruszczak-Żbikowska, 2008).

> rarely can they count on born Muslims to help them, and they can't count on Poles to help them. (Magda)

In this statement, Magda alludes to the difficult in-between position of Polish Muslim converts, similar sentiment was expressed by a convert who described how her children were met with rejection from born Muslims:

> As a Polish convert I am in between. When I came to Birmingham, for example, I noticed, that something is wrong with those [born] Muslims. My children at school, when they went to school in Birmingham, they heard from other Muslim children that they cannot be Muslims, because they are not brown. They are white, so they cannot be Muslims. And I noticed that some born Muslims look badly at us, Muslim converts. We are fakes. (Angelika)

The stories about rejection are complemented by a narrative themed around religious indifference, ignorance and conflation of Islam with ethnic practices among born Muslims. In creating these narratives, converts challenge the privileged status of power and authority of Muslims who were born to Islam:

> [There are] many people who do not study Islam, do not learn Islam, just, for example, as children they learn to recite the Qu'ran. They read it only in Arabic, without any [awareness of] its meaning. And later they believe anything. Because they do not know anything. [...]. I haven't seen anybody, almost anybody from among born Muslims I met for whom Islam would be everything. (Lidia)

> I do not know that many born Christians who open the Bible and read the Bible and learn. It is the same with born Muslims, they don't do that. (Arleta)

The "moralization" of religious practices and representations apparent in converts' narratives is the action taken in religious field in order to acquire moral and religious capital. Calling a practice "ethnic", or "cultural" is a type of "classification struggle" that disrupts the status of born Muslims.

### *Mosques – between Material and Social Lived Islam*

Arguably, converts choose different strategies to express their Muslim identity, from keeping religious identity private, to conveying a hypervisible Muslim identity in all social contexts (Zebiri, 2008). However, for those converts who chose to engage in practices that make them visible as Muslims, the socio-cultural context of the UK seems to be more conducive. Mosque attendance is one such practice.

While in Poland mosques remain scarce,[9] in the UK, the local discourse of multiculturalism is embraced by city councils and reflected in the growing success rate of planning applications for the construction of purpose-build mosques. These buildings are increasingly endorsed and celebrated as signifiers of "cultural diversity" and became an important feature of the British urban landscape (Gale, 2009). The presence of Polish converts in mosques is mediated by the amount of their cultural capital. For some converts a mosque is an unfamiliar setting, a place where they do not feel at ease and lack the sense of ownership. Some experience a form of alienation in a mosque, as one of the converts observed:

> I remember when I came to this circle, I was a bit … I only just started going to a mosque, I was a bit scared, I was so … there were so many sisters there. That was so overwhelming, you know, I was on my own, they all knew each other, you enter and there are so many sisters. (Arleta)

The ethnic boundaries seem to be important and mediate the sense of ownership of the religious space and accessibility of mosques for converts (Krotofil, 2011; Woodlock, 2010). This was evident in some our respondents' narratives:

> When somebody goes to a mosque that they are not familiar with, they will feel their different identity, they will feel like guests. Well, you are always a guest where you have people mainly from Pakistan, or when you are in a Somali mosque, or some other. You are always, always a bit distanced. (Magda)

The choice of a particular mosque is very often determined by the converts' spouses' preferences. As great number of mosques in the UK do not have adequate provisions for women (Brown 2008) (this is true especially for small local mosques situated in converted buildings which do not have the required separate entrances for women), they do not attract women. Therefore, when possible, Polish converts tend to visit larger mosques with a diverse ethnic makeup. Good command of English facilitates the process of joining a mosque community. Many converts who do overcome the initial unease, eventually

---

9  For more detailed discussion on the controversies and protests that unfolded with regards to the plans to build a mosque in Warsaw, see A. Nalborczyk (2011).

have largely positive experiences. "In most mosques they treat you well", stated Lidia, "when we pray in the mosque, no matter what status one has, who she is, everyone bends to the same level". Similarly, Arleta, quoted above, concluded her reflection on going to the mosque with an emotional statement. "But the way they received me, it made me cry. They were so warm, I had never been so warmly received in my life, anywhere", she said.

Another woman recalled the moment she went to the mosque for the first time and said the *shahada*. She felt welcome and developed a strong sense of belonging to the Muslim community:

> I felt something beautiful in Islam, that we are all one. There is no difference in the mosque, no matter where you come from, whether you are rich or poor, white or pink. We are all oneness and when I took the *shahada*, they all would come and congratulate me, and were crying. (Alicja)

These fragments highlight the intertwined character of different dimensions of religion and the intersectional position of Polish converts in the UK. The material and the social work together in these examples, generating intense spiritual experience and shaping identities.

Another material aspect of the plausibility structure is the better access to other resources facilitating religious development. Some converts felt that they were better able to live a "fully Islamic" life in the UK, than they would have been in Poland. This was particularly salient before the advent of online shopping, as the multicultural consumer market of the UK granted converts better access to books or Islamic objects used in everyday life, such as clothing. Many women took the advantage of the availability of Islamic education in the UK and attended classes in mosques.

### Negotiating Patterns of Belonging

As converts are very familiar with the anti-Muslim views, for many of them the moment they embraced Islam is reminiscent of "coming out" (Zebiri, 2008). In their narratives, becoming Muslim is also akin to finally making sense of the spiritual dispositions they recognized they had for a very long time, recalibrating and integrating them (Krotofil et al., forthcoming). This also means that modes of thinking, feeling and behaving that were private for a very long time become more public and socially embedded in the religious community. In this process, converts strive to preserve the continuity of biography and to establish new connections. For migrant converts, this labour takes place on the transnational plane. They negotiate their position as Muslim converts in relation to significant others from multiple socio-cultural contexts.

### *Maintaining the Old and Establishing New Close Connections*

Although typically, converts perceive Poland as a non-Muslim or even an anti-Muslim country, only a few women in our sample explicitly distanced themselves from their heritage. The vast majority cultivated the connection with Poland in diverse ways. Most of the women maintained relationships with their families of origin and periodically visited their parents in Poland. While intentionally scheduled their trips to avoid Catholic holidays and celebrations, others found creative ways to share some of the festive customs with their families (see Krotofil, 2011, also chapter 1 in this volume). The attachment to the Polish culture has a transgenerational dimension which often reveals the gendered nature of the ethnic boundary making (Yuval-Davis, 1997). The women who have children take upon themselves the task of transmitting and preserving the Polish ethnic identity of their children by, for example, familiarising their children with Polish customs and teaching them to speak the Polish language:

> We speak Polish and I want my children to have a close relationship with my family. And my husband wants that too, because we have to be good to our parents, we cannot give up on that. It would be one of the greatest sins, if we were to damage the relationship with our family. So we have to preserve our family ties. (Lidia)

Indeed, many women painstakingly maintained a connection with the family of origin interpreting this as an Islamic requirement. Loubna made a reference to Islamic canonical texts which portray parents, and especially mothers, as objects of veneration deserving love, respect and the kindest companionship (Oh, 2010; Schleifer, 1996). Some of the converts experienced conflicts in the relations with their parents who struggled to fully accept their choices, such as the decision to embrace Islam or marry a man from a Muslim majority country. Arleta described her situation as follows:

> In addition to my conversion, my husband is from India and I am a Pole. There are no mixed marriages in my family, or anything like that. So the very fact that I am with a man who comes from another culture was something they could not accept. They always had something against him. My father said he was too old for me although the age gap between him and my mother is the same as between my husband and I. (Arleta)

The most important milestone in negotiating the relationship with parents in the context of conversion does not seem to be the decision to embrace Islam, or the moment *shahada* is taken, but the point at which converts become visible as Muslims, usually after the adoption of the hijab. At this point the "discreditable" status of a convert changes into that of "a discredited" person (Goffman, 1963: 56) in the interactions with those who are hostile towards Muslims. The negotiation of the stigma attached to being Muslim in Poland, therefore, is not bounded to a single individual who converts, but involves also their close families. For Polish converts living in the UK, has a profoundly transnational character. In this context, some converts make a decision to "spare" their parents and do not express their religious identity publicly when visiting Poland.

Almost all of the women we spoke to had close relationships with other Polish converts at some stage of their conversion journey, some of them lasting many years. In line with research on Western converts from other countries, the Polish women agreed that they received most support from other Muslim converts from their country of origin (see Bourque, 2006) with whom they share the same "moral career" (Goffman, 1963: 44). The relationship with other Polish converts was highlighted in most interviews. The following examples reveal the dynamic character of convert groups based on collective learning and shared experiences:

> Only later I met many sisters from Poland. And it was because of them that I started reading more, and learning more. We were all on this Internet forum. There, everyone is together, if somebody learned something new, we were sharing this. We were dispersed all over Britain, Europe even. We were in touch and some of them I met in person. Later on, we created this network; "I know this [sister], she lives next to you, you can meet". And it was like ... I liked it very much, everybody was so open. You don't know them, but that doesn't matter, we can meet, we have similar experiences. Come to my house, we will meet, no problem, without any barriers. (Lidia)

> I met [name], [name], other sisters, and I remember the atmosphere. This was affecting you and pushing you to act. But I knew they did not have the knowledge about Islam that I did. And I thought that their intentions were good, but the intention on its own will not help you cross the street safely. You need to look right and left, so the knowledge is needed. So I said ok, we need to organize something, meet and talk about Islam. Every one of us can prepare lessons, choose a book and say something

about it. [...] I stick to other [converted] Muslims because I know every one of us experiences a difficult journey at the beginning. (Ola)

While these contacts are very important for Polish converts, the relationships evolve over time, as members of the group change jobs, move to other locations or start families. With time, many groups limit their interactions to online discussions and only occasional face to face meetings. As converts advance in their conversion journey, the initial generalized enthusiasm towards other women who share the national background and the experience of conversion to Islam may fade. Although the religious identity remains central to many converts' self-understanding, over time, other social roles and identities gain importance and impact their positioning within the group. The differences, such as class, the marital status, the professional status, or the level of involvement in religious practice, become more important than the shared conversion experiences. Often, these social differences lead to more selectivity in interactions within the group:

> At the beginning, when I was in London, I wanted to be friends with everyone, I thought it was worth to maintain these relationships with everybody. Later, I had less time and I wasn't looking for these encounters any more. Other various [women] came to me. I have a few relationships, I maintain a few relationships with sisters who occupation-wise, are at least on a professional pathway. With such women, I have more topics in common. (Magda)

### *Distancing from the Ethnonational Group of Origin*
The shortcomings of the "multicultural project" on the level of individual experience are reflected in the fact that Polish converts in the UK are often subject to intersectional stigmatization (discrimination or prejudice against an individual or group based on perceivable social characteristics that serve to distinguish them from other members of a society) and racialization (ascribing racial identities to a relationship, social practice, or group that do not identify itself as such). They are stigmatized as Eastern European migrants and perceived as "suspicious" as converts to Islam. At the same time, their status as Muslims is questioned by some born Muslims. Finally, they are very often rejected by their own ethno-national group – other Polish migrants in the UK (Pędziwiatr, 2017). In the popular ethno-nationalist discourse, conversion to Islam is often viewed as a form of national betrayal (Özyurek, 2009). In response to these experiences, converts adopt different strategies to negotiate their position in

this complex socio-cultural milieu. In relation to the British non-Muslims, for example, many Polish converts foreground their identity as Muslims and divert attention from the Eastern European migrant status (Ryan, 2010), despite the potential racialization and exclusion as members of the "non-white" religion (Moosavi, 2015, Galonnier, 2015). This strategy allows them to navigate the anti-Polish sentiments (Rzepnikowaska, 2019). This is illustrated by the following quote:

> [...] As I live here, it is not very often that I admit that I am Polish. I do not have relationships with other Poles. [...] So at work I wear more sparkly headscarves and everybody thinks I am from Turkey, or Iran. It is not very often that people think I am from Poland. (Ola)

With regards to their fellow nationals, most converts in our study cut off, or limit interactions with non-Muslim Poles living in the UK in order to avoid tense, ambiguous social interactions positioning them as stigmatized persons:

> Luckily, I never had to work in Polish environment in the UK. I say "luckily", because I heard lots of negative stories and I also usually did not meet with, I never met with positive ... Ok, in the Polish shop, I go there because I am attached to Polish products, there are nice ladies and one man, so its ok in there. But when I was still living in London, I went with other girls to a Polish festival. We went there only once, you could sense the *looks*. (Magda)

The experience of hostility from other Poles has a strong emotional resonance, as illustrated by the following quotes:

> On my previous estate I stopped going to the Polish shop, because back then I already had children. My daughter was able to understand, luckily not this kind of stuff. One Polish gentlemen commented that something was stinking [in the shop], "what are they doing in our shop", or something to that effect. (Lidia)

> On the one hand you are not quite a Pole – according to Poles – because you have other symbols and generally other beliefs. On the other hand, you are not quite a Muslim, because you are a new Muslim. [...] Some sisters still have good relationships with Poles, but the majority have met with negative, Islamophobic reactions. (Magda)

These interactions have significant bearing on how converts to Islam feel about their national identity, as I discuss in the next section in more depth.

### *Re-negotiating the National Identity*

Recent research reports suggest that Polish migrants in the UK have mixed attitudes towards their national identity (Adamczyk, 2019; Kapinos, 2018). Migratory experience is often related to foregrounding, questioning and sometimes rejecting the ethnic and/or national identity, as it becomes an externally ascribed aspect of personhood (Ryan, 2010). While some migrants embrace the Polish identity and express pride in their origins, others distance themselves from their ethno-national group (Drinkwater, Eade and Garapich, 2009). Both of these strategies can be linked to the complex power relations and the dominant identity discourses in the receiving and host societies. A similar pattern of reflexive engagement with national identity has been observed among Western converts to Islam (Wohlrab-Sahr, 2006; Shanneik, 2011; Younis and Hassan, 2017). For some, their nationality gains importance, while others reject it as a meaningful aspect of identity.[10] Thus, convert migrants are confronted with the issue of the national identity through a double movement: out of the country and out of the religion of their birth. The externally motivated engagement with one's nationality and ethnicity is even more pressing for Polish migrants who converted to Islam due to the positioning of Catholicism as an essence of Polishness in the discourse of right-wing political elites (Porter-Szűcs, 2011) that equates conversion out of Christianity with the betrayal of the nation.

Most women in our study identify as Polish challenge the Islamophobic, exclusionary discourses about ostensible incompatibility between Polishness and Islam and their status of migrants:

> I live in England, but in Poland I feel Polish. I feel I am a Pole, I don't have this thing that I am afraid of people. I was born in Poland, I was brought up there. I had my grandparents there, who are already dead, I lived my youth there, my memories are there. I feel Polish, I still feel Polish. (Ola)

> I see myself, most of all I feel Muslim. And right after that I feel Polish, because I grew up in Poland, I have been in touch with Poland for all this time. Many of…, all my friends are Polish Muslims. So you know, I feel Polish, British – not so much. (Angelika)

---

10   Blanka Rogowska (2017) observed in relation to Polish converts that the more they are rejected as Polish citizens, the more they emphasise their Polishness and patriotic attitudes.

> I was born in Poland, I lived in Poland almost 20 years. It would be difficult for me to feel like anything else than a Pole. For sure, I feel Polish and Muslim and these are inseparable. [...] When we came to England, it was because of money. There was this ease to practice too, of course. But I miss Poland, I miss the mountains, where I used to live. This will never change. I feel like a migrant here, although I know it's not that easy in Poland, for sure not for Polish Muslims. Here also it is not that easy. Polish migrants have their problems too and they cannot feel at home, like they do in Poland. Often I feel I don't belong here, Poland is my country. (Agata)

In the above fragments, the respondents highlight that being Polish and Muslim does not need to evoke identity conflicts or competing loyalties. Some other women in our sample, however, reject the category of national membership as a basis for their identity: "If everybody understood – like I did – this truth – we would all be one nationality [...] People ask me, when they ask me where I am from, I say: 'from God'". (Eleonora) In this statement, Eleonora rejects the national identity by evoking religious discourse about all people coming from God. A similar view was expressed by Alana, who emphasised the spiritual dimension of a personhood:

> I think we are all souls. And because we identify with some things or ideas, we create problems. We have to accept ourselves as souls. As a should that wants to know God. And what others do is of no interest to me. I chose my way, I strive for God. [...] I would put it like this: I have been here for such a long time, and I am Silesian [an ethnic minority in Poland], so I do not have a typical Polish accent. Very often, when people talk to me, they don't realize that I am a Pole. I do not admit that I am Polish. It is not like I am ashamed, but, when the stereotypes come out, why would somebody treat you differently for this reason. (Alana)

Other strategies used in the process of distancing oneself from the national identity included focusing on a regional ethnic minority identity contested in some Polish nationalist discourses, as is illustrated by Fatimah's statement:

> I am the worst case when it comes to this, because I do not feel so much Polish myself and there is not much to pass over [to children]. I come from Silesia, from a typically Silesian family, they are proud of being Silesians. We practised, maybe not practised, we cherished it; the language – all my childhood I spoke Silesian. They [my family] were proud of the history. (Fatimah)

It is worth noting, that the foregrounding of the Polish identity does not translate into a rejection of the host country. It is more likely that the British nationality and identity are not the significant point of reference for Polish Muslim converts. Typically, they do not aspire to become British, or to be seen as such.

## Conclusion

Identities are constructed through multiple social relations within various spaces and places. Belonging is multi-layered, territorial and dynamic (Yuval-Davis, 2011). Polish converts in the UK are a part of religion that is not only embraced in private, but also publicly contested and politicised. Therefore, their experiences need to considered as an interplay between the macro-level structures, institutions and policies and the micro-level identities and everyday lived realities. The longstanding approach of the British government of inclusion of all ethnic and religious minorities, and respecting and protecting their right to participate in all aspects of British life has been compromised by more hostile discourses which emerged during the EU referendum (Brexit). Many commentators argue that anti-Muslim racism have been conflated with intensified anti-immigrant populist sentiments mainstreamed during the Brexit campaign and following revisions of migration policies (Burell and Hopkins, 2020; Redclift and Begum Rajima, 2021). These developments exposed the fragility of multicultural project and demonstrated beyond doubt that multiculturalism has not been fully implemented. In consequence, in the UK, adherence to Islam continues to produce the spoiled identity in many social interactions. The "established" status means, however, that Muslims are represented, and to some extent, recognized at all levels of governance, and able to influence public policies (Tatari and Shaykhutdinov, 2014). Despite the ambivalent "special status" (Cheeseman and Khanum, 2009, p. 41) and "securitization" (Brown, 2008), they are less marginalised by the political elites than Muslims (converts and Muslims of immigrant origin) in Poland. This is reflected in the experiences of converts who feel more at ease about adopting a publicly visible religious identity in the UK.

The high level of religious pluralism in the UK facilitates migrants' reflexive engagement with the community of born Muslims and the wealth of ethnically mediated expressions of Islam. In the UK, Polish converts come into contact with the lived Islam more often than in Poland, and many of them change their perception of the imagined Muslim religious community as a result. Through the direct contact with born Muslims some converts face additional challenges in managing their identities and strive to pass on as "real" Muslims when their authenticity is questioned. The presence of material Islam and the aesthetic community allows them also to develop and recalibrate their religious practices, including mosque attendance.

The settlement in the new country locates the negotiation of converts' old and new social relationships on the transnational plane. Converts maintain their biographical continuity through the cultivation of their links with the culture of origin and close relationships with significant others. The discontinuities in their biographies are managed in such a way, as to not discredit who they were prior to embracing Islam and who they became (Goffman, 1963). At the same time, they establish new connections. As far as the relationships with diverse ethnic and religious groups are concerned, those with other Polish converts to Islam seem to be particularly prevalent and important for the respondents. Their specific position as both migrants in the UK and converts to a minority religion foregrounds their national identity. As a result, some women reaffirm their Polishness, while a handful of others reject it almost completely and try to pass on as non-Poles.

## References

Adamczyk, T. (2019). Wartości patriotyczne w doświadczeniu polskich migrantów w Wielkiej Brytanii. Zeszyty Naukowe KUL, 4(248), 71–90.

Adams, G. & Markus, H. R. (2001). Culture as Patterns: An Alternative Approach to the Problem of Reification. Culture Psychology, 7: 283–296.

Amin, A. (2002). Ethnicity and the multicultural city: living with diversity. *Environment and Planning*, 34, 959–80.

Barth, F. (1996). Ethnic groups and boundaries. In J. Hutchinson & A. D. Smith (Eds.), *Ethnicity* (pp. 75–82). Oxford University Press.

Baumann, G. (1999). *The Multicultural Riddle: Rethinking National, Ethnic, and Religious Identities*. Routledge.

Berger, P. L. (1990). *The Sacred Canopy: Elements of a Sociological Theory of Religion*. Anchor Books.

Birt, J. (2009). Islamophobia and British Muslim identity politics. In P. Hopkins & R. Gale (Eds.), *Muslims in Britain. Race, Pace and Identities*, (pp. 210–227). Edinburgh University Press.

Brice, K. M. A. (2010). *A Minority Within a Minority: A Report on Converts to Islam in the United Kingdom*, Faith Matters. Retrieved November 30, 2021, from https://www.researchgate.net/publication/309616357_A_minority_within_a_minority_A_report_on_converts_to_Islam_in_the_United_Kingdom.

Bolognani, M. & Mellor, J. (2012), British Pakistani Women's Use of the 'Religion versus Culture' Contrast: A Critical Analysis, *Culture and Religion*, 13(2), 211–226.

Bourque, N. (2006). How Deborah Became Aisha: The Conversion Process and the Creation of Female Muslim Identity. In K. van Nieukwerk (Ed.), *Women Embracing Islam* (pp. 233–249), University of Texas Press.

Brown, K. (2008). The Promise and Perils of Women's Participation in UK Mosques: The Impact of Securitisation Agendas on Identity, Gender and Community. *The British Journal of Politics and International Relations*, 10(3), 472–491.

Buchowski, M. &and Chlewińska, K. (2012). Tolerance of Cultural Diversity in Poland and Its Limitations. Adam Mickiewicz University. Retrieved November 30, 2021 from https://cadmus.eui.eu/bitstream/handle/1814/24381/ACCEPT_WP5_2012_34_Country-synthesis-report_Poland.pdf.

Burrell, K., & Hopkins, P. (2019). Introduction: Brexit, race and migration. Environment and Planning C. *Politics and Space*, 37(1), 4–7.

Cap, P. (2018). From 'cultural unbelonging' to 'terrorist risk': communicating threat in the Polish anti-immigration discourse. *Critical Discourse Sturdies*, 15(3), 285–302.

Cheeseman, D. & N. Khanum, (2009). 'Soft' segregation: Muslim identity, British secularism and inequality. In A. Dinham, R. Furbey & V. Lowndes (Eds.), *Faith in the public realm: Controversies, policies and practices* (pp. 41–62). Policy Press.

Collins, P. J. (2002). Habitus and the storied self: Religious faith and practice as a dynamic means of consolidating identities. *Culture and Religion*, 3, 147–161.

Collett, E. (2013). The Integration Needs of Mobile EU Citizens. Migration Policy Institute Europe. Retrieved November 30, 2021 from https://www.migrationpolicy.org/pubs/MPIEurope-FreeMovement-Integration.pdf.

Drinkwater, S., Eade, J., & Garapich, M. (2009). Poles Apart? EU Enlargement and the Labour Market Outcomes of Immigrants in the United Kingdom. *International Migration*, 47(1), 161–190.

Dziekan, M. (2005). Historia i tradycje polskiego islamu. In A. Przymies (Eds.), *Muzułmanie w Europie*. (pp. 199–228). Wydawnictwo Akademickie Dialog.

Eade, J., Drinkwater, S. & M. Garapich (2007). Class and Ethnicity: Polish Migrant Workers in London: Full Research Report. ESRC End of Award Report, RES-000-22-1294. Swindon: ESRC. Retrieved November 30, 2021 from http://doc.ukdataservice.ac.uk/doc/6056/mrdoc/pdf/6056uguide.pdf.

Erdal, M. B. & Oeppen, C. (2013). Migrant Balancing Acts: Understanding the Interactions Between Integration and Transnationalism, *Journal of Ethnic and Migration Studies*, 39(6), 867–884.

Farrar, M. (2002). *The Struggle for 'Community' in a British Multi-Ethnic Inner-City Area*. Edwin Mellen.

Farrar, M. (2012). Multiculturalism in the UK: A Contested Discourse. In M. Farrar, S. Robinson, Y. Valli & P. Wetherly (Eds.) *Islam in the West* (pp. 7–23). Palgrave Macmillan.

Gale, R. (2009). The multicultural city and the politics of religious architecture: urban planning, mosques and meaning-making in Birmingham. In R. Gale & P. Hopkins (Eds.), *Muslims in Britain. Race, place and identities* (pp. 30–44). Edinburgh University Press.

Galonnier, J. (2015). The racialization of Muslims in France and the United States: Some insights from white converts to Islam. *Social Compass*, 62(4), 570–583.

Goffman, E. (1963). *Stigma: Notes on the Management of Spoiled Identity*. Penguin Books.

Goffman, E. (1969). *Strategic interaction*. University of Pennsylvania Press.

Goffman, E. (1972). *Interaction ritual*. Penguin Books.

Goździak, E. M. & P. Márton. (2018). Where the Wild Things Are: Fear of Islam and the Anti-Refugee Rhetoric in Hungary and in Poland. *Central and Eastern European Migration Review*, 7(2), 125–151.

Grzymala-Kazlowska, A. (2018). From connecting to social anchoring: adaptation and 'settlement' of Polish migrants in the UK. *Journal of Ethnic and Migration Studies*, 44(2), 252–269.

Grzymała-Moszczyńska, H., Hay, D. & J. Krotofil (2011). Between universalism and ethnic particularism: Polish migrants to the United Kingdom; perspective from the psychology of religion. *Studia Migracyjne-Przegląd Polonijny* 37,1, 223–236.

Hann, C. (2000). Problems with the (De)Privatization of Religion. *Anthropology Today*, 16(6), 14–20.

Harris, A. (2004). *Future Girl. Young Women in the Twenty-first Century*. Routledge.

Hermans, H. J. M. (2001). The Dialogical Self: Toward a Theory of Personal and Cultural Positioning. Culture & Psychology, 7:243–281.

Jeldtoft, N. (2011). Lived Islam: Religious identity with 'non-organized' Muslim minorities. *Ethnic and Racial Studies*, 34(7), 1134–51.

Kapinos, S. (2018). (Nie)dylematy tożsamościowe Polaków w Wielkiej Brytanii na przykładzie badań w hrabstwie Hertfordshire. *Studia Migracyjne – Przegląd Polonijny*, 1(167), 117–143.

Kinnvall, C. (2004). Globalization and Religious Nationalism: Self, Identity, and the Search for Ontological Security. *Political Psychology*, 25(5), 741–767.

Krotofil, J. (2011). 'If I am to Be a Muslim. I Have to Be a Good One'. Polish Migrant Women Embracing Islam and Reconstruction Identities in Dialogue with Self and Others. In K. Górak-Sosnowska (Ed.), *Muslims in Poland and Eastern Europe. Widening the European Discourse on Islam* (pp. 154–168). University of Warsaw.

Krotofil, J. (2013). *Religia w procesie kształtowania tożsamości wśród polskich migrantów w Wielkiej Brytanii*. Nomos.

Krotofil, J. and D. Motak (2018). Between traditionalism, fundamentalism, and populism: A critical discourse analysis of the media coverage of the migration crisis in Poland. In U. Schmiedel, G. Smith (Eds.), *Religion in the European refugee crisis* (pp. 61–85). Palgrave Macmillan.

Krotofil, J., Górak-Sosnowska, K., Piela, A. & Abdallah-Krzepkowska, B. (forthcoming). Being Muslim, Polish, and at Home – Converts to Islam in Poland. *Journal of Contemporary Religion*.

Kulpa, R. (2014). Western leveraged pedagogy of Central and Eastern Europe: discourses of homophobia, tolerance, and nationhood. *Gender, Place and Culture*, 21(4), 431–448.

Lewis, P. (2015). From Seclusion to Inclusion: British 'Ulama and the Politics of Social Visibility. In G. Jonker and V. Amiraux (Eds.), *Politics of Visibility* (pp. 169–190). Transcript.

Lipiński, A. (2020). Constructing 'the Others' as a Populist Communication Strategy. The Case of the 'Refugee Crisis' in Discourse in the Polish Press. In A. Stępińska (Ed.), *Populist Discourse in the Polish Media* (pp. 155–180). Uniwersytet im. Adama Mickiewicza.

McGhee, D. (2008). *The end of multiculturalism? Terrorism, integration and human rights*. Open University Press.

Milewski, M. & Ruszczak-Żbikowska, J. (2008). Motywacje do wyjazdu, praca, więzi społeczne i plany na przyszłość polskich migrantów przebywających w Wielkiej Brytanii i Irlandii. *Centre for Migration Research Working Papers*, 35/93.

Mitchell, C. (2006). The religious context of ethnic identities. *Sociology*, 40(6), 1135–1152.

Modood, T. (2003). Muslims and the Politics of Difference. *The Political Quarterly*, 74(s1), 100–115.

Modood, T. (2013). *Multiculturalism*. Polity Press.

Mol, J. J. (1971). Immigrant Absorption and Religion. *International Migration Review*, 5 (1), 62–71.

Moosavi, L. (2015). The Racialization of Muslim Converts in Britain and Their Experiences of Islamophobia. *Critical Sociology*, 41(1), 41–56.

Nalborczyk, A. (2011). Mosques in Poland. Past and present In K. Górak-Sosnowska (Ed.), *Muslims in Poland and Eastern Europe. Widening the European Discourse on Islam* (pp. 154–168). University of Warsaw.

Narkowicz, K. and Pędziwiatr, K. (2017). Saving and fearing Muslim women in 'post-communist' Poland: troubling Catholic and secular Islamophobia. *Gender, Place and Culture*, 24(2), 288–299.

Oh, I. (2010). Motherhood in Christianity and Islam: Critiques, Realities, and Possibilities. *Journal of Religious Ethics*, 38(4), 638–653.

Öyzurek, E. (2009). Convert Alert: German Muslims and Turkish Christians as Threats to Security in the New Europe. *Comparative Studies in Society and History*, 51(1), 91–116.

Pasieka, A. (2014). Neighbors: About the multiculturalization of the Polish past. *East European Politics and Societies*, 28(1), 225–251.

Pankowski, R. (2012). *Right-Wing Extremism in Poland*. Friedrich Ebert Stiftung. Retrieved November 30, 2021 from https://library.fes.de/pdf-files/id-moe/09409-20121029.pdf.

Parekh, B. (2000). *Rethinking Multiculturalism: Cultural Diversity and Political Theory*. Harvard University Press.

Petley, J. & Richardson, R. (2011). Introduction. In J. Petley & R. Richardson (Eds.), *Pointing the finger. Islam and Muslims in the British Media*. Oneworld Publications.

Pędziwiatr (2011). "The Established and Newcomers" in Islam in Poland or the Intergroup Relations within the Polish Muslim Community. In K. Górak-Sosnowska (Ed.), *Muslims in Poland and Eastern Europe* (pp. 169–182). University of Warsaw.

Pędziwiatr, K. (2017). Conversions to Islam and Identity Reconfigurations among Poles in Great Britain. *Studia Religiologica*, 50(3), 221–239.

Piela, A. (2020). Peace versus Conflict-Journalism in Poland: Representation of Islam, Muslims and Refugees by Progressive and Right-Wing Polish Media. In K. Radde-Antweiler & X. Zeiler (Eds.), *The Routledge Handbook of Religion and Journalism* (pp. 279–295). Routledge.

Porter-Szűcs, (2011). *Faith and Fatherland: Catholicism, Modernity, and Poland. Faith and Fatherland: Catholicism, Modernity, and Poland*. Oxford University Press.

Rambo, L. R. (1995). *Understanding Religious Conversion*. Yale University Press.

Redclift, V. M. & F. Begum Rajina (2021). The hostile environment, Brexit, and 'reactive-' or 'protective transnationalism'. *Global networks*, 21(1), 196–214.

Rogowska, B. (2017). *Wpływ Polaków nawróconych na islam na społeczności lokalne w Polsce*. [Unpublished doctoral dissertation]. University of Łódź.

Ryan, L. (2010). Becoming Polish in London: negotiating ethnicity through migration. *Social Identities*, 16(3), 359–376.

Ryan, L. (2018). Differentiated embedding: Polish migrants in London negotiating belonging over time. *Journal of Ethnic and Migration Studies*, 44(2), 233–251.

Rzepnikowska, A. (2019). Racism and xenophobia experienced by Polish migrants in the UK before and after Brexit vote. *Journal of Ethnic and Migration Studies*, 45(1), 1–17.

Schielke, S. (2009). Being good in Ramadan: Ambivalence, fragmentation, and the moral self in the lives of young Egyptians. *Journal of the Royal Anthropological Institute* 15, 524–540.

Schielke, S. (2010). Second thoughts about the anthropology of Islam, or how to make sense of grand schemes in everyday life. *ZMO Working Papers*, 2, 1–16.

Schleifer, A. (1996). *Motherhood in Islam*. Fons Vitae.

Scott, J. W. (2007). *The Politics of the Veil*. Princeton University Press.

Sealy, T. (2017). Making the "Other" from "Us": The Representation of British Converts to Islam in Mainstream British Newspapers. *Journal of Muslim Minority Affairs*. 37(2), 196–210.

Sealy, T. (2018). *Identity, Difference, Religion: Multiculturalism and British Converts to Islam* [Unpublished doctoral dissertation]. University of Bristol.

Shanneik, Y. (2011). Conversion and Religious Habitus: The Experiences of Irish Women Converts to Islam in the Pre-Celtic Tiger Era. *Journal of Muslim Minority Affairs*, 31(4), 503–517.

Staiger, N. (2014). 'To be a minority or not': multiculturalism in Poland between Europe and the past [Unpublished Master's thesis]. Uniwersytet im. Adama Mickiewicza. Retrieved November 30, 2021 from https://repository.gchumanrights.org/handle/20.500.11825/477?show=full.

Tatari, E. & Shaykhutdinov, R. (2014). Muslims and Minority Politics in Great Britain. *Journal of Muslim Minority Affairs*, 34 (1), 22–44.

Taylor, Ch. (1994). The Politics of Recognition. In A. Gutmann (Ed.), *Multiculturalism. Examining the Politics of Recognition*. Princeton University Press.

Trzebiatowska, M. (2010). The advent of the 'EasyJet Priest': Dilemmas of Polish Catholic integration in the UK. *Sociology*, 44(6), 1055–1072.

Valentine, G. (2008). Living with difference: reflections on geographies of encounter. *Progress in Human Geography*, 32(3), 323–337.

Vertovec, S. (2007). Super-diversity and its implications. *Ethnic and Racial Studies*, 30(6), 1024–1054.

Werbner, P. (2002). *Imagined Diasporas among Manchester Muslims*. James Currey.

Włoch, R. (2009). Islam in Poland Between Ethnicity and Universal Umma. *International Journal of Sociology*, 39(3), 58–67.

Wohlrab-Sahr, M. (2006). Symbolizing Distance: Conversion to Islam in Germany and the United States. In K. van Nieuwkerk (Eds.), *Women Embracing Islam* (pp. 71–92). University of Texas Press.

Woodlock, R. (2010). Praying Where They Don't Belong: Female Muslim Converts and Access to Mosques in Melbourne, Australia. *Journal of Muslim Minority Affairs*, 30(2): 265–278.

Younis, T. & Hassan, G. (2017). Changing Identities: A Case Study of Western Muslim Converts Whose Conversion Revised Their Relationship to Their National Identity. *Journal of Muslim Minority Affairs*, 37(1), 30–40.

Yuval-Davis, N. (1997). *Gender and nation*. Sage.

Yuval-Davis, N. (2006). Intersectionality and feminist politics, *European Journal of Women's Studies*, 13(3), 193–209.

Yuval-Davis, N. (2011). Power, Intersectionality and the Politics of Belonging. FREIA *Working Paper Series*, Working paper, 75.

Zebiri, K. (2008). *British Muslim Converts: Choosing Alternative Lives*. Oneworld Publicationis.

CHAPTER 4

# Polish Platonic Islamophobia

*Katarzyna Górak-Sosnowska* | ORCID: 0000-0002-1121-6240
SGH Warsaw School of Economics

## Introduction

Islamophobia is a highly contested and discussed term which poses challenges for defining, operationalising, measuring and monitoring it. Some scholars critique the term "Islamophobia", arguing that it is too broad and, therefore, imprecise, while at the same time it offers only one explanation – an irrational fear against Islam (Cesari, 2011, p. 21). In this chapter, we focus on Islamophobia as a "real and tangible discriminatory phenomenon" (Allen, 2020, p. 8) as experienced by our respondents emotionally and sometimes physically. We will also refer to Islamophobia as a politically and publicly conceived phenomenon that provides the context for how Islamophobia is understood, experienced, and addressed. Despite the contested nature of the term 'Islamophobia' we use it consequently throughout the chapter as this is the word used by our respondents and the only one used in the Polish public discourse.

Given the marginal number of local Muslim population, their degree of integration with the mainstream society and the fact that there has never been a single terrorist attack inspired by radical Islamists in Poland, Polish Islamophobia seems to be simply unreasonable. Unlike many West European countries, Poland is not very attractive for Muslim migrants (Goździak and Márton, 2018) and most probably will stay this way – if not due to the level of economic development, then because of being culturally homogenous, which makes acculturation challenging as ethnic, national or religious Others will simply stand out.

Despite all these factors that ought to prevent prejudice against Islam or Muslims in Poland, Islam and Muslims are constructed as the key threat to Polish nation (Pędziwiatr, 2019), interchangeably (and sometimes jointly) with LGBT+ people. For a significant segment of the Polish political scene, the existence of Muslims in Poland signifies a cultural divergence from both Polish "traditional values" and European/Western values of freedom, equality or liberalism.

This situates Polish Islamophobia in a complicated setting for two reasons. First, due to the small size of local Muslim community the vast majority of Poles have never been in a direct contact with a Muslim person (Stefaniak, 2015, p. 3). A Muslim in not a colleague from work or school, a neighbour or a friend. In most cases it is the essentialised "global Muslim" (Allen, 2007, p. 98), attributed with all possible kinds of negative features. The Polish female converts to Islam – especially if they are "visibly Muslim" (Tarlo, 2010) – may the first Muslims Poles ever met. Thus, the former become the reference point for Islam (Frisina, 2006, p. 83) for people who have only essentialised knowledge about Muslims.

Second, Islam and Muslims are a counterpoint to how Polish ethnic and national identities are constructed and fetishized (Goździak and Márton, 2018, p. 4). In fact, Polish Islamophobia functions in a somewhat different way from the Western Islamophobia. While the latter is used as a way of achieving control over Muslims who are perceived as a challenge to Western liberal identity (Jackson, 2018, pp. 145–146), in case of Poland presenting Islam as the enemy serves to strengthen the Polish national identity. At the same time, the Polish Islamophobia is a manifest that aims to oppose Western values of democracy and liberalism. There are also similar ethnic and nationalist anti-Muslim discourses in the West, but they are overshadowed by post-colonial narratives, which are largely absent from Central and Eastern European intellectual thought (Balogun, 2020). This puts Polish female converts to Islam in a particularly difficult position as they are doubly stigmatised due to being Muslim and being seen as betraying the Polish nation (of which the Catholic religion is a significant element).

In this chapter, we are presenting the complexity and diversity of Polish platonic Islamophobia – an Islamophobia that in the last two decades has been steadily growing despite the marginal size of local Muslim population (Stefaniak, 2015)[1] and is a clear example of the "tribal stigma" according to Goffman (1963). Strong anti-Muslim sentiments and the fear of "Islamisation" of Poland make the Polish and Central and Eastern European Islamophobia puzzling. Over a decade ago Strabac and Listhaug (2008, p. 283) have noticed that individual anti-Muslim and anti-immigrant prejudice is higher in Eastern Europe compared to Western Europe, while the independent variables (such

---

1 The scarce Jewish community is the target of platonic anti-Semitism in Poland (Samuels, 2012, p. x). Anti-Semitism however, in contrast to Islamophobia, has a long history in Poland. Currently however, both communities – Jewish and Muslim – are very small, yet they provoke strong and widespread negative sentiments. Thus the reference of platonic feelings towards non-existent subject.

as level of education, or occupational status) have weaker effect on these prejudices. The cultural legacy of communism has been suggested as a potential reason for low acceptance of difference in these contexts.

### Being the Only Muslim

Among the EU countries Poland is one of the most homogenous in ethnic and religious terms. In fact, over 97% of Poland's inhabitants declared Polish nationality, while only 1.5% declared a non-Polish ethnicity or nationality. Of those who answered the question about religious belief (over 91%), almost everyone declared their religion as Catholicism (over 95%; GUS, 2013, p. 89, 99). This cultural homogeneity is often highlighted in national discourses and Polish converts to Islam locale their experiences within this framework. While Polish female converts to Islam are not the only Muslims in Poland, they may well be the first Muslim an average Pole meets. As one of our respondents says, it has a profound impact on how Polish female converts to Islam are being perceived in the public space:

> In Poland, everyone is the same. The only differences are the differences between the countryside and the city. Because those from cities believe that they are better than those who are living in the countryside. In Poland people live according to a schema, all are the same, all follow the same religion, and have the same vision of how life should be. If you stand out, they cannot understand you, and so you hear comments. (Daria)

According to Pickel and Öztürk (2017), exposure to migrants and/or Muslims is the decisive factor limiting anti-Muslim prejudice. It means that Eastern European countries are bound to be more Islamophobic, as their local Muslim communities are very small. As a result, Polish female converts to Islam encounter stares, questions, or remarks that constitute microaggressions – sometimes subtle negative and denigrating messages sent to the marginalised group (Nadal et al., 2012, p. 16). At the same time, our respondents said that they feel the need to embody the counter-example of all the negative stereotypes linked to Muslims and Islam (Ghalaini, 2020) which is a difficult identity to embrace.

Quite a few of our respondents recalled at least one situation in which they may have been the first, or one of the first Muslims ever met. Sometimes stares or question asked by strangers are not perceived as a form of microaggression. Our respondents take into account the lack of knowledge and familiarity with

Muslims that explain strangers' behaviour. As one of them explains: "many people don't want to do anything bad, it's rather their lack of knowledge, they don't know what to do, how to react ..." (Lidia). Being the only Muslim, one has encountered offers the family, colleagues or complete strangers a rare opportunity to see what a Muslim looks like and interact with them. Sometimes being possibly the first Polish Muslim met has an additional advantage as the following story illustrates:

> I was standing at the bus stop in [town name] and there comes a woman with groceries and I see that she is looking and lurking, and so she starts talking to me about her groceries (...) and then she says: "Are you a Muslim from Islam?", "Well, yes ...". "And can I ask you something?", "Sure" and so we are waiting for the bus and she says "coz my daughter lives in England and has a Muslim husband, but you tell me because he hates me. Tell me, how it is, what is a woman allowed to do in Islam?" (Franciszka)

The situation was not offensive for the respondent, even though she was singled out because of her hijab. The woman was civil, and thanked her for providing the information. This illustrates the limited access to reliable information about Islam and Muslims in Poland. The education system offers very limited information about Islam, religious instruction at schools is in fact Catholic religious instruction for Polish Catholics. At the same time, the Internet, especially social media is full of content that demonises and dehumanises Muslims. While generally the level of prejudice increases with age, in case of the attitudes towards Muslims in Poland, the opposite is true – many more young Poles are prejudiced against Islam and Muslims, and social media is often thought to be the reason for this (Stefaniak, 2015: 32). Another respondent (Iza) recalled a situation when a Somali husband of her friend's, dressed in a *galabiyya* (a loose-fitting traditional garment), started to pray at home and left the window open. An alarmed neighbour called the anti-terrorist squad. In both described cases, the individuals were singled out as Muslims, but they were perceived differently: Franciszka was met with curiosity and the interlocutor's willingness to learn about Islam, while the Somali man was considered to be a security risk. Both examples can be located at the intersection of racial and religious prejudice. In this case, the Somali man was considered as alien and thus threatening, while Franciszka was Polish – a fellow countrywoman. In this manner Polish females converts to Islam have a moral career to fulfil (Goffman 1963: 44–46). However, sometimes being Polish works against female converts to Islam as we will discuss it in the subsequent section.

In the plethora of individual cases and experiences attribution plays a significant role. It is about the meaning that Polish female converts to Islam give to the fact that they are singled out as the Muslims, and to how the non-Muslim public attempts to organise their knowledge about Islam gained from earlier encounters with a handful of Muslims.

> ... when a Muslim woman came to the recruitment office they [her colleagues] said to me: "She is smoking". They were so outraged, because they were used to me and it was so strange to them, or when I had my period and didn't pray they asked: "aren't you going to pray?" This is how it was – they were pointing it out to me. (*laughter*) (Kornelia)

> I am perceived through the lens of this religion all the time and it is Islam that is being judged, not me. (...) A person met me once and said: "Excuse me, can I ask you something, because I am so confused. Once I've seen you wearing a grey dress, another time a blue one, then a black one ... and so I try to figure out, because last Monday you wore a blue one, and now it's a blue one too, but it's Friday. What does it depend on? How do you have to dress?" So it was a great shock, as these people tried to figure out some religious rules. Instead of asking me directly, they were making up these patterns. (Czesława)

The two quotations presented here demonstrate how contextual Islamophobic behaviour is. Kornelia did not mind to a referent of Islam for her colleagues, and actually enjoyed it. Czesława was frustrated to have her behaviour interpreted exclusively through the lens of her religion.

Their individual choices or other dispositional features became less significant attribution factors compared to their culture and religion. This type of cultural determinism that explains an individual's behaviour, attitudes or opinions as the result of culture rather than individual dispositions seems to be common in the Polish context for two reasons. The first one is the monocultural environment and limited contacts with 'Others', what makes people prone to generalise knowledge gained from one case onto the whole population – thus the only Muslim becomes the image of Islam. While the first reason is cognitive, the second is systemic and refers to lacking post-colonial reflection and relevant studies or discourse. The post-colonial reflection occupies only the periphery of the Polish academic discourse and thus means to transcend the essentialised cultural framework are limited (Markowska-Manista, 2016, pp. 321–322).

Conversion to Islam means that one becomes a religious minority within the mainstream Catholic Polish society. Hijab wearers embrace an identity marker that carries a stigma. For many people from the converts' social circles, the conversion was significant enough to renegotiate, reconfigure, or sometimes even break existing relations. These reconfigurations occur on different levels – in the local community, among friends and extended family.

Despite their religious and sometimes visual difference, converts usually successfully manage to fit in. The familiarity is negotiated depending on the setting. In case of Ewelina it was achieved through constant small interactions in the same space with a group of strangers. They were a group of men standing around and drinking alcohol by her house, a common sight in Polish less-affluent areas. In the beginning, she would cross the street to avoid them. When they greeted her, she always greeted them back, when they spoke to her, she always replied politely. After a while, they got used to her and stepped off the pavement to make space for her when she was walking past. According to Simon and Grabow (2014) respect ought to be characterised by mutuality, and so experience of civility results in less negative feelings to the giver. In Poland (and beyond), individuals drinking alcohol in public are looked down on. Ewelina acknowledged them civility, and they were civil in return.

Large cities have been usually perceived as more open and friendly to social diversity then rural areas. According to Maxwell (2019) the reasons of the urban-rural divide in this respect are mostly compositional rather than contextual, that is, it is not the experience of living together with Others, but rather higher education, the choice of profession, or self-selection into a large city. Contrary to these findings, Herbert (2018, p. 48) observes that in Russia urban areas emerge as less tolerant than rural areas which have less experience with diversity. Our data seems to confirm this observation as our respondents tend to experience Islamophobia when they travel to larger cities rather in the towns or villages where they live:

> In bigger cities, at the airports I feel such negative vibes, people stare at me a lot with such a ... with such an anger, and they don't know me. And in my town, it is not the case (Aleksandra)

> In my town I never had any problems. It is worse if we travel somewhere to Poznań or to Gdańsk. There are always groups of young males who enjoy taunting me (Angelika)

It seems that living in rural areas gives many converts two assets – familiarity with the local community and the shared space. Interestingly, many of our respondents, regardless of where they're from, believe that it is much harder to be a visible Muslim in a city. In her Polish home town, Czesława became "the Muslim", who was locally known, recognized and protected by community members. If anyone stared at her or said anything unpleasant, the locals stood up for her and said "What are you looking at? This is *our* Muslim!". Angelika is well known in her local community – they know that she has been Muslim for 15 years, they remember her as a child, and despite converting, she is still perceived as "one of them". Both women became normalised in their local communities (Goffman, 1963: 43).

In some cases, the hijab worn by some of our participants invited unwelcome attention. Some women were approached and asked personal questions, as if wearing hijab was a clear indication of permission to engage or challenge them:

> When people saw that I wear hijab they allowed themselves to ask all possible questions, starting even from with whom do I sleep, because that was also the case. (Anita)

> It is that everyone claims the right to criticise your choice, talk about it, or ask. You have to explain yourself constantly and it is f****g frustrating. (Marysia)

A similar invasion of privacy occurs when women are visibly pregnant. Their pregnancy becomes the subject of public attention and as such, a social phenomenon. In a way a pregnant body becomes publicly owned with people daring to ask questions, comment or even touch it (Jakubowska, 2016, p. 104). In the case of converts, it is their journey to Islam that becomes the subject of public attention with people daring to ask things that they would have otherwise never ask a stranger. It also indicates that hijab is perceived as a stigma symbol and so, stigmatised individuals always have to explain themselves to the public (Goffman, 1963). However, some of our respondents used this opportunity for *da'wah* (proselyting). One of them was Czesława. When people asked her about her religion, she welcomed it:

> I was really happy and perceived it as a chance for dawah. It was quite funny to see that people keep looking at me. So I smile to them and sometimes someone dares to ask: "Sorry, can I ask you something?", "No problem". People apologised for asking questions that related to religion, but I told them that religion is not a taboo for me, I am free to talk. So I was very often stopping on the street, while I was going home and had an

hour or two, and talked with people – they were curious. And if someone had commented on something then I smiled and kept going my way. (Czesława)

### Familiar Strangers – Family Reactions to Conversion

Embracing Islam usually meant a significant decline in relationships with friends, colleagues and extended family members. Unlike the close family who often tried to understand and make peace with the convert's decision, many of these more distant significant others did not wish to continue the relationship. Although the relation usually depends on the two (or more) parties, and the converts also have their part in shaping these relations, rarely their was the convert who decided to distance herself. It was rather the non-Muslim majority who had the power to define who belonged to their (Ramahi and Suleiman, 2017). Many of our respondents did not understand this decision, especially as they had believed their relationships with the people who rejected them were strong. One of them said: "I don't regret it at all, because I can see now that they were not my friends, but at the time, I felt very sad, because nothing had changed!" (Marlena).

According to her, only one aspect of her identity had changed – her religion. For others, the change was much more profound. She was perceived as so different that multiple people simply cut her off. The same happened to Kornelia:

> It is so strange to me that when I wore no [head]scarf I was ok for my friends, but when I put on the scarf, I was not ok anymore. And I wonder why. When I take off the scarf, I am exactly the same person. My scarf gives me only the possibility to interpret myself, but I have the same stuff in my head, nothing changes. (Kornelia)

While conversion to Islam is a personal choice, it has significant consequences for the non-Muslim family in terms of dealing with the conversion in cognitive terms, but also the way family is perceived by their local community. In her now classic work, Zebiri (2008) identified three categories of family reactions: negative followed by acceptance, negative without much hope for a change, and supportive. In this chapter, we focus on the first two types of reactions.

The new rules that came together with embracing Islam are often hard to accept for non-Muslim family members. Sometimes, the non-Muslim family members postulated for a change in the boundaries between the old and new life by negotiating with the convert or by trying to make them more implicit

(Vroon, 2014). These include the brother of Franciszka, who kept offering her alcohol each time they met, or the mother of Paulina who tried to negotiate with her the length of her blouses. Sometimes these boundaries are set, even if not reconciled. For instance, the mother of Anita did not agree with her decision to convert to Islam, but at the same time she sewed niqabs and abayas for her.

It is often not the decision to embrace Islam, but to adopt the hijab that triggers the most hostile reactions. Since in the context of Islam, the hijab is the most powerful symbol of Otherness (Zebiri 2011), it is the ultimate proof that the decision to embrace Islam is firm, and at the same time, it communicates this decision to the public. Ola was verbally attacked at home when she turned up wearing a headscarf. Similarly, Anna's mother was horrified and outraged at her conversion 'A Muslim daughter? I did not raise you this way, I had you baptised, didn't I?'. The parents of Anna (a woman in her early 20's) prohibited her from wearing the hijab, but – as she lives away – she only takes the hijab off when they are around. The mother of Lidia looks at her with regret and keeps saying 'God, my child, what do you look like?.'

Some family reactions were particularly appalling. By the time she told her parents about conversion, Otylia, a woman in her 40s, learned from them that she had been adopted. She was told: "So we adopted you, and you ##hurt us so badly!". Extended family members of Daria believe that by converting, she rejected both them and their religion. Iza has no contact with family members on her father's side. The parents of Otylia threatened her that they would inform her employer about her conversion, so she would be sacked. Otylia works with children, and her conversion rendered her unsuitable for this role according to her parents. Thus, they argued, she would have to re-embrace Christianity out of economic necessity.

Some of our respondents were worried about the opinions of neighbours and extended family. Many of them struggled to follow their Muslim principles – especially wearing the hijab – and not embarrassing and confusing their parents. According to Goffman (1963: 44) this is called normification and indicates how far can a stigmatised individual go in order to present themselves as an ordinary person. When Daria visits her parents, who live in a small village in Poland, she covers her head with a cap or a hood, so her parents do not have to face inquiries from their neighbours. Kornelia decided to take off her hijab when she visited her patents, because, she reasoned, they did not deserve to be ostracised in their community. It was not the idea of her parents, but rather Kornelia's fear that her hijab might not be welcome in the home community. Her parents are active community members, respected in their village and having a veiled daughter could render them outcasts. Arleta decided to wear hijab while being at her parents' place, but before that she explained a lot about Islam to her parents, so that they knew how to respond if they heard any remarks from their neighbours. Paulina has a similar dilemma and what frustrates her the most is that community members ask her parents about her conversion, and not her. Matylda reported her father was ashamed when others found out about her conversion.

Our respondents adopted a variety of strategies to cope with negative family reactions. One was to give them time to come along with their decision. Sometimes it was followed by a visible change in convert's behaviour which was meant to be viewed as positive by their family members. As Julianna admits:

> There was a time when they were very aggressive and didn't want to listen to any arguments, so I thought that the only way was to show them how can I live, and I thought that I should change, do something about myself. Because I'd been awfully ... I'd acted only on my self-interest. I was very selfish in how I picked friends. I treated people like crap, you know it was very hurtful – now I can see it. (Julianna)

With time, Julianna became more open and helpful so that her family members could learn that her religion led to a positive character change. In similar manner, Daria commented on the importance of persistence, and being understanding and open to conversation. She knew her parents hoped to maintain a good relationship, so she visited them as often as possible. Eleonora is estranged from her family, but feels this strengthens her religious commitment, just as Sadek (2017) elaborated on her own case. The strong focus on positive family relations in Islam, the so called "Islamic capital" (Franceschelli and O'Brien, 2014) inspires another coping strategy among our respondents:

> I didn't know how to start, to tell my mother, to tell my sister that I am Muslim. Once I embraced Islam, and I prayed to God, I asked him to help me, to make it easy (...). And while praying I asked, 'God, please make it easier for me to tell my closest family', because I know that I have to keep close family relations, because God wants me to. I told God: 'How can I maintain close relations, if my mother knows, she will maybe not get furious, but still ... my sister has a good heart, but she is also a hothead and when she starts screaming ... I was so afraid. So I kept praying, and praying to God, and at some point, my mother called me and said: "What are you doing? Calm down, I already know everything"' (Ewelina)

### Racialization of Polish Female Converts

Racialisation is a process of alienation of certain social groups through their essentialisation and devaluation of their uniqueness. Racism as many other ideologies can be easily adapted to local settings and socio-political conditions (Bobako, 2017). When it comes to Islam, it is a religion that has a high potential to be racialised both in Western Orientalist discourse and by Muslims themselves (Alam, 2012). This, in turn, puts the converts to Islam in a vulnerable and ambiguous position, summarized by Angelika:

> Some born Muslims look down on us, on us, Muslim converts, because we are apparently fake Muslims. At the same time, in Poland they don't like us either, because we betrayed our Catholicism, our Polishness, you know – and so we are turncoats, half-breeds. We have to defend ourselves among born Muslims. We have to explain to them that we are for real, that we are as Muslim as they are. And when we are in Poland, we also have to prove, explain, that we are as Polish, that we have not betrayed Poland, and you know, this is so ... we are standing at a crossroads. (Angelika)

Galonnier (2015) has showed that the process of racial assignation works in a similar manner according to national settings, yet the experiences of white converts to Islam are different and mean different things. Poland is one of the Europe's least culturally diverse societies, what makes people of different ethnicity visible in the public sphere. Polish female converts to Islam are being racialised as if they were relegated from their ethic category. Moreover, the troublesome logic of Polish-centrism, as it is called by Balogun (2020, p. 2) makes the attempts to racialize Polish female converts to Islam even stronger. It is because the essence of being Polish is framed by biological racism, religiosity and language (Balogun, 2020). By giving up Catholic religion Polish converts to Islam become less than Polish, as if religion determined their national identity.

The way Polish female converts to Islam are racialised in Poland bears similarities to the already well described racialisation of white Muslim converts in other contexts, such as the UK (Franks, 2000; Moosavi, 2015a). In case of our respondents who live in Poland, racialisation occurred through ascription of other ethnicities (mostly Arab). This was tested by inquiries about their Polish language fluency:

> People believed that I [converted] for an Arab, what was not the case, but I am not going to explain it to every single person that they are wrong.

> So they were saying that this is the one who's hooking up with Arabs, the one who travels to Egypt to have sex for money, Bin Laden's whore – this is what I have heard. (Alice)

> When we were living with my parents, they were teasing me, saying that I was not an Arab, that I have my culture and tradition, that I am Polish. (Angelika)

> Some people try to see whether I will answer them in Polish. (Iza)

The above cases seem to illustrate what Moosavi (2015a) called as re-racialisation of white converts due to associating Islam with a non-white religion. In Poland, the dominant ethnic association with Islam is "Arab" – not so much due to the number of Arab Muslims in Poland, but rather as a result of a mixture of geographic proximity, media discourses and Orientalist clichés (Górak-Sosnowska, 2012).

The peculiar logic of Polish-centrism seems to stand behind an observation made by several of our respondents. Namely, they believe that Polish or Slavic looking converts to Islam who wear hijab are particularly vulnerable in the public sphere, compared to women who are perceived as born Muslims.

> Girls who look non-Polish have it a lot easier, because they are actually tolerated in Warsaw (…), but Poles who were a scarf – not at all. (Faustyna)

> Most women who are attacked are converts, due to our Slavic looks (…) native Muslims have more freedom than the converts, because the converts have sold themselves out. (Alice)

The explanation offered by Alice refers to the notion that converts to Islam are traitors entertained by some non-Muslims. This is particularly harsh for female converts, due to socio-biological notions, according to which they will give birth to non-Polish, non-Catholic children. Polish males appear to be particularly offended by this idea. It stands in a sharp difference to Alam's findings (2020, p. 132). Her respondents were called a "traitor" mostly by other women, who treat conversion as a form of betraying the emancipatory women's rights movement. The particular vulnerability of Slavic-looking female converts led them to adopt more "Oriental," "Arab" looks (achieved by applying heavy, black make-up) or pretend not to speak Polish in in the hope of distracting their abusers. This in turn seems to be a different strategy from the one that Özyürek

(2015, pp. 56–58) observed among many German female converts who did not want to be perceived as migrants and made a lot of effort to not look like a Turkish woman.

Racialisation of converts to Islam occurs also among born Muslims (Moosavi, 2015a). We have not recorded any such incidents or examples among our respondents who lived in Poland, except for one peculiar case of a Tatar female, who accused Aleksandra of not being a "real" Muslim, but a traitor. As Aleksandra narrates:

> I got into an argument with a Tatar lady, who said I wasn't a Muslim, because you had to be born Muslim. She said I was a traitor and a poor imitation. But I didn't have anyone to betray, so I told her to buzz off. I also heard the same thing from Arabs, that if you didn't have Muslim relatives, then you're s**t, not a Muslim. What can you do?

In this case, the Tatar woman had combined two types of racialisation – one deployed sometimes by non-Muslim Poles ("you are a traitor") and one deployed by some born Muslims ("you are not a Muslim"). These two narratives are usually articulated in different contexts.[2]

Some of our respondents who live in the UK were racialised by born Muslims in similar ways which are well described in extant literature (Moosavi, 2015a, 2015b; Alam, 2012). As one of our respondents said: "Muslims are also prejudiced, they don't trust us. They don't treat me as a real Muslim, because I am white." (Daria)

Daria's husband is of Bangladeshi origin and they have children. She chose for them a diverse school, not a Muslim-majority one, because of the race issue – she was afraid that her children would not be considered real Muslims because they did not look as 'real Bangladeshis'. Moreover, she wants them to be socialised into diversity. Angelika's children who go to school in Birmingham were taunted by their peers that they could not be Muslim, because they were not dark-complexioned.

---

[2] Relations between the Polish Tatars and converts are complex and often difficult, despite the fact that both groups are native Polish. The Tatars are the indigenous Muslim community of Poland who are referred to as "the Polish Muslims". The converts are newcomers within the Muslim community. Tensions between the migrant and Tatar Muslims in Poland have situated the converts closer to the former rather than the latter group.

## Institutionalised Islamophobia

2015 was the milestone in the rise of Islamophobia at the institutional level. For the first time in Polish modern history, the issue of projected mass immigration from Muslim-majority countries became an effective political campaign tool (Pędziwiatr, 2016, p. 430). Soon after, Poland stubbornly refused to accept refugees from Muslim majority countries. As Piela and Łukjanowicz summarized (2018, p. 479), "the Polish government and the state institutions are reluctant to acknowledge and challenge Islamophobia, instead trying to cast Islamophobic acts as hooliganism, ignoring the rise of Islamophobic crime and often fuelling it". This statement illustrates the troublesome attitude of the Polish state to Islamophobia – on the one hand, it ignores its existence in public space settings, while on the other hand – it actually deploys it in politics.

Polish leading politicians, just as the Hungarian president, Viktor Orbán, are known for their Islamophobic rhetoric (Górak-Sosnowska and Molodikova, 2018). Moreover, the bulk of Islamophobic content is produced by state media (Piela, 2019) which is recognised as problematic by many Polish Muslims. According to Matylda:

> You feel a stranger in your own country. So what, if your closest friends accept you if your own country is ... In your own country, the Islamophobic discourse works so well (...) Most people I know are very patriotic. Some are right-wing. And you feel that you experience this terrible tension and it is bound to affect you. It affects you every day. (Matylda)

The data about institutionalised Islamophobia that affects Muslims in Poland is very scant and anecdotal as many of them do not report these incidents to keep a low profile. The marginal number of Muslims in Poland and the long history of institutionalised presence of Polish Muslims – the Tatars – might explain, why no laws aimed to obstruct Islamic religious practice have been passed in Poland.[3] At the same time, and for the same reason, Islamic practices have not been recognized or protected to the same degree as the Catholic ones (for example, getting a guaranteed day off for Eid celebrations; Piela, 2020). This leaves Islamic practice in Poland in an institutional vacuum. On the one

---

[3] The case of Anita offers an interesting perspective in this regard. She was working at a French-owned supermarket in Poland when she was asked to remove her hijab. According to the supermarket, internal regulations meant that the employees could wear no visible religious symbols. She refused to discard her hijab, quoting the Polish constitution which safeguards the freedom of religion.

hand, there are no legal or institutional limitations to practicing Islam, on the other, there are no tools to counteract Islamophobic practices at the institutional level – at school, at work, or in a church.

Most of our respondents' experiences of discrimination are related to their work environment – both in the public the private sectors. Working as a Muslim, in particular a "visible Muslim" (Tarlo, 2010), is challenging in Poland – in particular, abstaining from alcohol at business events.[4] This is explained by Kornelia: "When you are at work, you represent work, so when you don't drink a glass of champagne with an agent or vice-president of the company, they will read it as slighting them". Eventually, Kornelia quit her job. As Piela (2019) observes, "born Muslims" often choose self-employment, so they are not expected to fit into the cultural role model related to being a Polish employee.

The adoption of the hijab at work caused the most problems for the participants. It often significantly aggravated relationships with colleagues and employers. Kornelia had to endure comments and teasing related to her religion at work, Ewelina was ostracised when one was talking to her or even returned her hellos. When Monika put on her hijab, she was called in by her manager who tried to persuade her to take it off. Kornelia was actually sacked, because, according to her manager, she "switched from a miniskirt to Islamic robes and started flaunting a halo". Fearing losing their job, some of our respondents decided to conceal their faith in their workplace.

The Polish school is another institutional space that provides a fertile ground for Islamophobia, as it provides little information about Islam or Muslim-majority countries. Religious as a taught subject occupied a prominent place in the curricula in actually religious instruction in pupils' own religion (mostly Catholic) rather than wider religious studies. History and geography textbooks offer essentialised and, sometimes biased content about Islam (Górak-Sosnowska, 2006). According to our respondents, there have not been many Islamophobic incidents at their children's schools. Some of them decided to keep their faith private in order not to expose their children, others' kids had not reached the school age. Two women told us about positive experiences in educational settings. At Angelika's children's daycare, children and teachers knew about her daughter's religion. Gradually, teachers and other children learnt to only offer pork-free foods and treats. Franciszka's daughter was asked by the religion instructor at school to give a presentation about

---

4  Comparing to other EU countries, Poland is the second country after Lithuania in pure alcohol consumption per capita. Drinking with colleagues, during work-related parties or even at business meetings has become established in Poland since ww2. (EC, 2020; Morawski and Swiatkiewicz, 1988).

Islam. Franciszka decided to go to school with her daughter and they gave the presentation together.

Two of our respondents experienced Islamophobic attitudes at the university level. Aleksandra was asked by her lecturer whether she had become interested in terrorism, after she skipped some of his classes. She made the following point:

> If I weren't Muslim, he would most probably have come and asked if everything was ok, and what had happened, but because I am Muslim he came and asked if I was, by any chance, interested in terrorism. And here my world was collapsing, because I thought I might lose both my mother and my grandmother. C'mon, I was experiencing serious personal issues and I did not expect anything like this. This guy had known me quite well, we'd had classes together. (Aleksandra)

Stanisława is an academic and took part in a public discussion on monotheistic religions with three senior male academics. As the discussion got more and more engaging, one of them – a professor – pointed at her and said: 'And so they are wearing these rugs on their heads'. She told us she had frozen at that point, saying that there must be something seriously wrong going on with Polish academia if a university professor felt it was acceptable to publicly make such statements.

Catholic Church is the next stop on the institutional map of Polish Islamophobia. Church authorities are very much divided on the matter, with some clergy promoting interreligious dialogue and some other forcefully opposing it. Right-wing Catholic media and some outspoken xenophobic clergy produce a significant part of Polish Islamophobic content (Pędziwiatr, 2016; Piela, 2019; Krotofil and Motak, 2018). According to a study carried out among Polish Catholic seminarians, their attitudes toward Islam area as negative as general Polish population's: eight out of ten believed that Islam encouraged violence to a larger degree than other religions, and that Muslims were more aggressive and less tolerant than members of other religions (Pędziwiatr 2018, p. 472). What is more, almost half of them sympathise partially or fully with the idea of "banning Islam" (2018, p. 475).

Our data indicates that Polish converts to Islam are not directly affected by the negative role that the Church plays in producing Islamophobic narrative. Negative experiences with Catholic clergy push them closer to Islam, or at least further away from the Catholic religion. When Julianna had doubts about her faith and tried to ask her some questions related to Catholic doctrine:

He swore at me and humiliated me, as if I was a piece of garbage. He did not even answer me, only told me to attend the mass later that day. And then he made the sermon all about me. He didn't say my name, but I was so humiliated that I left in the middle of it and I never went back to church, I will never set my foot there again. (Julianna)

Polish female converts to Islam, especially those who live abroad or have husbands of other nationalities are bound to have contact with airport and embassy employees. It seems that airports are particularly difficult to navigate. It is somewhat surprising that our participants did not refer to British or other Western airports – despite their bad reputation for the surveillance of Muslim citizens (Blackwood, 2015) – but only the Polish ones. For example, Marlena keeps being pulled out for extra checks only at Polish airports. She is already used to it and says she purposely picks the longest hijab and abaya to retaliate for being harassed that way. An employee at the Polish embassy refused to receive the Polish citizenship registration for Maria's son because his name was Muhammad and his father was not Polish. Maria became so frustrated that for a while, she would not claim Polish nationality for any of her children (later however, she sought legal help and successfully obtained the passports).

### From Microassaults to Violence: the High Level Islamophobia

Microassaults are explicit derogations that are verbal or environmental and are meant to hurt the person. Unlike other types of microaggressions – microinsults and microinvalidation – they are generally deliberate and conscious (Sue et al., 2007). They can start with a verbal abuse, such as a text ("Now if there is a bomb at school I know where shall I go" – as experienced by Kornelia), verbal provocations (such as "Terrorist!", "maybe you'll hijack a plane?", "Bin Laden's wife" – as experienced by Czesława; "What Muslim are you if you don't kill? You should follow the rules, right?" – as experienced by Eleonora), insults: ("Arab pig" – as experienced by Matylda), and offensive sexualization ("look, an Arab whore" – as experienced by Alice).

For many years, Polish Islamophobia was latent – it was there, as indicated by essentialised representations of Islam and Muslims – but there were hardly any Islamophobic incidents in Poland. The situation deteriorated after the 9/11 terrorist attacks, but even more so after the 2015 so-called "refugee crisis" that coincided with the electoral victory of the right-wing and conservative Law and Justice Party (pl. Prawo i Sprawiedliwość). The combination of these internal and external factors triggered explicit Islamophobia, which seeped into the Polish mainstream narrative. For the Polish public, the "refugee crisis" became real enough to activate fears of and hostility against Muslims (Kalmar, 2018). The current wave of anti-Muslim hatred is not only understood as an expression of patriotism, but also meant to violate Muslims.

Political shifts in Poland have changed the way Islam and Muslims are narrated: once an external enemy, they have become "domesticated". While this word bears positive connotations, in this context it means that it was not enough for Poles to articulate Islamophobic narratives, they have also put these narratives into actions directed against Polish Muslims. This has serious consequences for the local Muslim community as well as the people who are perceived as Muslims. One of our respondents has reflected on this difference in the following way:

> You know, actually Poland before the "refugee crisis" and after the crisis have been two different countries. Before the crisis, there were no problems. We were living in Poland normally. I wore the scarf, people were actually very interested. Sometimes they asked why I wore the scarf. What is Islam? They chatted, they were friendly. And after the crisis, there is more hostility, sometimes when I walk with my husband, there are these silly quips [from strangers], like: "Oh God, what is going on here in Poland?" (...) Not always, but there are many more hostile incidents. (Angelika)

A peculiar feature of Polish Islamophobia is its "banalisation" – the representations of Muslims are omnipresent and unquestionable – deployed without any further reflection, showing them as dehumanised beings (Pędziwiatr, 2017a, p. 421). Embracing Islamophobia in the mainstream discourse, negative media representations have led to a significant rise in crimes motivated by racialized or xenophobic hate.

According to the crime registry of the Prosecutor's Office there were 835 such cases, including 14 with a victim who was a Muslim (+9 Arab, 8 Chechen, 4 Turkish, 1 Pakistani, Palestinian, Egyptian, Iranian each in 2012; Prokuratura Generalna, 2013). In 2017, the number of hate crimes rose to 1149 cases, including at least 328 where a Muslim (+24 Syrian) individual was targeted (Prokuratura Krajowa, 2018). In other words, while there was a 37% increase in hate crimes, in case of hate crimes targeting Muslims there was a 23-fold increase (provided that the data is accurate, as it might be hard to distinguish a crime directed at an Arab from one that targets a Muslim, especially as these two categories overlap for many Poles).⁵ Moreover, as often police authorities refuse to record such acts, many of them are not even officially reported (Piela and Łukjanowicz, 2018: 479).

Some of our respondents were affected by such hate crimes. A friend of Angelika and her husband were insulted and assaulted on public transport. Marlena's brother-in-law was beaten up several times. Matylda's husband was insulted while driving his car, and followed by the perpetrator who claimed that he wanted to kill his wife and children. A wall next to the home of Daria was covered with vulgar slogans that clearly targeted her. When she was painting it over, police were called on her.

Employees of kebab restaurants are particularly vulnerable at work, usually in customer-facing roles. They are perceived as Arabs or Muslims, regardless of their actual ethnicity or religion. As kebab restaurants offer cheap fast food, their clientele usually represents lower socio-economic groups. While kebab restaurants used to be "a place that helped Poles to learn about other cultural groups" (Nowaczek-Walczak, 2011, p. 123) they have recently become a dangerous workplace. Anita's husband was beaten four times, and then he was threatened to have his throat cut at a kebab restaurant he was working at – as the harasser claimed, to mirror ISIS's crimes. Matylda's husband was regularly insulted with racist expletives by drunk customers.⁶ For some of the respondents, experiencing hate crimes was a reason for emigrating from Poland, some decided to be more careful (and to live in fear). When Daria and her friend decided to paint over Islamophobic slogans scrawled on her building, someone reported them to the police who then questioned them for vandalising the property.

As in Western Europe (Zempi and Chakraborti, 2014), converts wearing the hijab – a visible marker of Muslim identity (or according to Goffman (1963: 122) "a highly visible sign that advertises his failing wherever he goes") – are also a particularly vulnerable target. Joanna was told to "go back to her country", because it was Poland and she must not wear a "rag on her head". Once her hijab was ripped off her head, she decided to stop wearing it for over a year. Matylda was assaulted on a bus by a man who stubbed out a cigarette on her arm. Daria's Muslim husband asked her to take off her headscarf. Marysia

---

5   Iza's story illustrates this: A wall in the building in front of her office window was covered with anti-Islamic slogans. When she reported it to the police, she was told that only the owner of the building could file a complaint. Moreover, the case was registered as an act of vandalism, even though the messages were clearly Islamophobic.
6   Interestingly, simultaneously with the political right turn, a new type of kebab restaurant has emerged: a "real Polish" kebab restaurant.

decided to take off the hijab in order to blend in with her surroundings – especially when out at night, when she was more likely to encounter inebriated, aggressive men.

Being a target of microassaults and religiously motivated violence is a significant burden that many converts in Poland have to bear. Some of them (like Maja) decided to lead a "double life" and conceal their Islamic identity. Often, the reason for that was not only their own safety, but also the safety of their families – especially if they were not ethnically Polish. For the same reason some participants' children changed their Muslim-sounding names to traditional Polish ones to avoid the harassment. In this case, children of Polish female converts to Islam are often "those who pass" and changing the name is used as a stigma management technique – not revealing the stigma to others (Goffman, 1963: 121).

### Polish Islamophobia Exposed (through the British Context)

Islamophobia is contextual. It depends on national, cultural and political settings that provide the framework for how it is expressed, manifested, but also created (Allen, 2020, p. 32). Our participants experience a Polish variety of Islamophobia, and that is regardless whether they live in Poland or the UK. All of those who had the experience of living both in Poland and the UK agree that living in Poland as a Muslim is much harder, and Polish-style Islamophobia is one of the reasons.

> What is now happening in Poland, how people perceive me, especially my family – it bothers me more than what is going on in England. Coz in England I guess that Islamophobia is specific to the underclass. Ordinary people don't act like this. (Balbina)

Our respondents attributed this difference to the diversity of cultures, religions and nations that one can engage with in the UK. Those who have lived in London enjoyed the anonymity that makes people feel invisible in the streets: "There is much greater diversity here, people know more about Islam. In London there is anonymity, you can walk down the street dressed in whatever and people don't stare" (Daria). Living in the UK gave them a sense of agency and freedom: "I get on a train, the underground, wherever I go I feel free, no one pays any attention to me, even though I came from a small town, with only a few Muslims." (Maja)

Interestingly, Polish immigrants in the UK rarely consider multiculturalism as something positive. They generally do not value the opportunity to interact with people of other cultures (Temple, 2011). Polish female converts to Islam perceived it as an opportunity that allowed them to express their identity. To use Pędziwiatr's words (2017b, p. 221): they "engage in construction of hybrid identities, linking elements of Polishness with super-diverse British Muslimness".

One could argue that their positive evaluation of life in the UK is contextual – it results from a greater anonymity and diversity compared to culturally homogenous Poland. However, it also seems that the way Islamophobia is manifested and expressed in Poland and in the UK is often different – at least according to our respondents' experiences. Only two participants described being harassed by British people due to their religion (Maja and Agata), the repertoire of Islamophobic harassment in Poland is much wider and its intensity stronger. The latter also refers to incidents involving other Polish migrants in the UK.

As already mentioned in the Chapter 2, United Kingdom was one of the top destinations for Polish people to emigrate. As of 2019 Poles are the second most numerous population in the UK born overseas, estimated at 0.8 million (Office for National Statistics, 2020). While their experiences in the UK varied, many of them did not have a positive experience of living in the UK. They had to compete with other economic migrants for the same resources (Goździak and Márton, 2018), and cope with negative attitudes; many British resented cheap Polish workers taking "British jobs" and allegedly abusing British welfare system (Fitzgerald and Smoczyński, 2015).

While the Polish diaspora is internally diverse and conflicted, Polish female converts to Islam are excluded from it in anyway. Polish migrants prefer to stick to their own socio-cultural environments. Their significant others and friends are usually Polish, and their identities are rooted in their home country – this is what Kapinos (2018) termed "identity (non)dilemmas". In addition, Polish migrants in the UK express strong social distance towards Muslims in comparison to other groups including the native British population (Korczyński, 2015). Moreover, according to Gawlewicz and Narkowicz (2015) at least some Polish migrants developed prejudice against Muslims after their migration to the UK.

Experiences involving the mainstream Polish diaspora in the UK have been frustrating for our respondents. According to Magda, some Polish female converts remain engaged with the Polish diaspora, but most are received negatively. The case of Lidia illustrates this point. She was insulted by Polish people on a number of occasions. Subsequently, she made a decision not to speak Polish in public in order to avoid being recognized as a fellow Pole.

A space that many Polish converts to Islam share with other Polish migrants is the famed Polish shop – a place that gives Poles comfort and helps them adjust to their new life. The goods traded or celebrated there are not only distinctive to the country of origin, but also implicated in the culture of the home country. They help migrants to maintain links to the home country and their national identity (Newland and Taylor, 2010, p. 15).

According to the study of Brown and Paszkiewicz (2017) Polish food is associated with the Polish heritage and gives Poles a sense of belonging, regardless of their background. The same applies to Polish female converts to Islam. However, encounters with other Poles at Polish shops proved to be a challenge, as one respondent described:

> When I started to wear the hijab I would go to the shop when the business was bound to be slow. Sometimes I felt ok, other times I felt so uncomfortable ... I also know that many people didn't know how to react, seeing me in a Polish shop. They were aware that I was Polish, but they were confused. Poles living here are the biggest problem. (Beata)

Another respondent (Magda) recalled going to the Polish Festival in London wearing the hijab The stares she and her Polish hijabi friends received made them deeply uncomfortable. Both the Polish shops and the Polish Festival are spaces that are symbolically defined as Polish – places where nostalgia abounds. The respondents felt that they were denied the right to participate in that collective celebration as they did not fit in with the mainstream imaginary of Polishness.

### The Uneven Battle: Challenging Islamophobia

Comparing the amount and affective power of Islamophobic narratives in Poland with the size of local Muslim population makes it clear that any attempt to challenge the narrative is costly, burdensome and unlikely to result in positive change. Opposing Islamophobia carries personal risks. As Matylda illustrates it: "All the time you are stuck between the willingness to take part in public and social life, and the instinct to hide and live just for yourself in your immediate environment".

Zempi (2014) distinguished between two different strategies of coping with Islamophobia – passive, when the response was to ignore the incident, or pretending that it did not happen, and active – when Muslims showed agency in the way they responded to the incident, either positively (by trying to educate the abusers), or negatively (by retaliation). Magassa (2019, p. 208) identified several coping strategies (avoiding contact, fitting in) and resistance strategies (countering, confronting, preventing). Both studies differ in terms of the sample, country, methodology of data collection, but also in their definitions of an Islamophobic incident. For Zempi, the coping strategy refers to an incident that has actually happened, while Magassa includes strategies that can limit potential Islamophobic incidents – that is, incidents that did not happen (yet). In our research we combined these two approaches and set the coping strategies on a continuum from passive coping strategies to actually challenging the possibility of Islamophobia.

Concealing identity is a coping strategy adopted by those female converts who do not present as visibly Muslim. Some decided to remove it for security reasons, or just to fit in:

> When I meet someone [when I wear the hijab], we usually spend the first two-three meetings with my working hard to prove that I am not f**** up. Then it's up to them to decide that I'm actually an ok person, but how many times do I need to accept this challenge? So I've had enough, I wanted to disappear and so I did. (Anita)

> I don't want to publicly declare that I am Muslim, because people have these preconceptions like Muslim = terrorist. They think I was brainwashed. I don't want to be perceived this way, I don't want to be seen as weird. (Małgorzata)

As Sadek (2017) noted, many Muslims, especially those of immigrant origin, are under suspicion, and have to prove that they share the same values, and have successfully assimilated into the dominant society. This expectation may create a sense of alienation and affect their identity.

Alana's coping strategy is a pre-emptive, dynamic negotiation that involves sometimes concealing, sometimes revealing her identity:

> Before I announce to anyone that I am a Muslim, these people get to know me as me (...) and then when I am already familiar to them as me, then, you know. This is a much better way to reveal it to people. (Alana)

This strategy is selective and conscious. She decides whether she feels comfortable enough to share this personal information about herself after she learns about her interlocutor's attitudes.

While the coping strategies discussed earlier were perceived as related to being a Muslim, the following ones refer to actual Islamophobic incidents. Some of our respondents chose to ignore the abuse in order to prevent escalation:

> People didn't really ask and it didn't really matter to me. I didn't care what were they thinking. I got a rep of a born-again convert and that's it. (Matylda)

> I think that in such a daily life we are all simply tired, because how many times you can explain, that if there is a terrorist attack, so what – I stopped to explain myself. (Faustyna)

Zempi (2019) observed that many women who were abused due to wearing a veil or niqab perceived it as something ordinary, a part of their daily life. They acknowledged Islamophobia but made a decision not to react. In similar manner, Matylda accepted her role as "the born-again convert", while Faustyna was too tired to explain Islam (and herself as a Muslim) to others. However, another respondent, Monika explained that Islamophobia was caused by a lack of knowledge about Islam and persistent misinformation:

> Sometimes I also got stared at in the street, but this is just that they have to have more interaction with other cultures, with other people … and also the media certainly doesn't help. (Faustyna)

While the repertoire of passive strategies is rather limited, the active strategies against Islamophobia are much more diverse. Polish female converts to Islam have enough cultural capital to actively engage in challenging the Islamophobic narratives in many different ways.

In our data we have encountered a only few active strategies which could be classed as negative: "If someone stares at me notoriously then I give them my 'special look'" – said Anna. Staring back is a way to get the other person confused. However, it is not the only strategy that she employs – when she is in a good mood, she smiles at them.

Unlike Zempi's (2019, p. 8) respondents whose active coping strategies sometimes take a form of responding with abuse, none of our respondents have admitted to that. Even if they actually mean to retaliate, they do it by showing civility to the abuser:

My aunt is a simple woman. She says: "This is how you pitch the carpet to pray? Why the hell are you doing it?" And for her it is funny. I say to her: "Listen, am I laughing at people who are kneeling in front of a piece of wood in a church? You know, it is a matter of civility. You know I respect your religion, or my ex-religion". (Franciszka)

Franciszka decided to educate their family members or colleagues. She did it however, by referring to what was familiar to them, rather to the tenets of Islam. Instead of referring to Islam, she used an example that her interlocutors would definitely understand.

Julianna followed the same pattern of educating a non-Muslim, but she juxtaposed her behaviour with the negative media images to make her point. She has told us the following anecdote:

Once an older man, who worked here for a long time, accosted me and he said: 'will you tell me, how it is possible that you are so good and nice? Don't be offended but I've heard that you are Muslim, and those Muslims are so bad'. And I say to him: 'A real Muslim is like me, you shouldn't not listen to what they say on TV'. And it felt so good that through my behaviour I could show it, that being a Muslim means an obligation to be good. (Julianna)

She felt gratified that she could contribute to fostering a positive image of Islam. It gave her strength to keep setting the right example as a Muslim. For the older man, she was primarily a good person. She used this impression in order to show what Islam is like. Moreover, she believes that her religion gives her strength to carry out good deeds.

Another strategy used by Polish female converts to Islam – maybe not as retaliation, but as prevention – is being civil. Matylda told us the following anecdote:

So once they brought me a sofa bed from Poland, so I offered the man a drink. And he said that usually he would leave the delivery at the door and get money through the mailbox. And I let him in and offered him something to drink. And he was like wow, a lady in a hijab and speaks Polish and it's so nice. (Matylda)

Taking into account the difficult interactions between Polish converts and the Polish diaspora, the strategy pre-emptive and educational. Matylda hoped that the man involved might change his opinion about Islam and Muslims. According to the classical exemplar-based theory of social judgement, specific past experiences with the target person are one of the factors that contribute to the core of stereotype of the target group, and so can influence their judgements and perceptions (Smith and Zárate, 1992). As another respondent indicated: "If we are nicer, then the next Muslim woman might have it better, because someone has already met good Muslims." (Czesława)

Significantly, neither respondent meant that being civil was about giving up their Muslim identity or trying to fit in. It was a part of their duty as Muslims, to be ambassadors of Islam. While this notion has been criticised by Mamdani (2005), even if he was referring to political identities, in case of Matylda and Czesława it had positive connotations.

Engaging in community work and increased involvement in broader society is another strategy used by Muslims to confront Islamophobia (Agrawal et al., 2019). The variety of these actions and events is impressive. Many Polish female converts are active in their local Muslim communities, but also engage with the non-Muslim society by organising and participating in events, discussions, seminars or open lectures, "living libraries".[7] Some of represent their mosques by attending events (Moosavi, 2015b), but many of these activities takes place outside of an institutionalised framework on the convert's own initiative. And there are a lot of such events – at least among our respondents, mostly active, well-networked converts to Islam: Daria co-organised an event during Ramadan to invite non-Muslims to fast with them. She managed to convince her sister to fast. It was a challenge for her but at the same time her sister began to understand why she was fasting. Marlena was asked by the imam of a local mosque to invite non-Muslims to her wedding. She invited a lot of colleagues from work, and since she worked at a supermarket, so many people came that they could not all fit into the mosque. For many of them, it was their first encounter with Islam. Many events for Muslims and non-Muslims are organised by the Women of Faith (Kobiety Wiary)[8] – a grassroots organisation of Polish Muslim women in the UK.

The reasons for organising are usually religious, as seen in the following quotation:

---

7  Living library is a project in which one can borrow a 'living book', that is, persons who belong to socially stigmatized or stereotyped groups in order to talk with them and ask them questions.
8  More at: https://kobietywiary.co.uk/.

Recently my dad suggested that I should maybe become a translator for Poles, that I do a course and translated for police forces and hospitals. I think hospitals are ok, but police stations make me uneasy. But then I think, golly, if I helped this that person in such a stressful situation, then maybe it would be a good opportunity to advocate for Islam and to say that there are Polish Muslims, we are ordinary women, we can work ... (Paulina)

Kornelia spends a lot of time with her grandparents and so she meets many older people. Sometimes mistakenly she is taken for a nun and asked for help: "'Sister, can you help me?', and I say: 'Sure, I can'. Without even explaining that I am a sister, but not in that sense ...". Both Matylda and Kornelia's actions are religiously motivated. For Kornelia, Muslim women have a duty to help those who are in need. However, she does not really treat her actions as a way to proselytise about Islam or improve the image of Muslims. It is, rather, her own religious commitment. In both cases, positive religious coping strategies are believed to lead to a greater post-traumatic growth and thus can smooth or absorb negative experiences of Islamophobia (van der Ven, 2012).

### Conclusions

Islamophobia is a global phenomenon. Localised in the Polish context it illuminates unique experiences of Polish female converts to Islam. Polish Islamophobia intersects with the Polish nationalist discourses and narratives imported from Western countries. yet they are not counteracted by any postcolonial reflection. For decades, it was uncritically accepted that Poland was "immune" to racism – unlike the Western countries (Balogun, 2020) – while xenophobia was understood only very narrowly as affecting local ethnic vulnerable groups, especially the Jews and the Roma. In terms of unacknowledged Islamophobia, this myth of tolerant Poland was strengthened by the small size of the local Muslim community. Until the political shift of 2015 – the so-called "refugee crisis" which coincided with the conservative Law and Justice party securing the majority in Polish parliament – Islamophobia in Poland was fairly latent. In recent years however, it has been incorporated into the mainstream political discourse from the right-wing political margins where it always used to thrive. The central location of Polish Islamophobic discourse in the mainstream politics makes Polish Muslim population vulnerable. On the Western European political scene, it occupies a more peripheral position (Hafez, 2018), therefore many of our respondents who had experiences of living as a Muslim in Poland and in the West tend to prefer living in multicultural, liberal, and democratic environments of Western Europe to Poland.

This political shift has significantly has impacted the life and daily experiences of Polish female converts to Islam, who – just as other Muslims, especially those 'visible' ones – experience various types of harassment – from microaggressions to hate crimes and violence. Female converts to Islam adopt a wide range of coping strategies against Islamophobia. Some of them are racialised and essentialised by people for whom they are 'the only Muslim' one ever encountered. Some women use this opportunity to positive aspects of Islam, others are frustrated by such essentialisation and decide to keep a low profile. Living as a minority and being socialised in Polish context gives them agency and power to negotiate their position in their families, among their friends and outside – in the public. Being the only Muslim or one of the Muslims ever met and living in the mostly homogenous Polish mainstream society, they had to work out their ways and strategies in order to challenge the dominant Islamophobic discourse. Despite the emotional, and sometimes physical burden, it seems that many of them have actually succeeded.

## References

Agrawal, P., Yusuf, Y., Pasha, O., Ali, S., Ziad, H., Hyder, A. (2019). Interpersonal stranger violence and American Muslims: and exploratory study of lived experiences and coping strategies. *Global Bioethics*, 30, 28–42.

Alam, O. (2012). 'Islam is a Blackfella Religion, Whatchya Trying to Prove?': Race in the Lives of White Muslim Converts in Australia, *The La Trobe Journal*, 89, 124–163.

Allen, C. (2007). *Islamophobia*. Ashgate.

Allen, C. (2020). *Reconfiguring Islamophobia. A Radical Rethinking of a Contested Concept*. Palgrave Macmillan.

Balogun, B. (2020). Race and racism in Poland. Theorising and contextualising 'Polish-centrism'. *The Sociological Review*, 68(6), 1–16.

Blackwood, L. (2015). Policing Airport Spaces: The Muslim Experience of Scrutiny. *Policing*, 9(3), 255–264.

Bobako, M. (2017). *Islamofobia jako technologia władzy. Studium z antropologii politycznej*. Universitas.

Brown, L. & Paszkiewicz, I. (2017). The role of food in the Polish migrant adjustment journey. *Appetite*, 109, 57–65.

Cesari, J. (2011). Islamophobia in the West. A Comparison between Europe and the United States. In. *Islamophobia. The Challenge of Pluralism in the 21st Century*.

In J. Esposito, I. Kalin (Eds.), *The Challenge of Pluralism in the 21st century* (pp. 21–46). Oxford University Press.

EC (2020). Daily and per capita alcohol consumption in European countries. European Commission. https://ec.europa.eu/jrc/en/page/alcohol-daily.

Fitzgerald, I. & Smoczyński, R. (2015). Anti-Polish Migrant Moral Panic in the UK: Rethinking Employment Insecurities and Moral Regulation. *Czech Sociological Review*, 51(3), 339–361.

Franceschelli, M. & O'Brien, M. (2014). 'Islamic Capital' and Family Life: The Role of Islam in Parenting. *Sociology*, 48(6), 1190–1206.

Franks, M. (2000). Crossing the borders of whiteness? White Muslim women who wear hijab in Britain today. *Ethnic and Racial Studies*, 23(5), 917–929.

Frisina, A. (2006). The Invention of Citizenship among Young Muslims in Italy. In G. Jonker, V. Amiraux (Eds.), *Politics of Visibility. Young Muslims in European Public Spaces*. Transcript Verlag.

Gallonier, J. (2015). The racialization of Muslims in France and the United States: Some insights from white converts to Islam. *Social Compass*, 62(4), 570–583.

Gawlewicz, A. & Narkowicz, K. (2015). Islamophobia on the move: circulation of anti-Muslim prejudice between Poland and the UK. In Y. Suleiman (Ed.), *Muslims in the UK and Europe* (pp. 90–100). University of Cambridge.

Ghalaini, S. (2020). Another F***ing Growth Opportunity: Overcoming Islamophobia and the Enduring Impacts. *Studies in Gender and Sexuality*, 21(2), 99–103.

Goffman, E. (1963). *Stigma: Notes on the Management of Spoiled Identity*. Simon & Schuster.

Goździak, E. & Márton, P. (2018, June 21). 'Where the wild things are' fear of Islam and the anti-refugee rhetoric in Hungary and in Poland. *Central and Eastern European Migration Review*, 7(2), 125–151.

Górak-Sosnowska, K. (2006). Wizerunek islamu w Polsce na przykładzie podręczników szkolnych. In K. Górak-Sosnowska, K. Pędziwiatr & P. Kubicki (Eds.), *Islam i obywatelskość w Europie* (pp. 237–251). Elipsa.

Górak-Sosnowska, K. (2012). *From Polish Muslims to Muslims in Poland: There and Back*. In H. Yılmaz & Ç. Aykaç (Eds.), *Perceptions of Islam in Europe. Culture, Identity and the Muslim 'Other'* (pp. 107–124). I.B. Tauris.

Górak-Sosnowska, K. & Molodikova, I. (2018). "Polish, Hungarian, cousins be". Comparative discourse on Muslims and refugee crisis in Europe. *Rocznik Instytutu Europy Środkowo-Wschodniej*, 16(5), 141–158.

GUS (2013). *Ludność. Stan i struktura demograficzno-społeczna*. Główny Urząd Statystyczny. https://stat.gov.pl/spisy-powszechne/nsp-2011/nsp-2011-wyniki/ludnosc-stan-i-struktura-demograficzno-spoleczna-nsp-2011,16,1.html.

Hafez, F. (2018). Street-level and government-level Islamophobia in the Visegrád Four countries. *Patterns of Prejudice*, 52(5), 436–447.

Herbert, D. (2018). A Different Dynamic? Explaining Prejudice Against Muslims in the Russian Federation: Islamophobia or Internalized Racial Hierarchy? Understanding and Explaining Islamophobia in Eastern Europe. *EEGA Leibniz ScienceCampus*, special issue 1, 45–52.

Jackson, L. (2018). *Islamophobia in Britain. The Making of a Muslim Enemy*. Palgrave Macmillan.

Jakubowska, H. (2016). Doświadczanie ciężarnego ciała jako ciała przekraczającego granice – studium socjologii ucieleśnienia. *Przegląd Socjologii Jakościowej*, 12(4), 100–117.

Kalmar, I. (2018). Islamophobia in the East of the European Union: an introduction. *Patterns of Prejudice*, 52(5), 389–405. https://doi.org/10.1080/0031322X.2018.1512467.

Kapinos, S. (2018). (Nie)dylematy tożsamościowe Polaków w Wielkiej Brytanii na przykładzie badań w hrabstwie Hertfordshire. *Studia migracyjne – Przegląd polonijny*, 1(167), 117–143.

Korczyński, M. (2015). Dystans społeczny emigrantów polskich w Wielkiej Brytanii wobec "Obcych" a ich poziom wykształcenia. *Pogranicze. Studia społeczne*, XXV, 151–174. https://doi.org/10.15290/pss.2015.25.09.

Krotofil, J. & Motak, D. (2018). A critical discourse analysis of the media coverage of the migration crisis in Poland: The Polish Catholic Church's perception of the 'migration crisis'. *Scripta Instituti Donneriani Aboensis*, 28, 92–115. http://dx.doi.org/10.30674/scripta.70069.

Magassa, M. (2019). How Muslim Students endure ambient Islamophobia on campus and in the community: Resistance, coping and survival strategies [Unpublished doctoral dissertation]. University of Victoria.

Mamdani, M. (2005). *Good Muslim, bad Muslim. America, the Cold Was and the Roots of Terror*. Harmony.

Markowska-Manista, U. (2016). Walka ze stereotypami odmienności kulturowej – szkolne i pozaszkolne pola bitewne. In M. Dudzikowa & S. Jaskulska (Eds.). *Twierdza. Szkoła w metaforze militarnej Co w zamian?* (pp. 315–339). Wolters Kluwer SA.

Maxwell, R. (2019). Cosmopolitan Immigration Attitudes in Large European Cities: Contextual or Compositional Effects? *American Political Science Review*, 113(2), 456–474.

Moosavi, L. (2015a). The Racialization of Muslim Converts in Britain and Their Experiences of Islamophobia. *Critical Sociology*, 4(1), 41–56.

Moosavi, L. (2015b). White privilege in the lives of Muslim converts in Britain, Ethnic and Racial Studies, 38(11), 1918–1933. https://doi.org/10.1080/01419870.2014.952751.

Morawski, J. & Swiatkiewicz, G. (1988). Alcohol in Employment Settings in Poland. *Employee Assistance Quarterly*, 3(2), 105–119.

Nadal, K., Griffin, K., Hamit, S., Leon, J., Tobio, M. & Rivera, D. (2012). Subtle and Overt Forms of Islamophobia: Microaggressions toward Muslim Americans. *Journal of Muslim Mental Health*, VI(2). https://doi.org/10.3998/jmmh.10381607.0006.203.

Newland, K. & Taylor, C. (2010, September). Heritage Tourism and Nostalgia Trade: A Diaspora Niche in the Development Landscape. Migration Policy Institute.

Nowaczek-Walczak, M. (2011). The world of kebab. Arabs and gastronomy in Warsaw. In K. Górak-Sosnowska (Ed.), *Muslims in Poland and wider Europe. Widening the European discourse on Islam* (pp. 108–125). University of Warsaw.

Office for National Statistics (2020). *Population of the UK by country of birth and nationality*. https://www.ons.gov.uk/peoplepopulationandcommunity/population andmigration/internationalmigration/datasets/populationoftheunitedkingdom bycountryofbirthandnationality.

Özyürek, E. (2015). *Being German, Becoming Muslim. Race, Religion, and Conversion in the New Europe*. Princeton University Press.

Pędziwiatr, K. (2016). Islamophobia in Poland: National Report 2015. In E. Bayraklı & F. Hafez (Eds.). *European Islamophobia Report 2015* (pp. 423–443). SETA.

Pędziwiatr, K. (2017a). Conversions to Islam and Identity Reconfigurations among Poles in Great Britain. *Studia Religiologica*, 50(2), 221–239.

Pędziwiatr, K. (2017b). Islamophobia in Poland: National Report 2016. In E. Bayraklı & F. Hafez, *European Islamophobia Report 2016* (pp. 411–442). SETA.

Pędziwiatr, K. (2018). The Catholic Church in Poland on Muslims and Islam. *Patterns of Prejudice*, 52(5), 461–478. https://doi.org/10.1080/0031322X.2018.1495376.

Pędziwiatr, K. (2019). Religious dimension of Polish fears of Muslims and Islam. In I. Zempi & I. Awan (Eds.), *The Routledge International Handbook of Islamophobia* (pp. 212–224). Routledge.

Pickel, G. &Öztürk, C. (2017). Islamophobia without Muslims? The "Contact Hypothesis" as an Explanation for Anti-Muslim Attitudes – Eastern European Societies in a Comparative Perspective. *Journal of Nationalism, Memory & Language Politics*, 12(2), 162–191. https://doi.org/10.2478/jnmlp-2018-0009.

Piela, A. (2019). Islamophobia in Poland: National Report 2018. In E. Bayraklı & F. Hafez, *European Islamophobia Report 2018* (pp. 659–680). SETA.

Piela, A. (2020). Islamophobia in Poland: National Report 2019. In E. Bayraklı & F. Hafez, *European Islamophobia Report 2019* (pp. 609–636). SETA.

Piela, A. & Łukjanowicz, A. (2018). Islamophobia in Poland: National Report 2017. In E. Bayraklı & F. Hafez. *European Islamophobia Report 2017* (pp. 463–482). SETA.

Prokuratura Generalna (2013). *Wyciąg ze sprawozdania dotyczącego spraw prowadzonych w 2013 r. w jednostkach organizacyjnych prokuratury z pobudek rasistowskich lub ksenofobicznych (tj. spraw zarejestrowanych, wszczętych w tym okresie oraz kontynuowanych w tym okresie a wszczętych, czy też zarejestrowanych we wcześniejszym okresie) sporządzony na podstawie danych przekazanych przez prokuratury apelacyjne*. PG II P 404/10/13.

Prokuratura Krajowa (2018). *Sprawozdanie dotyczące spraw o przestępstwa popełnione z pobudek rasistowskich, antysemickich lub ksenofobicznych prowadzonych w 2017 roku w jednostkach organizacyjnych prokuratury*. PK II P 404.4.2016.

Ramahi, D. and Suleiman, Y. (2017). Intimate strangers: perspectives on female converts to Islam in Britain. *Contemporary Islam*, 11, 21–39.

Sadek, N. (2017). Islamophobia, shame, and the collapse of Muslim identities. *International Journal of Applied Psychoanalytic Studies*, 14, 200–221.

Samuels, S. (2012). Foreword. In. Baum, S., *Antisemitism Explained*. University Press of America.

Simon, B. & Grabow, H. (2014). To be respected and to respect: The challenge of mutual respect in intergroup relations. *British Journal of Social Psychology*, 53, 39–53.

Smith, E. & Zárate, M. (1992). Exemplar-Based Model of Social Judgement. *Psychological Review*, 99(1), 3–21.

Strabac, Z. and Listhaug, O. (2008). Anti-Muslim Prejudice in Europe: A Multilevel Analysis of Survey Data from 30 Countries. *Social Science Research*, 37(1), 268–286.

Stefaniak, A. (2015). *Postrzeganie muzułmanów w Polsce: Raport z badania sondażowego*. Centrum Badań nad Uprzedzeniami. https://www.mowanienawisci.info/post/postrzeganie-muzulmanow-w-polsce-raport-z-badania-sondazowego/.

Sue, D., Bucceri, J., Lin, A., Nadal, K. & Torino, G. (2007). Racial Microaggressions and the Asian American Experience. *Cultural Diversity and Ethnic Minority Psychology*, 13(1), 72–81.

Tarlo, E. (2010). *Visibly Muslim: Fashion, Politics, Faith*. Berg Publishers.

Temple, B. (2011). Influences on integration: exploring Polish people's views of other ethnic communities. *Studia migracyjne*, 1(139), pp. 97–110.

Ven, van der, C. (2012). Experiences, coping styles and mental health of Muslims following 9/11. *Social Cosmos*, 3(1), 76–82.

Vroon, V. (2014). *Sisters in Islam. Women's conversion and the politics of belonging. A Dutch case study* [Unpublished doctoral dissertation]. Universiteit Amsterdam.

Zebiri, K. (2008). *British Muslim Converts. Choosing Alternative Lives*. Oxford: OneWorld.

Zebiri, K. (2011). Orientalist themes in contemporary British Islamophobia. In J. Esposito & I. Kalin (Eds.). *Islamophobia: the challenge of pluralism in the 21st century* (pp. 173–190). Oxford University Press.

Zempi, E. (2014). *Unveiling Islamophobia: The Victimisation of Veiled Muslim Women* [Unpublished doctoral dissertation]. University of Leicester.

Zempi, I. (2019). Veiled Muslim women's responses to experiences of gendered Islamophobia in the UK. *International Review of Victimology*, 26(1) 96–111. https://doi.org/10.1177%2F0269758019872902.

Zempi, I. & Chakraborti, N. (2014). *Islamophobia, Victimisation and the Veil*. Palgrave Macmillan.

CHAPTER 5

# Language of Polish Female Converts to Islam

*Beata Abdallah-Krzepkowska* | ORCID: 0000-0003-4370-8095
University of Silesia in Katowice

**Introduction**

Previous research on to 'Western' conversions to Islam has often overlooked the issue of the language used by new Muslims, foundational for studying identity. Bucholtz and Hall (2005, p. 1) argue that 'among the many symbolic resources available for the cultural production of identity, language is the most flexible and pervasive'. Therefore, including Polish linguistic aspects of converts' identities enables us to enhance those discussions. Here, we address the construction and negotiation of identity in a process of linguistic interactions within a community of converts to Islam.

Sociocultural linguistics (linguistic anthropology) views identity as social positioning of 'myself' and 'others' produced in linguistic practices. This is related to the role of language as a fundamental source of cultural production, and therefore also a vital source in the production of identities (Bucholtz and Hall 2004a, 2004b, 2005, 2010). In this chapter, we refer to the linguistic practices as 'the religious language of Polish Muslim converts'. We consider converts to Islam whose native tongue is Polish a 'speech community'. A speech community is defined as 'a group of people who maintain constant contact and share both a variety of language and social conventions of its use, the latter being called sociolinguistic norms' (van Herk 2012, p. 1).

The Humboldt-Sapir-Whorf hypothesis views language as a factor influencing the way individuals perceive and express their reality, thus playing a significant part in the process of cognition and constitution of the world. Therefore, one of the tasks before the converts is an adequate linguistic rendering of the new reality of religious life. In order to create a new religious language, they must decide on the new elements it will include, such as such as translations of the Qur'an, the language of Polish Muslim organisations and, above all, the Internet and the virtual ummah. They learn new words, as well as the usage of non-Qur'anic and Qur'anic (Arabic) idiomatic phrases. Many Muslims deem the use of the latter, considered God's own words, to be the most appropriate in their linguistic practice. Converts often learn their meaning in a rather random manner. It can be while learning the Arabic language, from the husband and his family, through contact with Muslims from other countries and linguistic traditions if the convert lives abroad, as well as through, very popular, online courses. Adopting such a manner of speaking on an everyday basis may lead to linguistic estrangement of the new Muslim in their non-Muslim social settings, which is why this language is mostly used within the *ummah*.

One can also use familiar building blocks to create the language – the Polish Christian religious language, Islamic borrowings long present in Polish due to close historical contacts with the Islamic world, and finally the language of Polish Islam created by the Tatars living in Poland for 600 years (interestingly, the last source is not used by the converts we interviewed at all). There are plenty of potential building blocks for a new language. The choice might be related to multiple extralinguistic factors, such as one's linguistic and cultural competence, sense of identity, understanding of the role of language in the sacred sphere of life, and finally social factors – the convert's relationships with fellow believers and her non-Muslim environment. It is the last factor in particular that causes the tensions that are reflected in the discourse of the Polish *ummah*. All these factors render the construction of the language a highly dynamic process.

This chapter presents an analysis of the discourse of Polish female converts and to discuss some of its characteristics significant in light of the identities the language helps to construct. The research material presented here consists of:

1. written language – websites; blogs; Facebook (FB) pages, ran by Polish Muslims in Polish, containing both original texts and translations; Polish female converts' content on FB and open groups; comments under publicly available texts about Islam (list of fan pages and groups is included in the appendix). The material was collected from 2018 to 2020.
2. spoken language – in-depth interviews with female converts and Polish female converts' vlogs.

Another research method we used is participant observation, as the author of this chapter has been an active member of the community for many years. The material constitutes a linguistic corpus consisting of 1057 samples (posts, comments, documents, and memes) collected from open groups, fan pages and open Internet profiles. The appendix includes the names of the fan pages and Facebook groups from which the material was collected. The sources of the anonymous quotes are coded as F (fan page), G (group) and P (person).

Our qualitative analysis was focused on the lexical and syntactic units, the stylistic devices applied, and the ways and manners in which the texts, as well as the terms, concepts and linguistic structures they use in the discourse of Polish female converts to Islam. Our research was focused on lexical units related to religious language. We also searched for the sources of linguistic inspirations and loans to be found in the language. We isolated several hundred lexical units which are borrowings, mainly from Arabic, thematically related to the dogmas, practices and ethics of Islam. Furthermore, our analysis concerns common structural borrowings. We were also interested in honorifics, linguistic self-awareness and reflection on language and its role.

This chapter consists of several sections. In the first one, we discuss the role of the Arabic language in the religious life of new Muslims. The second section consists of a presentation of Internet material which provided the basis for our analysis. The third section concerns loans, which are a characteristic feature of the religious language of Polish female converts. In the last three sections, we present issues related to 'spoiled identity' by showing such linguistic behaviour as changes in the use of rules of honorifics and, above all, linguistic attempts at defining the group's identity through polonization of the religious language.

## Does One Have to Speak Arabic as a Convert?

Conversion to Islam, a religion which places the core of the sacred in text believed to be divine in origin, is also followed by a shift in one's conception of the status, the role and the meaning of language. The sacred meaning of the Arabic language for the faithful stems from the belief that God revealed the Sacred Book in that language and *i'jaz al-Qur'an*, the idea of inimitability and untranslatability of the Qur'an. The Qur'an replaces the institution of the Church, which used to be the depositary of the language of religion. The sacred character of language lends special significance to the meaning and the form of a word, as well as the place, time and circumstances of the use of religious language.[1]

For converts, the acceptance of the new religion is also a change at the level of language, and in the case of conversion from Catholicism to Islam, also a revolution in the perception of its understanding and use. While the status of Arabic as the language of the Revelation, as well as the extraordinary weight of the Word containing the sacred within itself, is nothing new for Catholics,

---

1 We understand religious language as 'a language aimed at seeking transcendence and finding it by lending a new dimension to empirically experienced subjective and objective reality (Termińska, 2015, p. 187), which is a subtype of general language, 'actually belonging to it, (...) a borderline type, one we separate a priori not basing on its form, but on the function it serves in social life. This function is serving the category of social life which we describe as religious life, i.e. life focused on communing with the supernatural world.' (Bajerowa, 1994, p. 11).

it is only the conversion to Islam and the necessity of rethinking the role of words that uncovers the essence of concepts and spurs the faithful to discuss meanings, functions and limitations in the use of words: 'When I started reading more and thinking about religion, it started to make less and less sense to me, and I kinda started to think about it, and I thought no, because I had always believed in God and I was surprised with myself, having repeated different things without reflection, not having thought them through. Even some of the words of the (Catholic) prayers were actually strange.' (Angelika)

Such deliberations are particularly important in the context of a lack of "keepers" of religious language, such keeper in Catholicism being the institution of the Church. With an awareness so awakened, both a revision of the "old" religious language related to the Catholic tradition and a careful examination of the words of the new language gain particular significance. Furthermore, the fear of committing accidental blasphemy by improper use of language becomes prominent. Questions concerning the ontic[2] status of language and its form arise, as the answer to the question of whether digital, phonographic or graphic records are God's word as well has ethical consequences for the converts.

Knowledge of the Arabic language, even at a basic level, becomes of particular significance. The acceptance of the thesis of the untranslatability of the Qur'an means that a believer ought to discover the sense of the words of the Holy Book, which cannot be rendered in other languages. This leads to the question of the acceptability and the meaning of replacing them with familiar equivalents. Multiple Internet discussions revolve around the meanings of Qur'anic terms, their adequacy and acceptability of use. Some Muslims also think that Arabic is the language to be used for the various Qur'anic formulas uttered in different situations throughout the day. The formulas, *dhikr*, have a sacred role (the faithful remember about God while performing any activity, they believe they will be rewarded for the utterances in the eternal life) and a social one – they are important in unifying the ummah as a code for communication. Linguistic socialisation also includes practical skills. This is how its significance is explained by one of our interviewees, Stanisława:

> (…) it is significant because the Qur'an, as we believe, has been revealed in the Arabic language only. We pray reciting the Qur'an in the Arabic language, so surely understanding the language and practising recitation of the Qur'an is something important and positive for every Muslim. However, it isn't, of course, a requirement that being a Muslim one must

---

2  Relating to entities and the facts about them.

> know the Arabic language. (...) yet, the Qur'anic language is worth learning. It is not the ability to communicate or to have some complex conversation in the Arabic language that is significant, but rather recitation and understanding of the Qur'an, because this is our foundation and that we pass the Qur'an on to future generations in the same form. (Stanisława)

The purpose of studying the Arabic language is predominantly learning to read in this language (understanding the script and mastering the pronunciation). The knowledge of grammar is useful and desirable, yet not necessary, while speaking in Arabic is not needed for converts with no personal connections to the Arab world. As undertaking to learn a difficult foreign language is a considerable effort, the learners focus predominantly on the sacred aspect of the language. Reading the Qur'an is an act of worship for which the faithful are rewarded in the afterlife. This is how Kornelia perceives it: 'I believe that, when we read as well, well, even when we look at the letters, because you devote your time to it, to looking and thinking about what it says, we have a reward for that then, so I believe in it.'

The learning consists of stages, usually beginning with learning prayers, through reading the Qur'an (this stage being perceived as the final one by most of the learners), to learning the Qur'anic recitation (*tajweed*), the actual final stage mastered by very few converts. Learning prayers starts at the very beginning of the conversion process (even though it sometimes continues for several years afterwards) – the new Muslim memorizes texts she does not understand yet, which is difficult for many beginners:

> I learnt to pray very quickly. (...), because I read somewhere that prayer is what you must start right away, because otherwise you go to hell and what not. (...) You can learn it not knowing Arabic, which makes it much easier. (...) Two, three suras in addition to al-Fatiha, so those two, three suras are enough to start with. So I studied with those notes and I learned it quite quickly. And that, generally was a priority for me, to pray. (Anatolia)

Most of the respondents want to be able to read out the Qur'an in the original language (even without comprehension, as reading the Qur'an aloud and reciting it are acts of worship for which the faithful will be rewarded; the Hadiths speak of rewards for the recitation of particular suras) and some of them also wish to be able to use Arabic-language sources, which is why most of them are learning or have wished to learn the language at a certain point. Usually, they were studying or are still studying the language in classes organised by mosques or in private women's meetings. Some of them came into contact with the language in an Arab country where they lived with their husbands (in such a case, it was usually one of the dialects that they were learning), while some also try studying on their own.[3] A vast majority of them are dissatisfied with their level of knowledge of Arabic – the lack of time as well as the lack of continuity in teaching the language at a mosque or in other meetings are the most common causes of discontinuation of studying the language. They also declare their willingness to continue studying in the future, time and opportunity permitting.

Yet it is not solely the meaning of God's Word that is valuable for the new Muslims – some of the respondents told us about their spiritual experiences evoked by the very sound of Qur'anic recitation:

> (…) I don't know Arabic, but I had already read the Qur'an, so I had known al-Fatiha as the first sura of the Qur'an. Besides, there are whole suras with Polish and English translations available on YouTube (…) The very sound of it, the pronunciation itself, such a recitation of the Qur'an reaches the heart and the soul, and it generally changes a person. (Cecylia)

Another stage for some of the converts is learning the *tajweed*, the art of reciting the Qur'an. Currently, it is being taught by several Polish converts. Our respondents informed us that a number of Polish converts have qualified as Qur'anic recitation teachers having completed courses abroad and share their knowledge with other Poles by teaching their own online courses. One of our respondents, currently residing in an Arab country, perceives a great deal of difference in the level of recitation between converts and born Muslims. This prevents her from participating in a course organised at the mosque. She says it is difficult for new Muslims to compete in Qur'anic recitation with women from Arab countries boasting rich traditions of recitation.

Listening to Qur'anic recitation or learning recitation might be an equivalent of the aesthetic function of the Catholic liturgy: 'I liked singing very much, so I was in that gospel choir and I generally liked singing in church, Christmas carols and such things, but actually, as for Islam, recitation of the Qur'an, I mean the *tajweed*, is something like that, 'cause *tajweed* has those various rules etc., which could, in a sense, be compared to music, right?' (Anatolia)

In recitation, Anatolia has found a remedy for a problem mentioned by many of our respondents. After they left the Church, many of them were left

---

3   Among our respondents, there were two Arabic philology university graduates and two graduates of Muslim theology programmes (the latter programme including an Arabic language course).

with their aesthetic needs related to religious life unfulfilled. Accustomed to enjoying sacred art and music, the new Muslims may seek to fulfil those needs mainly through spoken word, as listeners and reciters of the Qur'an. The active role, however, is very difficult and requires years of practice with professional recitation teachers. This is unlike singing during the Mass or other religious services, in which everyone is allowed and encouraged to sing.

## Polish Virtual Ummah

For Polish converts, geographically dispersed both at home and abroad, the virtual umma, which often gives Polish female converts to Islam a sense of belonging (Górak-Sosnowska, 2015), is a Muslim *agora*, the space for daily meetings and exchange of knowledge and opinion. It is predominantly there that the common language of the group is constructed.

The richness of Muslim texts available online, representing the variety of genres generally available from the Internet, offers insight into the construction of the language of Polish Muslims' community. The specific language of the Polish *ummah* is one which has been developed as a constant work-in-progress project directly arising from its communicative practices. We divided the linguistic material gathered in the realm of Polish Muslim Facebook into two types (the division is not, however, a strict one, as the character of Facebook comments themselves is not always specified): didactic texts and comments.

The aim of the texts we call 'didactic' is, as their authors claim, 'to share knowledge about Islam' (it is not uncommon for the knowledge or Islam to be described as true/authentic). In addition to texts communicating information on dogmas, ethics, practices and Islamic law, the category also includes texts of moralizing character. The 'didactic' texts are predominantly translations of authors of content originally found on the English-language internet, yet there is also no dearth of Polish authors' original thoughts, accompanied by Qur'anic quotations, Hadith, and excerpts from scholars' writings. Most of the texts are of primarily online character, that is, they were created with the internet as the medium of communication in mind (Grzenia, 2006: 45). Published as posts and documents in publicly available groups or (most commonly) on multiple pages, they represent the authors' views, often disputed by the readers. Memes, containing their authors' own reflection as well as fragments of Hadith or other longer statements, also translated by the memes' authors, are a form that has a particular potential of dissemination; thus, they play a significant role in the reproduction of language. The other type of texts are comments on Islam and all matters related to it, left by Polish converts in public groups and pages. They are dialogic and often polemical, revealing the contributors' personal experiences, but also (quite commonly) sharing aims similar to those of the didactic texts.

The readers of both types of texts are Polish converts and potentially also (as intended by the authors) non-Muslim Poles. The didactic texts are often amateur translations or compilations thereof. They are most often sourced from English-language websites[4] and Facebook pages ran by Muslim scholars, popular preachers, or lay people. The translation strategy of choice is authenticity, sometimes articulated through 'reproduction without explanation' – a strategy adopted in face of cultural foreignness, resulting in a significant foreignization[5] of the text itself. Widespread use of such an approach leads to changes in linguistic norms and in canons of the target culture (Krysztofiak, 1999). In this case, the target culture is that of the religious language of Polish Muslims and a result of the process is their dogmatic-ethical system being based on selected parts of the Islamic conceptual system. The 'selectiveness' of the parts is dependent on the converts' commitments, which is why the linguistic practices in the context we studied included more terminology specific to the Salafist movement than Sufism.

Little attention is paid to the expressive function (the aesthetic aspect) of the text, often overlooked by the translators as insignificant in light of the informative and sacred functions considered by the authors to be primary for the reader. The authors of the translations are predominantly concerned with theological accuracy, which is why they most commonly apply translocation – retaining certain features or elements of the source text unaltered in the target text (Balcerzan, 2011: 147), and only partial adaptation to the grammatical-lexical system of the Polish language (the adaptation most commonly applying to the categories of gender and number). Structural loans, or calques, are common as well. The translators rarely attempt to find an equivalent in their native language. When both words are commonly known, they either both occur with similar frequency or one of them prevails. For instance, the Arabic word denoting adultery, *zina*, is chosen much more often than the Polish *cudzołóstwo*. When the Polish term is a rare word, as is the case with *suplikacja* (supplication), the equivalent of *du'a*, the Arabic term becomes a commonly used one, while the Polish word is not used at all. A high frequency

---

4   The source is not always credited, yet an English-language source can usually be inferred either from a high number of structural calques from English or from the fact that the English-language materials are relatively easy to find on the Internet.
5   Foreignization is the strategy of retaining information from the source text, and involves deliberately breaking the conventions of the target language to preserve its meaning.

of exotisms[6] and linguistic calques, the former derived mainly from Arabic, but also from English, leads to code-mixing.[7] The translators' and users' attitude to the Polish language appears to be indifferent, while their attitude to the meaning and form of the loanwords from Arabic could be described as a peculiar understanding of purism, focusing almost exclusively on their meaning, function or, sometimes, even spelling (Markowski, 2006).

While some Polish converts do not speak English sufficiently well, such online works constitute a response to their demand for knowledge of Islam. The whole content of this body of texts constitutes a narrative alternative, also linguistically, to that of the official message of Polish Muslim organisations. The organisations shape discourse through publications (written language, predominantly compliant with linguistic correctness norms) and lectures/classes/meetings (spoken language, far from linguistic correctness, rich in loans and linguistic calques, mostly ones derived from Arabic). The narrative of the 'internet minbars' could be deemed constitutive for Polish Muslims' discourse and its language due to the range of its influence and the ability to reproduce new lexical units or even whole sentences of conventional structure.

The second type of texts are Polish Muslims' comments in open Facebook discussion groups and FB pages, as well as blogs and pages where the authors share their personal thoughts on religion and experiences of Islamic life. Such texts also include a high density of loanwords from Arabic (yet fewer linguistic 'meteors'[8]) and more well-assimilated borrowings, already known to and used by a wide circle of readers belonging to the umma. The texts are not always originally produced in writing, but also spoken (lectures, sermons, conversations with other Muslims), hence the presence of various spellings of such popular lexemes. We noted over a dozen spellings of such commonly used Qur'anic phrasemes as *As-salamu alaykum* (peace be upon you), *mashallah* (what God has willed), or *insha'Allah* (God willing) and dialectal forms.

---

6   In Polish, unassimilated loanwords, mostly from Arabic especially ones maladapted to the syntax of the target language are called "islamism" (islamizm). For an English-speaking reader, this word could only bring in associations with political Islam. Therefore, for the sake of clarity we will refer to "islamisms" as loanwords from Arabic throughout the text. Moreover, the term is far from unambiguous in Polish too. Turek (201, pp. 87–88) remarks, the term is an imprecise one, which is why "islamisms" would need to be assessed quite arbitrarily.

7   Code-mixing is a term for hybridization of two or more languages.

8   Meteors are, therefore, words, similar in their nature to nonce loans (Kuźniak, 2009), the presence of which in corpora, and thus their degree of assimilation in the target language, is so insignificant that it is difficult to call them borrowings proper. (Kuźniak & Mańczak-Wohlfeld, 2014, p. 69)

Although colloquiality is a prominent feature of netspeak,[9] the colloquial style of the texts in question is often mixed with the grandiloquence of religious language and the posts often employ homiletic rhetoric.

### A Language Borrowed Twice

One of the most characteristic features of Polish Muslims' religious discourse is an unusually large number of loans, predominantly occupying the semantic field related to Islam. We define loans – units adopted into a new system (the target language) from a foreign system (the donor language) as 'words, expressions, types of derivation, inflection, syntactic constructions, and phrasemes foreign to the structure of a given language' (Markowski, 1999). Foreign terms are borrowed in a situation of no adequate terms being found in the mother tongue. Therefore, in the case of converts, with their need to name new practices and dogmas, the presence of culturally marked lexemes of foreign origin with no equivalents in the target language (Witalisz, 2016, p. 26) seems necessary. However, the fact that a vast majority of the borrowed words has its equivalents, ones that are well established in Polish, raises questions about the function of such loans, as from a 'linguistic correctness' perspective using them might be seen as an error.

A high number of loan words designating basic terms from the semantic field of religion, such as *iman* used instead of the Polish *wiara* and *haya* instead of the Polish *skromność* (with the English modesty also appearing in the latter case), comes as a surprise. They include ones used interchangeably with their Polish equivalents, such as *jahanna* with *piekło*, as well as haplax legomena[10] such as *muhasaba* and *taghut* (especially in the 'didactic' texts), secondary loans, for example *masjid* used instead of the well-established Polish *meczet*, and arabisms not directly related to the sphere of Islam, such as *shifa* and *dars*. Some of them find users' acceptance and even when they are (extremely rarely) replaced with Polish equivalents, they can still be deemed perfectly well-established in Polish Muslims' language, such words being, for instance, *iman, shirk, nikah, kufr, tawhid, sabr, nafs* (see Glossary for explanation of all the terms in this paragraph).

While assessing lexical loans, we may adopt the criterion of sufficiency, checking whether the borrowed word names something new or simply

---

9    On features of Polish Internet language (netspeak) see Górska-Olesińska (2010).
10   A word used once in a text.

replaces a term already existing in language. It is not always easy to resolve whether a given loan is redundant, as the loan word: a) might undergo semantic modification, b) might be marked for a style different from that of its Polish equivalent, c) becomes a euphemism as compared with the domestic term. An analysis of more extensive material is usually needed to establish semantic shift basing on idiomaticity. (Dunaj & Mycawka, 2017, p. 70)

Polish linguists have developed a set of criteria for assessing the correctness of linguistic forms. Walczak (1995, 4–17) distinguishes six useful ones among the many available: the criteria of sufficiency and economy of language, the functional criterion, the usage criterion, the cultural authority criterion, and the aesthetic criterion. Markowski (2006, pp. 49–54) added a seventh one, the national criterion (Markowski, 2006, p. 54). However, the influence of correctness assessments formulated by linguists on linguistic reality is rather limited than essential and the linguistic usage can be the decisive factor (Markowski, 2006, pp. 168–177).

The linguistic decisions in question are likely based on extralinguistic factors. The use of borrowed terms might indicate the new Muslims' assessment of the Polish equivalents as inadequate and finding the Muslim and Christian systems of dogmas, ethics and practices incompatible and therefore requiring different means of linguistic description. The choice of a loan over a mother-tongue term also indicates the distinctness of the designate – *talaq* will mean a Muslim divorce, *janaza* – a Muslim funeral, and *Jannah* will not be an equivalent of Paradise the way it is understood by Christians.

Another aspect important for a Muslim is also using the same words as those God used in the Book God sent to people. That results from their understanding, as religious people, that the sacred is to be found in God's Word itself, impossible to be rendered in any translation. Yet another aspect which might play a part is the connotative meaning of a word and the expressive function it has in a text. Loan forms might intensify the meaning of a word, as a foreign term sounds more definitive and carries with it a stronger evaluation of an aspect of reality than a native one (*haram* – forbidden, *halal* – allowed, *Jahanna* – hell, *Eid* – holiday, etc.). Moreover, many such loan words give the impression of their user being an expert and understanding them as requiring acquisition of certain knowledge of Islam. Those loans also include lexemes designating actions, states, objects and people (such as *wudu, aqiqa* and *ghusl*) the replacement of which would require functional equivalents, which in turn are not the best solution from a perspective focusing on economy and precision of language.

A comparison of 'native word-loanword' pairs consisting of a broadly understood analysis of the meaning and connotations of words (Leech, 1981, pp. 9–23) would certainly reveal a superficial synonymity of many of them. A good case in point is the meaning of *hidżab*, virtually the only term used by converts to name a *hijab* (*chusta*, the Polish word for headscarf, is used very rarely and *chustka*, its diminutive, is used hardly at all). The Internet authors often define it as follows: *Hijab* is not a headscarf, *hijab* is a way of dressing and *haya* (modesty).

On a socio- and psycholinguistic level, the use of loanwords from Arabic in place of their native synonyms is not an insignificant operation. Especially in religious language, where a foreign word will reinforce its character as distinct from colloquial language. It might evoke a sense of wonder, mystery, and transcendence, but also, especially in readers who are not believers themselves, a sensation of strangeness, resentment, or, in certain cases, especially when overused, ludicrousness.

Possible reasons for such a great number of loan words being absorbed into the converts' language might include a need to be close to 'true' Islam, a need to be part of a greater *ummah* (which, particularly among converts, has adopted English with Arabic loanwords for key terms as its language of choice), a search for their own authorities (linguistic ones included) originating from a lack of centralised authority, and finally, ignorance of the native Polish vocabulary. The use of Arabic loanwords might also suggest that their user is an expert on Islam, resulting in achieving a distinguished status among other members of their group pursuant to the mechanisms of symbolic and cultural capital described by Bourdieu (1986).

While for some converts, the foreignness has the desired effect, as it constitutes their own way of talking about God, thus creating foundations for a separate religious language of Polish Muslims, it also brings about negative effects, both inside and outside their community. The negative effects stem from foreignness being ascribed negative value at the society-wide level, because it is related to otherness of value systems and perceived as one which disrupts order and unambiguity (Znaniecki, 1990; Bauman, 1995). Foreignness of words implies foreignness of their designates in the reader's mind, which is why a non-Muslim Pole will see the confirmation of their opinion about the inherent foreignness of Islam here. Some converts perceive locking themselves up in a fortress of a language impenetrable to the wider society as a poor solution in the context of Islamophobia and xenophobia, and the exoticisation of language as an unnecessary and harmful barrier: 'We enclose ourselves in this *mashalling* (sic) and the *shirks*, nobody understands that the texts are sometimes comical, while they're doing some great *da'wah*.' (Maja)

It is possible that the converts feel a need to separate themselves from their former religious language of Christianity, simultaneously attempting to create their own as a code understandable for the members of their group. The loans might have the function of consolidating the group through creating its identity-based language which distinguishes it from other groups, in particular from the religious group to which the converts belonged before. Thus, they would serve as a distinctive factor. However, a considerable proportion of didactic texts on the Internet is created and intended not only for converts who wish to study Islam, but also for non-Muslims, aiming to encourage them to convert or at least to regard the religion more kindly.

Yet another explanation could be the prosaic one of sloppiness and linguistic nonchalance which, after all, characterise multiple online texts, the hurry and reliance on automated translation characteristic for amateur translators (Janikowski, 2008), insufficient linguistic competence and insufficient knowledge of the Polish religious language. A factor of no mean significance could also be a high number of Polish Muslims living abroad who participate in the online umma, especially those living in Great Britain, for whom the English language is the main medium of absorbing Islam. Many of our respondents and Internet users also report using Anglophone literature and claim to read the Qur'an in English or even in two or three languages (Polish, English, Arabic) to compare translations. Even though the high frequency of borrowings from English in Polish is a nationwide phenomenon which took on unprecedented scale after 1989 (e.g. Bańko, 2008, 2011, 2013, 2014, 2015; Mańczak-Wohlfeld, 1992, 1993, 1994, 1995, 2006, 2008, 2010; Markowski, 2000, 2002), the written language of Polish Muslims is so rich in both lexical loans (from Arabic in the context of religious language and English more generally) and structural loans (mostly calques from English, more rarely from Arabic) that it is closer to contemporary language of the media than to religious language.[11]

Nouns are the most commonly borrowed words in general (Mańczak-Wohlfeld, 1992, p. 20). So it is in the case of the Arabic loanwords in Polish converts' language, most of which are nominal: nouns, substantivized active and passive participles (*kafir*, *munafiq*, etc.), and verbal nouns – *masdars* (*iman*, *muhasaba*), adopted into Polish as nouns by substantivization. The source of a vast majority of the loans is Arabic, with English serving as an intermediary. The route of borrowing is sometimes that of direct contact (other Muslims and imams, mostly of Arab descent), yet the most common source is the Internet, the space of the global virtual umma with English as its *lingua franca*. This is

---

11  This speaks to the concept of 'banalisation of religion' associated with the role of the media in communicating religious content (Hjarvard, 2008, 2013).

complex communication, resulting in lexemes that penetrate the Polish language having previously been mediated by languages other than the original donor (Fisiak, 1962, pp. 287–288).

Depending on the mode in which a word is communicated, it can be differently rendered in the target language. When the word to be borrowed is heard in spoken language (phonetic/auditory loan), the pronunciation of the foreign word is usually accepted, but its spelling is not. When the word is found in written texts (graphic/visual loans), the spelling remains unaltered, but the foreign pronunciation does not. Borrowing from spoken language usually concerns high-frequency terms and phrasemes, such as *as-salamu aleykum, subhana Allah, mashallah, inshallah*. Due to the nature of such a mode of transmission, there can be multiple graphic forms of a single phraseme circulating on the Internet (the longer and more frequent the phraseme, the more forms can be found). The large number of forms is most commonly due to mishearing and lack of attention paid to reproducing the word. This is also how the (occasional) dialectical forms of Arabic terms are loaned. In the case of spoken language, the source of new words are lectures, sermons and, predominantly, contact with other members of the *ummah* – Polish converts and Muslims from other countries. The spelling can vary significantly, particularly in the case of frequently used words or phrasemes which the converts have heard before. Although Polish phonetic transcription ('spelt-as-pronounced', with minor exceptions such as the spelling of sounds subject to devoicing) is sometimes used, even in such cases the spelling is based on English transliteration. The most numerous loans are ones derived from written, predominantly English-language, texts.

The loan encompasses both the term itself and its spelling, that is, a simplified (and, as the texts are often written by amateurs, quite arbitrary) transliteration of Arabic terms. The overarching rule for transliteration in Polish is phonetic notation, yet after 1989, with the linguistic change, (the influence of English and English-related notation, increased with the rise of Internet), incorrect notation is ever more often to be found even in publications from renowned publishers. Such notation not only misleads the reader, but also affects orthographic coherence of the text. In the case of words borrowed as a result of translations of online texts, the transliteration usually depends on how the word was transliterated in the English text (often itself a translation of a text originally produced in Arabic or other languages). Once a word has been introduced into the Polish umma, it acquires a life of its own and becomes adapted by subsequent users.

We could also divide loan words into those which occur in a (usually translated) text without having appeared in the discourse of the Polish ummah before and those which have already been commonly used. As for the former, only some of them have a chance of becoming more widespread and blending into the religious language of Polish Islam. As for the former, they are already spelt in a multitude of ways, depending on individual users' preferences.

In the case of texts published by Polish converts on the Internet, the transcriptions and transliterations (both frequent) are not usually uniform ones. The authors apply their own modifications, which not only increases the relative difficulty to be experienced in the reception of the texts, but may even preclude comprehension. There are different spelling forms to be found in single texts, which might result from a disregard for established transcription systems. Certain Arabic sounds are rendered with Polish and English spellings interchangeably, which adds to the confusion, as is the case with *dżummuah*. This transcription usually has the letter *j* instead of the Polish diphthong *dż*, *y* instead of *j*, *sh* instead of *-sz*, *-kh* instead of *h/ch*, *w* instead of *ł* (even in the case of simplified Polish transcription, *w* is still used instead of *ł* – *wa alejkum assalam* – despite the letter never signifying the desired sound in Polish). The simplified French transcription with ch instead of sz, and ou for the long Arabic vowel u is much more common. Long vowels in Arabic are rendered with doubling the letter representing the vowel (aa, uu, ou or oo, ee or ii), which is partly a seemingly arbitrary modification. Sometimes, the length of the vowel is not marked at all. There are also the rare cases of the Turkish mark for a lengthened vowel as in *Allâh, Tauhîd, Du'â, Kâfir*, usually in translations from Turkish or translations of texts which had already been translated from Turkish. The apostrophe is often used to represent the hamza or the letter *'ayn*. Texts by Polish Shiites include transcriptions of Persian terms (*Ayyam-e-Beez, Masjid-e-Kufa, Eid-e-Zehra Eid Zahra, Eid e Ghadeer*). One can also find, albeit rarely, transcriptions using the Arabic chat alphabet (Arabizi) used by Arabic speakers to communicate on the Internet and in text messages, with figures representing the letters ayn, hamza, and the three h-like consonants – *Allah yar7amuhu*. There are not many Polish converts skilled in using this system, which is why it is not effective in this context and its occurrences are usually accidental rather than intentional. Even for individuals who speak Arabic, it is entirely unnecessary to render Arabic sounds and long vowels in any special manner, as both the vowel length in particular and the whole of the phonology of the loan words in general become adjusted to the requirements of the target language. Moreover, even converts who speak Arabic adjust the pronunciation of loanwords from Arabic to the phonological system of the Polish language while speaking the latter. The Arabic feminine final *ta marbuta* letter can be rendered with *-a*, *-at* or *-ah*, but using either *-at* or *-ah* makes it more difficult to establish the gender of a word, which is a significant feature of the Polish language. It is sometimes difficult for the writers to accept Allah being spelt entirely in lowercase, which is required by transcription rules when the word is preceded by a preposition. This is why they split the prepositional phrase, e.g. replacing the most common spelling of *alhamdulillah* with *alhamdu li Allah*, or *fisabilillah* with *fi sabil Allah*. The application of such a spelling might result in the *bi* or *li* preposition being removed. It is also common in transcription prepared by people who do not speak Arabic, when the transcript is based on a spoken text, that the article is separated from the noun it relates to – *Ar-rahmanur rahim, salatul Eid, salatul jumma, Dabbatul Ard, ummul muminin, ahlul beyt, Ibnul Qayyim*. It is quite common that capital letters are incorrectly used at the beginning of common nouns. It is common in Internet texts, particularly memes, that Polish, English and Arabic text, also using the Arabic alphabet, is used together (*Robimy Du'a*, or *by Allah* تعالى *prowadził nas do tego, co Mu się podoba* – "We're doing Du'a," or "so that Allah تعالى leads us to things of His liking").

Thus, we can speak of double borrowing – that of the Arabic word and that of its English graphic form. Moreover, the complete arbitrariness of transcription and the copying of English transcription patterns are not useful for any language users. The Polonised graphical form of the Arabic loanwords may diminish much of the wonder, uniqueness, and even sacredness they would carry. If the foreign variant harmonizes better with the connotative meaning of a word, the writers will prioritise it. Logically speaking, if the adapted variant was judged to be a better vehicle for the content, one would expect it to gain predominance.

### A Convert's *Savoir vivre*; Honorifics in Polish Female Converts' Language

Polish rules of linguistic politeness require strangers to be addressed with *pan/pani* (historically roughly equivalent to the English Sir/Madam, currently to Mr/Mrs) and a third-person form of a verb. Currently, due to the influence of Americanisation and pop culture generally, the rules are treated less rigorously. Members of multiple groups in various environments, both in workplaces and private situations, switch to the direct form of address, *ty* (you), until recently reserved for close friends, *en masse*. Before, in a public situation when participants in the conversation are strangers to one another, the use of such a form would have constituted an intentional act of disregard, a form of verbal aggression. However, the polite forms of *pan/pani* remain the default form in communication between adults. The internet requires a different mode of communication, thus democratising social relations. Polish netiquette advises users to address one another with the 'ty' form. The Polish Internet, however, often evidences the use of *pan/pani*, especially on Facebook, predominantly when interlocutors know their respective identities and can often be parties to professional relationships, which is a situation of social hierarchy not being levelled down by online communication.

In spoken language, converts replace the *pan/pani* forms with *brat/siostra* (brother/sister). These can either be used with a third-person verb, which results in the address being more polite and official (*z jakiego Siostra jest miasta?* "What city are you from, Sister?" or *Niech Brat z nim porozmawia na ten temat.* "Please talk to him about this, Brother."), or a second-person verb – more informal and familial, used for people with whom the speaker would use *ty* (*Siostro, zrobić ci kawę?* "Sister, would you like some coffee?" *Bracie, podaj mi tę książkę!* "Brother, pass me that book!"). The former version sounds very formal due to the use of the third-person verb and the use of the vocative (*Siostro! Bracie!*), a case which has fallen out of popular use. It leaves the impression of archaicity and rather excessive politeness. Currently, the only other widely accepted uses of such structures are addressing nuns and monks; previously frequent addressing nurses as *siostra* (sister) has fallen out of favour with Poles (the nurses themselves arguing against the form as they find it depreciating) (Sosnowski, 2015, p. 328).

The English equivalent 'sister' and, even more commonly, its short form 'sis' are used as often as the Polish *siostra*. It is worth noting that the short form itself, contrary to its singular-only English use, is used by Poles to denote either the singular or the plural. One may also observe adding both singular and plural Polish feminine suffixes to both forms (*siska, siski, sisterka, sisterki*). These forms are examples of the rare morphological adaptations to be found in our material. The resulting word has a jocular sound to it, which lends it a positive emotional timbre that evokes the unofficial and friendly relationships between the young women (playing with English loans is a domain of young people). Another common form is the Polish diminutive for sister, i.e. *siostrzyczka*, pl. *siostrzyczki*. *Uht/ukht* (from *uht*, the Arabic for sister) is quite common as well, yet it is often incorrectly rendered as *ukhti*, while in Arabic the final i is not an integral part of the noun, only a first-person possessive pronoun and the Poles use it in strictly nominative functions (*jaka powinna być idealna ukhti?* – what should an ideal *ukhti* be like). Both the *sis/sister* and the *ukht/ukhti* pairs are described with Polish adjectives (*Kochana uhti! Droga sis!*). It is not uncommon for the English *sis* to be joined by Arabic terms (*wa iyaki, sis!*). Interestingly, men are almost exclusively addressed with the Polish *brat*, pl. *bracia*, the Arabic *ah* being almost, and the English *brother* and *bro* entirely, absent.

As forms of address are evaluated using the criterion of appropriateness (Sosnowski, 2015, p. 322), one may ask how they are perceived by the interested parties themselves. Certain women are vocal on the Internet, expressing their opposition to such forms, deeming them artificially grafted into Polish from Arab culture and probably to diminish social stigma and manage spoiled identity (Goffman, 1963). However, even people who do not use them as forms of address will from time to time describe somebody as their *siostra/brat w islamie* (sister/brother in Islam): 'I don't like those forms, they are weird and artificial for me. That's not how we speak, we are not Arabs, are we!'[12]

Some converts express dislike for the sister/brother form as it is often used by new Muslims: 'I have only one sister, and her name is Basia. Calling people sister/brother doesn't sound appropriate to me, I do not use it and I do not wish to be called that. It is something artificial and untrue for me, that's not how you speak in Poland, we are not nuns.'[13] The honorifics are, however, used very often, particularly by 'fresh' converts. A great number of posts in women's groups begin with *Kochane (Dear) Sis, Kochane Siostrzyczki, Kochane Sisters, Kochane Siostry*. The converts use the forms in multiple comments as well as, with high frequency, in spoken language, which justifies the assumption that they have been accepted as a way of communicating. It appears that this convention, at least silently accepted if not used by all participants, serves the function of building a sense of belonging to a group.

### In Search of Their Own Way

The picture emerging from the material we gathered in our conversations with women who had accepted Islam is one of a Polish convert for whom Polishness, a feeling of belonging, both to a nation and to a culture, and feeling 'at home' are important constituents of her identity. They perceive Islam as a universal religion which can be followed without giving up one's cultural identity. Moreover, they feel the religion ought to, or even must, feel 'familiar'.

---

12  From https://www.facebook.com/Islam-po-polsku-229308817105396, Retrieved March 7, 2019.

13  Ibidem. Retrieved March 9, 2019.

> Nobody is saying 'Mosques for Poles' here (a paraphrase of the nationalist slogan 'Poland for Poles'). If Islam is to spread in Poland at least a little bit as it has been the case with other non-Arab countries, it must also be Poles' religion, one for Poles and by Poles. This has nothing to do with xenophobia, but with acknowledging the role of language in religion gaining a foothold on new soil. It is not about nation but about language and culture. I would not underestimate those things, because we have a strong emotional bond with our mother tongue. Islam is universal, it is not Arab, it is not exotic, it is not from Arab countries, it is from heaven. The more it is our own, the more place will it have in our hearts. Should we not build, or at least try to build, an Islam without sediments? (Maja)

Some of them are aware that their religious feelings and experiences are rooted in the Polish language. They wish to use the feelings of closeness and homeliness and adapt the language to the narration of the new religion.

> R. You know, we'd need to translate that Islam more into our Polish conditions. For someone who lives in it, how much of the Arabness can you take? (...) I am with Muslims on Facebook on an everyday basis and we use Arab expressions there. But in that normal language you speak Polish, don't you? I have equivalents: *jak Bóg da* (God willing), *mój Boże* (my God), you know.
> A. And do you use that type of phrases, but in Polish?
> R. Well, I do.
> A. Not in Arabic?
> No. Normally and in conversation usually in Polish when I talk to a Muslim you will sometimes say *alhamdulillah* unreflexively, but also *jak Bóg da*. With Rysio (a convert friend) I often talk and say *z Bogiem* (with God) or *Szczęść Boże* (God Bless). (Franciszka)

> I find it annoying when new sisters are always saying – *Oh Subhanallah* (Praise be to God), how much my stomach's hurting today, a word like that all the time, it's funny, nobody speaks like that ... Who are they imitating? It's impossible to talk like that. If you have to say such things, can't you say – *O Boże* (Oh, God)?[14]

Converts seek lexemes which they could use to replace Arabic loanwords in the tradition of Polish religious language. Inspiration is found in Polish translations

---

14  Ibidem. Retrieved May 12, 2019.

of the Qur'an and other religious writing, lectures and sermons, but also, to a very large extent, in the amateur translations present on the Internet and the vernacular of Polish Muslims. Some of the new words are of episodic character, yet some have already found recognition in the language of Polish Muslims.

This is exemplified by the expression *radiya Allahu*, uttered after the names of prophets, being replaced with the very common calque *Oby Allah był z niego zadowolony* ('May God be pleased with him'), despite the existence of a particularly suitable version of that – *Niech Bóg rad będzie z niego*. Not only is it phonetically close (with little chance of establishing whether anyone had intended it) to the Arabic original (*rad – radiya*), but it also carries, due to the Polish adjective *rad* being somewhat archaic, a greater emotional valence than the banal and not nearly as emotional word *zadowolony*.

The phraseme *subhana wa ta'ala* ('the most glorified') is rarely translated, most often left in the original (transcription or, much more rarely, the Arabic alphabet). Polish Shi'ite texts utilise the Polish phrase *Allah jest uwielbiony i wywyższony*, with the *Allah Najwyższy* and *Allah Wzniosły* occurring as well albeit less often respectively.

The prophet Muhammad is most often called *Wysłannik Allaha/Boga* (Allah's/God's Envoy), *Prorok Muhammad* (the Prophet Muhammad), and (albeit rarely) *Święty Prorok* (the Holy Prophet) (while *Święty Koran* (the Holy Qur'an), as well as *Szlachetny Koran* (the Noble Qur'an), and *Święte Hadisy* (the Holy Hadith), even though usually restricted particularly to the so-called *qudsi* Hadith (holy hadiths), this phraseme occurs much more often), *Szlachetny Prorok* (the Noble Prophet) and *Apostoł Boga* (God's Apostle). The form *nasz ukochany Prorok* (our beloved Prophet) is also common. A vast majority of Polish Muslims use the Arabic form of the Prophet's name – Muhammad, instead of the traditional Polish form *Mahomet*, the latter felt by many Muslims to be derogatory and associated with Christian Europe's historic hostility towards Islam. Both describing the Prophet or the Qur'an with the adjective *święty* (holy) and calling the Prophet *Apostoł* might be considered uses of the terminology of the religious language of Polish Christianity, even though it employs a translation of the English Apostle. The phrase *salla Allah alayhi wa sallam*, which traditionally follows the Prophet's name in Muslim discourse, is most often replaced with *Pokój z Nim* (Peace with Him), abbreviated as PZN, a Polish equivalent long accepted in Polish Muslim literature. Other translations to be found are *pokój i błogosławieństwo Allaha z Nim* (Allah's peace and blessing with Him), *niech będzie z Nim Pokój i Błogosławieństwo* (may Peace and Blessing be with Him).

The *rahimahu(a) Allah* phrase is sometimes replaced with the Polish *oby Bóg się nad nim/nią zmiłował* (pray God has mercy upon him/her). When giving condolences, Polish Muslims most often use the *inna lillahi wa ilayhi raji'un* phrase, yet some replace it with the Polish translation (*Zaprawdę*) *do Boga należymy i do Niego powrócimy* ((indeed) to God we belong and to God we shall return). We have also noted *Od Allah*[15] *pochodzimy i do Allah powrócimy* (From Allah we come and to Allah will we return) and *Niechaj odpoczywa w ramionach Litościwego Allah* (May s/he rest in the arms of the Merciful Allah).

In the case of common religious formulas, the converts use both the Arabic originals (most often in English transcription) and traditional Polish phrasemes of a certain equivalence (most often calques). Phrases of the highest frequency, such as *in sha' Allah* or *alhamdulillah* are often replaced with Polish equivalents: *jak Bóg da* (God willing), *dzięki Bogu* (thanks be to God), *daj Boże* (may God allow), *jak Bóg pozwoli* (God allowing), *chwała Bogu* (praise to God). In the Polish Catholic context, the latter have either become limited to elderly people's language (*jak Bóg da, daj Boże*) or remained in popular contemporary use albeit as devoid of religious intent (*dzięki Bogu, chwała Bogu*). There are also new phrases, created as calques: *Chwała Allahowi* (Praise to Allah) instead of *alhamdulilah*, a *Allah wie najlepiej* (and Allah knows best) instead of *Allahu a'alam*, *niech Ci/Cię Bóg błogosławi* (may God bless you) instead of *Allah yubarik feek*, *pokój, błogosławieństwo i miłosierdzie Boże niech będą z Tobą/Wami* (may God's peace, blessing and mercy be with you) instead of *assalamu aleikum wa rahmatullahu wa barakatuhu, niech Ci Bóg ułatwi* (may God facilitate (it) for you) etc.

However, the extremely common phrase *jazak Allahu khayran* is not replaced with the traditional Polish *Bóg zapłać* (may God repay you), which would seem a perfect equivalent. Most likely, the reason for the rejection of such a phraseme is its strong emotional and social connotation – it is too strongly associated with the greedy attitude of the Catholic Church towards material goods, commonly criticised in Poland. Currently, the only use of this phrase outside of the church is the ironic use in jokes. We have not encountered a Polish translation of the *jazak Allahu khayran* phrase.

Polish Muslims wish to use the terms in their everyday life, but some of them perceive the use of Arabic terms as strange and would like to replace them with Polish equivalents. Many converts use the Arabic terms (and even their Polish equivalents) only among their fellow Muslims, as they find it inappropriate to confuse non-Muslims with vocabulary or style which is unknown to them. They also usually apply Polish translations in Internet communication with

---

15   One of the most characteristic features of the language of Polish converts is a specific 'sanctification' of language which one of the signs is lack of declension while using word 'Allah'.

Polish Tatars, for instance the condolences expression *do Boga należymy i do Niego powrócimy* (to God we belong and to Him we shall return), while they would rather choose the original when addressing converts.

> A. Do you use such phrases as "inshallah"?
> R. Yes, but because now I have limited contact with Muslims, maybe I can enjoy using them (...) and *do my inshallahs* when Zosia (the respondent's friend, a fellow convert) is around (...) (Alana)

> I use them for example when children sneeze, then we say *alhamdulillah*. It is also because we often have really diverse company that I do not confuse them, I am not this kind of person. Then, you'd need to remember, with Muslims I will of course say *salam aleikum, inshallah, alhamdulillah, mashallah*. I only use them at home and among Muslims. I am drenched with the expressions. Oh yes, surely my husband (who is an Arab) inserts them after every other word (...) So when I hear my husband say *inshallah*, he is really saying – this will never be done. This is why I don't like it. (Danuta)

> I speak Arabic, so I am used to the expressions. But I think it is for that reason precisely. If I didn't know Arabic, maybe I would be using *daj Boże* or *chwała Bogu*. Now, they have become a part of me and I feel weird not having said *alhamdulillah* or *inshallah*, so when I am talking to non-Muslims, I add them in my thoughts. (Maja)

In Internet texts, one may find attempts at replacing the Arabic terms with Polish translations, such as *suplikacja* instead of *du'a* (supplication), *tradycja* (Polish for tradition) instead of *Sunnah*, *wyznanie wiary* (declaration of faith) instead of *shahada*, *nawoływać do islamu* (call to follow Islam) instead of the rather clumsy calque from English, *robić dawah* (do dawah), *Noc Przeznaczenia* (the Night of Destiny) instead of *Layla al-Qadar* (the term *Noc Mocy*, meaning the Night of Might, can also be found), or the blend of *noc Qadr*. We have also observed a translation of *Layla al-Qadar* as *Noc Dekretu* (Night of the Decree). There are also new terms based on the Arabic ones or their English translations, for instance *ludzie Księgi* (people of the Book) in addition to *ludy Księgi* (peoples of the Book), a phraseme earlier established in Polish.

Another example of such calques is *kara grobu*, a phraseme long-present in Polish Muslims' language, which is an equivalent of the Arabic phrase *adhāb al-qabr* and the English 'punishment of the grave' (it is difficult to establish whether the Polish phraseme was based on the original or on the English translation). We have also noted an episodic occurrence of the phraseme *życie grobowe* (gravely life), based on the phraseme *życie pozagrobowe* (life beyond the grave).

Not all Polish terms replacing the Arabic ones, however, are fit for purpose. Sometimes, their lack of suitability lies in the connotation of a word or in using a word from an unsuitable register. Among such terms, one might list *decyzja* (decision) instead of *fatwa* (not reflecting the meaning of the Arabic term and even falsifying it), *ignorancja* (ignorance) instead of *jahiliya* (even though a more fortunate term, *czasy niewiedzy*, the times of lack of knowledge, is used too), *przerwanie postu* (the breaking of the fast) instead of *iftar*, *czysty monoteizm* (pure monotheism) instead of *tawhid* (the term implies the existence of an impure, thus untrue monotheism). Calling scholars' opinions or *fatwas orzeczenie* (verdict), which implies an authoritative and final character of such statements, seems an abuse or misinterpretation of the original Arabic term. Another example in this category is the formula *szukać zadowolenia Allah* (seek Allah satisfaction), made very popular by the Polish Muslim League lectures. It is a calque from Arabic which is not only grammatically incorrect (Allah is used in the nominative, instead of the genitive form, which would be appropriate in Polish for seeking Allah's satisfaction), but also represents very poor style. A similar phrase, also made popular by the Muslim League lectures, is *przypodobać się Allah* (earn Allah's favour, this time the nominative form of Allah used instead of the dative which would be appropriate in Polish), also incorrect in Polish. Other popular phrases in the language of Polish converts are: *życie to test* (life is a test), instead of the better-sounding *życie to próba* (life is a trial) (also: *zostałem poddany testowi* – I have been subjected to a test). An example of a more fortunate neologism is *robić dżihad na* (to do jihad on), an interesting, original and somewhat jocular one created by a convert. Attempts at replacing the Arabic terms *dawa* and *dai* have not been successful until now – a small number of Internet texts use the phrasemes *wzywać/zapraszać/nawoływać do islamu* (call/invite/exhort to Islam) (verbal forms), *wezwanie/zapraszanie/nawoływanie do islamu* (calling/inviting/exhorting to Islam) (verbal nouns) and the participle form thereof for *dai* – *nawołujący do islamu* ((one) calling to Islam). All the forms, based on translations of the verb *daa*, are relatively rare in Polish Internet texts.

The converts often use ready-made phrases and slogans disseminated by popular pages (I love Allah more than his creation), their Polish translations/adaptations (*Islam jest idealny, muzułmanie nie są* – Islam is perfect, Muslims are not), and code mixing (*Be sabr!*).

There are very few examples of Polish word-formation processes affecting the loans. We have only noted five new verbs – three of them created from borrowed nouns, one from an Arabic verbal noun (*masdar*), and two based on phrasemes: *iftarować* (to eat the *iftar* meal), *maszallować/pomaszallować* (to say mashallah), *inszallować/poinszallować* (to say inshallah), *takfirować* (to call somebody a *kafir/a* (nonbeliever), to call somebody's actions/beliefs kufr/disbelief), *haramować* (to pronounce somebody's actions forbidden – haram). There were also verbal nouns derived therefrom: *takfirowanie, haramowanie, inszallowanie, maszallowanie*. All of these except *iftarowanie* are used in ironic and jocular contexts in the circles of Polish female Muslims who contest the Polish Salafi discourse: 'Oh, again, another one who'd *takfir* everyone!', 'They *haram* everything – Peppa the Pig, listening to music, makeup, well, everything!', 'It is always like that – the *shahada*, they'll all *mashallah*: "Oh sister, sister, *mashallah*," and bite you in the back a moment later'.[16]

Other hybrids formed by morphological adaptation are ones which denote female Muslims: *hidżabka*, pl. *hidżabki* (women wearing hijabs), *nikabka*, pl. *nikabki* (women wearing niqabs), *muslimka*, pl. *muslimki* (the most common word beside *muslima* used to denote female Muslims), *sis/siska* pl. *siski*, and *haramitka* pl. *haramitki* (women who 'haram' often and without a reason). *Nikabka, hidżabka. muslimka* and *siska* are words with positive connotations, yet might be perceived as somewhat childish. *Haramitka* is undoubtedly a jocular and depreciating term, similar to such hybrids as described above.

Another example of morphological adaptation is *hasanaty* – a noun existing only in a plural form. Formed from the Arabic *hasanat*, 'good deeds', by adding the Polish plural suffix. The word has gained immense popularity and, being currently the only one used instead of the Polish phrase *dobre uczynki*, has even become part of the official written language of the Muslim League (at least on their Facebook page). this loan seems fairly justified – *dobre uczynki*, a term from the semantic field of Christian ethics has also gained secular meaning and currently it is not precisely clear what it denotes. It is somewhat archaic, with a possibility of a shade of irony in its meaning. The term *hasanaty* is unambiguously characteristic for religious Polish Muslim contexts. Furthermore, the economy of language might play a part here.

As for other interesting neologisms, a noteworthy one is *szejkija*, denoting a female Muslim scholar. This form, contrary to the masculine forms occurring on Polish Internet sites, such as *sheykh*, was given not only a feminine ending, but also Polish spelling. An additional point of interest is that the ending is not a Polish feminine ending, but an Arabic one used technically incorrectly – to form a noun, while in Arabic this ending is used exclusively to form adjectives.

---

16  Ibidem. Retrieved January 27, 2019.

## Language as a Battlefield

The process of the Polish ummah taking shape is parallel to that of its language being formed. The latter, in turn, becomes a basis for reflection on the community's identity and the conflicts it breeds. Facebook groups and walls become venues for disputes pertaining to the accuracy of Polish translations of the Qur'an and the adequacy of translation of Arabic terms and replacing them with Polish equivalents. All these phenomena can be seen as linguistic forms of managing spoiled identity (Goffman 1963).

The Polish Internet *ummah*, and particularly the part of it which discusses the perspectives of Polish Islam and finds the influence of Polish converts on the shape of Polish Islam to be insufficient (we discuss the issue of representation of Polish Islam in Chapter 1), is particularly interested in the language which Polish Muslims should be using in sermons and public appearances. The discussion referred to the damage to the community's image caused by the community representatives' lack of Polish language skills. According to the critics, the Polish umma suffers substantial damage to its image Polish society due to being represented by Arab immigrants, whose presence makes tribal stigma more visible and acts of "passing" harder. The Arab Muslims ostensibly do not experience stigmatizing trauma in Polish society in the same way as Polish converts because there is no contradiction between their virtual and actual social identity (Goffman, 1963).

The Muslim League claims it has the right to represent Polish Muslims by presenting its activity as complementary to that of the Muslim Religious Association, which represents the Tatars. Their website says the League was created as a "Polish Muslims' initiative". Polish Muslims claim that the perception of them as an exotic group culturally foreign to Poles is increased by the insufficient command of Polish and deficiencies in cultural competences found among representatives of the Muslim League. Polish female Muslims often need to defend themselves against the charge of being strangers in their own country. This is why, for some, the use of the Polish language in the life of the umma, especially in its contacts with the non-Muslim majority, seems to be very important. As one of the Internet users puts it: 'As long as we are represented in the media by organisations led by Arabs and the Arabs speak instead of Poles, we will be treated as strangers.' (Maja)

Polish female converts, long-time victims of Islamophobia, are also critical of the community's self-proclaimed representatives appearing in the media. They are sometimes individuals completely unknown to the *ummah*, representing fringe views, whose incompetence in Islamic teachings or inexperience in media appearances does nothing else than, in most converts' opinion, entrench Polish society's lack of sympathy towards Muslims.

A topic discussed on the Internet equally frequently is that of the believers' experience of lack of Friday *khutbahs* (sermons) in Polish and (even more importantly), the lack of Polish imams. The Internet users complain about the *khutbah* being limited to a short summary in Polish, only a few sentences long. It must be observed, however, that there are also opposing voices – some see nothing unusual in the fact that the sermon is delivered in Arabic, and even perceive it as a necessity:

> The *khutbah* should be given in a language understandable for those coming to the mosque – in the language of the country it is located in, 'cause most people use that language and other languages in accordance with the needs of the local *ummah*. If it is in Arabic, nobody will understand a thing and will just be siting there like an idiot. A *khutbah* in Polish, what's more, delivered in beautiful Polish by an imam from Poland, could attract more locals to Islam, 'cause the barrier for them is the language which creates a sense of foreignness. On the other hand, the level of many of those sermons is miserable, so maybe we shouldn't worry about missing the Arabic part.
>
> Personally, I believe that the fight for our mother tongue in mosques makes sense. My identity is within the language. I cannot imagine talking about God in broken English or some strange mix. As long as we do not speak of God in our mother tongue in our mosques, it will be, both for ourselves and for people from the outside, some exotic fashionable faith, something foreign in its essence.
>
> I also dream of Polish imams. An Arab, a Turk, etc., no matter how religious and pure in their faith, (…) is prone to multiple cultural influences which are impossible to root out. Besides, despite living in Poland for, in general, at least 30 years, they speak terrible Polish.[17]

The opposing voices argue for using the Arabic language in Friday sermons as necessary and (as one of the Internet users wrote in her comment) providing a degree of sacralisation:

---

17   Ibidem. Retrieved November 21, 2019.

It must be in Arabic, there is no *khutbah* whatsoever without that, and then translation. If the non-Arabic speakers in a given umma care for it, they may help the imam provide such a translation. A *khutbah* is not meant to be a battle call, like those of Khalid bin Walid, nor to satisfy somebody's niche linguistic needs. If you don't understand the *khutbah*, you are supposed to listen or you may draw circles on the carpet with your finger.[18]

Attempts at exerting influence on and changing the linguistic shape of Polish Islam meet resistance from Muslim League decision makers, who are predominantly native Arabic speakers. Although the Muslim League's publishing activity has been, from its start, marked by a significant participation of Polish converts (as it would be impractical without their linguistic competences), the data we have gathered shows that they do not shape the official language of Polish Islam. The convert input could, for instance, result in Polonization or domestication of the language, as it has been suggested by one of the converts:

> At the League's Convention in 2001 or in 2002, (…) there was a discussion, which consisted of saying what the organisers wanted to hear (…). This is not a style for people from Europe (…) There are some people who find it attractive. I, however, find it offensive, treating adult people this way. It is not (…) suitable for Polish conditions at all. (…) I raised my hand, I'm standing up and I thought that (…) I might help, I'm saying excuse me (…) it seems to me, because you are using the word "Allah", brother, yet in our publications, when we are writing some texts for Poles, we could use the (Polish) word *Bóg* (…) to avoid exoticisng, so that people do not feel that it is some polytheistic religion with Allah as its main deity, that we are someone foreign. (…) I thought they would eat me alive. They trampled me into the floor, treated me disrespectfully, like an idiot. The one chairing it was a doctor, (…) his Polish was incomprehensible, and such was the Convention. (…). (Maja)

There are voices appearing among the converts which are saying that the overuse of Arabic terms, so common in the language of new Polish Islam, especially the use of words which have Polish equivalents, is an aspect of unnecessary Arabisation of the local *ummah*.

> I prefer saying *chwała Bogu* to *alhamdulillah*. After all, it means the same. (…) I can see it in all the new ones, it is very important for them to learn all

---

18    Ibidem. Retrieved November 10, 2019.

the rules: "My, I don't know all the vocab yet. I am not a good Mus ...", and I'm saying: "but what does vocab have to do with it?". There is that certain conviction that, at least in the very beginning, that Islam is 'Arabness' only and nothing more. (Franciszka)

Some converts consider the activity of the Muslim Religious Association an excellent example to follow, thanks to how much the imams in the mosques operated by the organisation care for good Polish language. The Tatar Muslims themselves are also sometimes considered by the Polish *ummah* to be an excellent example of preserving their own religious and ethnic identity and simultaneously reaching a high level of integration with the Polish society.

We have the tradition of a few hundred years of Islam in the lands of the Polish Republic, there is something to refer to. In the old days, *khutbahs* in mosques of the Polish Republic were delivered in Polish as early as in the 16th century. (…) Many Poles are not aware of the fact that there have been Muslims living in our country since the 14th century. The Tatars (…) since the 18th century are simply Poles like us, so a continuity is preserved. The traditions are shared, there is no 'us' and 'them'.

I wish we had a spokesperson, preferably one like that of the MZR, their spokesperson is Musa Czachorowski, a poet, see how well he does in interviews and what statements he writes!

Thus, some of the converts, particularly ones who converted a longer time ago, acknowledge the significance of their mother tongue in their religious practices and the need for using the language in their community, not only for emotional reasons ("my identity lies within the language"), but also because of the expressed desire to be accepted by the Polish society.[19]

### A Language Recovered

The narrative of Polish Islamophobia targets the converts painfully, denying them a sense of identity and their emotional relationship with the land and Polish culture, which we discuss in Chapter 4. Therefore, their counterarguments are usually reaction to such charges. Polish converts emphasise their

---

19   Ibidem. Retrieved October 3, 2019.

relationship with Polishness on the Internet (in Facebook groups, profiles and fan pages which serve as a medium for shaping their image) with national symbols, images referring to a common national imaginary (the Polish Independence Day, the Warsaw Uprising Day), referring to Islam's relationship with Poland (Tatars, famous converts – national heroes), trying to find their place in the dominant patriotic-historical discourse forced upon the Polish public sphere by the political right. The above does not mean however, that such an attitude is the only one among Polish converts – it ought to be mentioned that there is a large group who are trying to 'Arabise' both their language and their Internet image, which is a certain declaration of self-identification. This pertains particularly to Muslims who have converted recently.

Another, more personal motive, is referring to traditional Polish religiosity – often nicknamed 'grandmas' faith'.[20] Many of our respondents, as well as Facebook groups' members, highly value the traditional Polish religiosity which, in their opinion, fades away with the generation of their grandmothers.[21] The grandmas, very warmly and affectionately remembered by the respondents, often provide their familiar model of religiousness. The respondents also talk about the bond they started to feel between themselves and their grandmothers after their conversion, a bond arising from a faith of equal strength, yet of a different name.

It appears that it has been very natural for the educated urban professionals, to find a sense of spiritual community with the elderly women, often originally from traditional rural areas, who exhibited, as the respondents put it, "deep faith".

> There are such people as, for example, my grandma, who is a very elderly woman and doesn't know [that I am a Muslim], or else her heart would break. Since I became a Muslim, I have been grandma's beloved granddaughter, 'cause her two other granddaughters are, you know, secularised, and all her daughters-in-law as well. So, she calls and says to my mum: "may God bless her" and my mum goes blank and doesn't know what to say, as she can't even pretend, and she passes the phone to me and I tell her: "granny, I pray for you", she answers: "I pray for you too", she says something and I tell her that I'll visit, and she replies: "God willing".

---

20    Which Hall (1997) described as "lived religion", religion rooted in practice and experience.
21    Although the traditionally understood 'folk religiosity' faded away together with Polish folk culture, with which it had been inseparably bound, some of its aspects have remained alive and their presence leads to creative reimagining of traditions. (Królikowska, 2014)

Yes, God willing (laughter). And my mother just keeps looking at me like that, but I am not lying when I say all that to grandma. (Marysia)

Placing one's spiritual way within the picture of one's family and its history, interweaving it with a tradition of generations of female believers, might be of no mean significance for the converts, as even if they are not rejected by their families, they are symbolically excluded from the society. It might also be of certain significance in the context of exclusion from the national community. The converts talk about the tradition of women wearing headscarves in the past in response to the accusation of 'non-Europeanness' of the Muslim headscarf. To counter this, Polish Muslim blogs and Internet groups feature old photographs of Polish women in headscarves and long skirts.

Some of the converts propose replacing Arabic phrases with their Polish equivalents which sound somewhat archaic and are associated with the older generation (*daj Boże* – God allowing, *jak Bóg da* – God willing), and restricted to conversing with the Catholic clergy (*szczęść Boże* – God bless), or ones which are still used colloquially but have lost their religious connotations by virtue of their popularity. 'Our grandmothers would always say *jak Bóg da* or *daj Boże* (equivalents of "God willing") when they were planning something, when they were talking about the future. It was beautiful. Now people don't speak like that anymore, but such is our tradition.' One of the respondents says:

> We went with the girls [fellow converts] to visit a mining museum. We were surprised, but also very happy to hear that they were still using the traditional miners' greeting *szczęść Boże* (God bless you), instead of *dzień dobry* (the usual Polish greeting, 'good day'). And those are not only the guides, who are retired miners, but young girls working there too. (...) Once I was working in the garden, and there's that elderly gentleman passing by saying: *Szczęść Boże*. And it was so sweet, Jesus, so moving. That's what you used to say, maybe what people still sometimes say in the country, to someone who is working. I replied *daj Boże* (God willing). Oh my, nobody speaks like that anymore today ... (Maja)

The phrases not only allow converts to communicate with their grandmothers' generation, but also to find a community code that is not obvious for others.

The new Muslims say that the phrases also enable them to communicate with Catholic clergymen without the feeling of 'faking something'. This might be deemed a specific type of linguistic camouflage. If the convert is not wearing a hijab, the clergyman may think he is dealing with a pious Catholic, while she – using the former linguistic forms filled with new meaning – may 'pass' and feel confident despite an awkward social situation.

> I said *Szczęść Boże* instead of *Niech będzie pochwalony Jezus Chrystus* (Polish for 'May God bestow happiness upon you' instead of 'Praised be Jesus Chris'), as I do pay attention to such things, and I didn't really excuse myself for anything in front of him, I just had the funeral organised. (Marysia)

> I enter (...) my neighbourhood shop, to which I would go several times a day, and I know all the people there, and there's a group of construction workers standing there. And they say to me *Szczęść Boże*, so I answer *Szczęść Boże*. *Szczęść Boże*, and not some *Niech będzie pochwalony Jezus Chrystus*, just the ordinary *Szczęść Boże*. (Franciszka)

## Conclusions

The selected features of Polish converts' language discussed here, predominantly sourced from online texts, illustrate the multifaceted character of the group's members' identity. They converted to a religion in which the divine intent had been revealed with a particularly strong bond to the language of the revelation itself. This fact, in conjunction with the language being a foreign one for them, draws the believers' attention to the weight and significance of words with a particular strength. The lack of tradition and continuity of religious language, insufficient religious infrastructure, Arab educators' lack of integration into the Polish society (both its language and culture), and the lack of strong social networks all contribute to incomplete religious and linguistic socialisation. The former religious language related to the Catholic tradition gains particular significance. Such a revision is accompanied by, on the one hand, a need to discard the old and create a language of one's own and, on the other hand, a need to be included in the global English-speaking umma.

Members of the Polish umma are rooted in the symbols, religious imagination and the language of Polish Catholicism. This can be seen in the willingness of mobilising that linguistic ecosystem in speaking about the new religion. Their efforts aimed at adapting the old forms to the new content demonstrate that Islam must be domesticated, which includes its linguistic layer. They do not perceive Islam as an exotic novelty, but rather as something that had always been present but has only now found its shape, as a continuation and completion of Catholicism they were brought up in, a return to a forgotten tradition of religious and social life. Thus, it is not only possible, but also necessary to fit it into old linguistic forms so as to make it more familiar. The ongoing battle in the linguistic field is oriented towards managing spoiled identity and reducing social stigma.

## References

Bajerowa, I. (1994). Swoistość języka religijnego i niektóre problemy jego skuteczności. *Łódzkie Studia Teologiczne*, 3, 11–17.

Balcerzan, E. (2011). *Tłumaczenie jako "wojna światów". W kręgu translatologii i komparatystyki.* Wydawnictwo Naukowe UAM.

Bańko, M., Drabik, L., Wiśniakowska, L. (2007). Słownik spolszczeń i zapożyczeń. PWN.

Bańko, M. (2008). Dlaczego wow? In G. Dąbkowski (Ed.). *Reverendissimae Halinae Satkiewicz cum magna aestimatione* (pp. 9–21). Plejada.

Bańko, M. (2011). Dlaczego polskie myszy klikają po angielsku? In A. Kwiatkowska (ed.) *Przestrzenie kognitywnych poszukiwań* (pp. 267–278). Uniwersytet Łódzki.

Bańko, M. (2012). Obcość jako istotny element charakterystyki wyrazów zapożyczonych. In H. Burkhardt, R. Hammel, M. Łaziński (eds.). *Sprache in Kulturkontext. Festschrift für Alicja Nagórko* (pp. 17–24). Peter Lang.

Bańko, M. (2013). Normatywista na rozdrożu. Dwugłos w sprawie tzw. kryterium narodowego. In J. Migdał & A. Piotrowska-Wojaczyk. *Cum reverentia, gratia, amicitia ... Księga jubileuszowa dedykowana Profesorowi Bogdanowi Walczakowi* (pp. 141–148). Rys.

Bańko, M. (2014). Czego bronimy, broniąc języka? O możliwych przyczynach niechęci do wyrazów zapożyczonych. *Poradnik Językowy*. 2014, 5, 30–42.

Bańko, M. (2015). Iconic effects in loanword adaptation, In K. Kosecki & J. Badio (Ed.) *Empirical Methods in Language Studies* (pp. 259–269). Peter Lang.

Bańko, M., Svobodová, D., Rączaszek-Leonardi, J., Tatjewski, M. (2016). *Nie całkiem obce. Zapożyczenia wyrazowe w języku polskim i czeskim.* Ostravská univerzita. Uniwersytet Warszawski.

Bauman, Z. (1995). *Wieloznaczność nowoczesna, nowoczesność wieloznaczna.* PWN.

Bourdieu, P. (1986). The Forms of Capital. In J. Richardson (Ed.). *Handbook of Theory and Research for the Sociology of Education,* (pp. 241–258). CT Greenwood.

Bucholtz, M. & Hall, K. (2004a). Language and identity. In A. Duranti (Ed.). *A Companion to Linguistic Anthropology* (pp. 369–394). Blackwell.

Bucholtz, M. & Hall, K. (2004b). Theorizing identity in language and sexuality research. *Language in Society*, 33(4), 501–547.

Bucholtz, M. & Hall, K. (2005). Identity and interaction: A sociocultural linguistic approach. *Discourse studies*, 7(4–5), 585–614.
Bucholtz, M. & Hall, K. (2010). Locating Identity in Language. In D. Watt & C. Llamas (Eds.). *Language and Identities* (pp. 18–28). Edinburgh University Press. Edinburgh.
Dunaj, B. & Mycawka, M. (2017). O potrzebnych i niepotrzebnych zapożyczeniach z języka angielskiego. Annales Universitatis Paedagogicae Cracoviensis. *Studia Linguistica*, XII, 67–80.
Fisiak, J. (1962). Złożony kontakt językowy w procesie zapożyczania z języka angielskiego do polskiego. *Język Polski*, XLII(4), 286–294.
Goffman, E. (1963). *Stigma: Notes on the Management of Spoiled Identity*. Simon & Schuster.
Górak-Sosnowska, K. (2015). Between Fitna and the Idyll, Internet forums of Polish female converts to Islam. *HAWWA. Journal of Women of the Middle East and the Islamic World*, 13(3), 344–362.
Górska-Olesińska, M. (2010). Retoryka w kulturach elektronicznych. Cyberdyskursywność. In W. Chyła, M. Kamińska, P. Kędziora & M. Kosińska (Eds.). *Kultura medialnie zapośredniczona. Badania nad mediami w optyce kulturoznawczej* (pp. 353–365). Uniwersytet im. Adama Mickiewicza.
Grzenia, J. (2006). *Komunikacja językowa w Internecie*. PWN.
Hjarvard, S. (2008). The mediatization of religion: A theory of the media as agents of religious change Northern Lights. *Film & Media Studies Yearbook*. 6(1), 9–26.
Janikowski, P. (2008). Obrazy religijności. Odmienność religijna w przekładzie. In P. Fast, P. Janikowski & A. Olszta (Eds.), *Odmienność kulturowa w przekładzie* (pp. 53–66). Wydawnictwo Śląsk & WSL.
Królikowska, A. M. (2014). Elementy "ludowe" w religijności współczesnej? *Opuscula Sociologica*, 4(10), 5–16.
Krysztofiak, M. (1999). *Przekład literacki a translatologia*. Wydawnictwo Naukowe UAM.
Kuźniak, M. (2009). *Foreign Words and Phrases in English. Metaphoric Astrophysical Concepts in Lexicological Study*. Uniwersytet Wrocławski.
Kuźniak, M. & Mańczak-Wohlfeld, E. (2014). Angielskie wyrazy okolicznościowe w polszczyźnie. *LingVaria*, 9(17), 69–79.
Leech, G. N. (1981). *Semantics: the study of Meaning*. Penguin Books.
Mańczak-Wohlfeld, E. (1993). Uwagi o wpływie języka angielskiego na polszczyznę końca XX w. *Język Polski*, LXXIII, 279–281.
Mańczak-Wohlfeld, E. (1995). *Tendencje rozwojowe współczesnych zapożyczeń angielskich w języku polskim*. Towarzystwo Autorów i Wydawców Prac Naukowych "Universitas".
Mańczak-Wohlfeld, E. (1992). *Analiza dekompozycyjna zapożyczeń angielskich w języku polskim*. Uniwersytet Jagielloński.

Mańczak-Wohlfeld, E. (2006). *Angielsko-polskie kontakty językowe*. Uniwersytet Jagielloński.

Mańczak-Wohlfeld, E. (2008). Morfologia zapożyczeń angielskich w językach europejskich. *Studia Linguistica Universitatis Iagellonicae Cracoviensis*, 125, 113–120.

Mańczak-Wohlfeld, E. (2010). Język polski w dobie globalizacji. In J. Gruchała & H. Kurek (Eds.). *Silva rerum philologicarum: studia ofiarowane Profesor Marii Strycharskiej-Brzezinie z Jej jubileuszu*, (pp. 213–221). Księgarnia Akademicka.

Markowski, A. (1999). *Polszczyzna znana i nieznana*. Gdańskie Wydawnictwo Oświatowe.

Markowski, A. (2000). Jawne i ukryte nowsze zapożyczenia leksykalne w mediach. In J. Bralczyk & K. Mosiołek-Kłosińska (Eds.). *Język w mediach masowych* (pp. 96–119). Upowszechnianie Nauki – Oświata.

Markowski, A. (2002). Zapożyczenia dawne – dziś (stan z początku i końca XX wieku). In W. Gruszczyński (Ed.). *Język narzędziem myślenia i działania* (pp. 76–85). Elipsa.

Markowski, A. (2008). *Kultura języka polskiego. Teoria. Zagadnienia leksykalne*. PWN.

Niedźwiedź, A. (2014). Od religijności ludowej do religii przeżywanej. In B. Fatyga & R. Michalski (eds.). *Kultura ludowa. Teorie, praktyki, polityki* (pp. 327–338). Instytut Stosowanych Nauk Społecznych.

Nowowiejski, B. (2001). Makaronizmy końca XX wieku. *Białostockie Archiwum Językowe*, 1, 93–111.

Sosnowski, W. (2015). Formy adresatywne: aspekt językowy i socjologiczny. In D. Roszko & J. Satoła-Staśkowiak (Eds.). *Semantyka a konfrontacja językowa* (pp. 319–332). Slawistyczny Ośrodek Wydawniczy.

Termińska, K. (2015). Wątek religijny w paradygmacie lingwistycznym. Niewysłowioność Tanachu a problem tłumaczenia. In K. Termińska (Ed.). *Studia z hebrajszczyzny biblijnej. Niedoczytanie moje* (pp. 187–198). Uniwersytet Śląski.

Turek, W. P. (2001). *Słownik zapożyczeń pochodzenia arabskiego w polszczyźnie*. Universitas.

Van Herk, G. (2012). *What is sociolinguistics?* Wiley-Blackwell.

Walczak, B. (1995). Przegląd kryteriów poprawności językowej. *Poradnik Językowy*, 9–10, pp. 1–16.

Witalisz, A. (2016). *Przewodnik po anglicyzmach w języku polskim*. Towarzystwo Miłośników Języka Polskiego. Kraków.

Znaniecki, F. (1990). Studium nad antagonizmem do obcych. In F. Znaniecki (Ed.). *Współczesne narody* (pp. 265–358). PWN.

CHAPTER 6

# Converted Bodies: Interior Life and Embodied Religious Practices of Polish Female Converts to Islam

*Anna Piela* | ORCID: 0000-0002-3589-1822
Northwestern University

## Introduction

Embracing a new faith is often associated with developing new concerns for material bodies. This chapter traces the ways in which Polish female converts approach Islam as an embodied religion, one that relies on spatial and material reconfigurations of the body as part of comprehensive religious practice. Inspired by Topal's (2017) strategic connection of Foucault's notion of the "technologies of the self" and Mahmood's (2005) and Asad's (1993) discussions of the modern project of Islamic ethical self, I draw from these theoretical constructs to situate the empirical data about Polish female converts' deployment of ritual Islamic practices that involve the body: the hijab (understood in the broader sense of modest behaviour, rather than just the headscarf, as it is used in modern parlance), prayer, and food-related practices. I pay particular attention to how these practices may carry with them social stigma and how the converts manage it discursively and through modified behaviour.

Simultaneously, I recognize that the study of Muslim lives, including those of converts', ought to acknowledge the ambivalence of everyday religious lives in which religious frameworks, aims and practices may be sometimes secondary or tertiary to other concerns (Schielke, 2009 and 2010). The data related to incorporating the body in the process of conversion, or, rather, living conversion through the body, presented in this chapter resonates with both the ethical self and everyday religion discourses; here, striving for perfection is shown as often intertwined with embracing imperfection as emblematic of human action across different social contexts. Butler described these intersecting aspects by stating that 'very often religion functions as a matrix of subject formation, an embedded framework for valuations, and a mode of belonging and embodied social practice' (Butler, 2011, p. 72).

In the recent decades, the body has emerged as the focal point of conceptualizations of ethical and religious meaning-making. McGuire (2006, p. 188) writes: 'embodied practices ... emphasise those ritual and expressive activities in which spiritual meanings and understandings are embedded in and accomplished through the body (e.g., bodily senses, postures, gestures, and movements)'. Indeed, embodied religious practices are increasingly seen as central to producing new moral selves in the process of conversion (Winchester, 2008). Practices such as wearing religious dress, praying, fasting, and keeping halal are fundamental in creating a religious or pious disposition in the believer (Mahmood, 2005). (In the past, religious practices were interpreted as a necessary step for developing moral virtues (Asad, 1993)). With the "bodily turn", the embodied practices are no longer seen as derivative of belief, but rather, mutually constitutive with it in the construction of religious realities (Winchester, 2008). This view is a departure from Kantian and liberal understanding of the moral self as an essentialized *a priori* notion (Mahmood, 2005).

For converts in non-Muslim majority contexts such as Poland or the UK, the task of developing an Islamic moral self, or a pious disposition, is multifold: they need to learn these practices over a period of time, and simultaneously dynamically manage them, recognizing various affordances and limitations of the social contexts they inhabit. While the Muslim identity is seen as spoiled within the mainstream Polish society, it becomes an asset in Polish convert communities, whether in-person or online. Significantly, these contexts may offer different degrees of allowances for Islamic practices, therefore sometimes converts are faced with a dilemma whether to adjust the levels of their practice or depart from the social setting that is perceived as stigmatizing.

This chapter maps out the process of developing, adjusting, and operationalizing the moral self that occurs within and through the body among the Polish female converts we interviewed. Thus, it shows how one's moral self cannot be divorced from the space in which it operates, or the ways in which the body of the believer is gendered, sexed, and racialized through the lens of religious practice. In this chapter, the headscarf and the niqab are intentionally discussed alongside prayer, fasting, and other practices, as I recognize that the intense focus on Islamic dress code in scholarship has, at times, obscured other gendered practices in Islam that may offer alternative conclusions regarding the place of the (female) body in Islam. By discussing how Polish converts to Islam variously negotiate prayer, fasting, and dress in a dynamic social context, I demonstrate the central role of the body in the process of conversion.

### Islam, the Gendered and Sexed Body, and the Process of Conversion in the Polish Context

The (gendered) body plays a central role in Islamic ethics. Delaney (1991, p. 26) wrote about the focus in Islam on "the meaning and comportment of the body in everyday life. Islam prescribes in minute detail how the body in its myriad activities must be presented." In this sense, the discussion of embodied Islamic practices cannot be separated from a consideration of the gendered and regulatory quality of these practices. In recognition of this, Anwar (2006, p. 102) notes: "while the ethical message of Islam promotes a balanced well-being of male and female bodies, women's bodies, their contours, suppressions, and concealments reveal good and bad, truth and falsehood, virtue and vice, honor and shame, and blame and responsibility."

Despite the existence of gender-based variation in religious practices in most faith traditions, the gender-specific character of some Islamic practices is perceived with fascination and indignation to an equal degree. In other words, it carries with it a particular kind of stigma. Alleged oppression of Muslim women is often expounded in order to obscure gender inequalities experienced by Western women. Thus, "[g]endered issues have been pivotal in the construction of Otherness between Islam and the West" (van Nieuwkerk, 2006, p. 1). The burka in particular became the symbol of Afghan women's plight during and after the US-led invasion (Khiabany and Williamson, 2011); the niqab-clad 'jihadi bride' continues to be resented and desired long after the collapse of the Islamic State in Syria (Owe, 2017; Ibrahim, 2019); the 'burka bans' have been instituted in seven European countries and have not been rescinded despite pandemic mask mandates that require populations of these countries to cover their faces (Zine, 2020). In the popular imaginary, the Islamic (headscarf) is a very, if not the most, symbolic gendered embodied practice in Islam (Ruby, 2006; Haddad, 2007; Byng, 2010). This is also recognized by Polish converts to Islam who sometimes adopt the hijab even before their formal conversion (Krotofil, 2011).

As mentioned in the Introduction, for many women, the process of conversion to Islam is narratively, constructed as entirely in harmony with their lifelong lifestyle choices, such as maintaining variously interpreted modesty, abstinence from alcohol, and enjoyment of prayer. This often applied to women who grew up as Catholics and were often active in lay religious movements. Other women talked about Islam as a final choice following a long spiritual search that often encompassed Buddhism or Hinduism, but even they were socialized into dominant discourses strongly inflected by Catholicism. After the conversion, the already existing attraction to an Islamic lifestyle among many participants could now be properly framed. The embrace of Islam is therefore constructed as a logical outcome, aligned with, rather than opposed to, their ethical disposition pre-conversion. This alignment is expressed by highlighting the continuity of embodied practices that simply gain increased religious significance post-conversion. Practices such as headcovering, sometimes seen as culturally foreign by Polish converts, may not necessarily be seen as significant for the reformulated religious identity. For example, Małgorzata (who does not wear the headscarf) commented:

> [after conversion] I wear the same kind of clothes. Always modest, unpretentious. It can even be short sleeves or shorts, but I'd never dressed seductively. I never liked it. Nothing has changed. I never dressed provocatively or enjoyed raucous parties. [Now] when I go out, I just sit with my friends, they're drinking beer, I'm not. I've never liked alcohol or getting drunk. (Małgorzata)

### Sexual Practices

A prominent subset of the "naturally Muslim" convert narratives in our dataset was related to developing a positive disposition to one's body image and, in particular, sexuality (within the bounds of Islam). This applied particularly to married, heterosexual respondents. Kinga remarked that she enjoyed the sense of well-being that Islam fostered for her, in particular being able to affirm her sexual needs:

> I've remained myself; I haven't changed. I didn't have to, because Islam didn't affect any of my needs; when I was with someone, as I said, I had a husband, I didn't suppress my sexual needs. Nothing changed. I really appreciate it, that Islam takes into account sexual needs, physical, biological ones. There are hadith traditions that say that you have actual responsibilities towards your body, just like you have responsibilities towards your family, your spirituality, your mental health … I love Islam for this balance. Living with this religion you do not have to deny yourself anything. (Kinga)

This participant speaks about Islam's recognition of believers' sexual needs from a particular position of a married woman. Contrary to her statement in the last sentence of this extract, Islam's teachings are generally understood to restrict sexual activity to marriage (traditionally defined as a union between a man and a woman), similar to Catholicism. In this sense, the shift to Islam did not affect the boundaries of sexual desires. However, it appears to reflect the notion, popular among the converts we interviewed, that within these boundaries, the attitudes to sexual activity are more open in Islam (which permits contraception and a wider variety of sexual acts) than in Catholicism (Krotofil et al., 2021). Alternatively, this statement could be interpreted as a sign of developing a disposition where bodily desires are refashioned according to Islamic ethics and unlikely to be a cause of a transgression. A statement that illustrated how discourse related to sexual transgressions may be refashioned and reintegrated into Islamic sexual ethics was offered by Renata, who was a widow, during a focus group. In response to the facilitator's question about different listed identities that the women in the group feel conflict with a Muslim identity, she pointed to "kochanka" (mistress or lover) and said:

> For my husband, I am supposed to be the lover – not a mistress, hidden somewhere. He's supposed to be the best lover for me, and I have four kids with him. You see, as a Muslim, I understand this word only in this way. This is the meaning of this word for me – lover, lover in marriage, for my husband – and I hope I was a good one. (Renata)

A juxtaposition of identities of a deeply religious woman and a "good lover" is unusual in the cultural context of Poland, where celibacy is associated with priests, nuns, or monastic vocations, and, by extension, with high degrees of religiosity. Polish Catholic religious language does not accommodate the notion of sexual satisfaction well; Joanna commented that her friend, a staunch Catholic, gratefully said once to her "You're the only person I can talk to about sex" after she got married and needed advice on the topic articulated from a religious perspective. Presumably, she appreciated the directness that the Muslim identity afforded Joanna with respect to discussing sexuality.

Narratives of spirituality, common sense, positive relationship to the body and sexuality are intertwined in Justyna's response. She contrasts the new dispositions explicitly with Catholic teachings that she received in the past and a sense of guilt related to sexuality that was inculcated into her as a Catholic. Strikingly, her story also recalls simultaneous pre-conversion pressures related to maintain a skinny body through dieting:

> I used to be under pressure to weigh very little; I haven't weighed 50 kilograms for a long time now and I don't mind at all. I don't feel pressure, I have started seeing [my body] as packaging for me. I look after it and don't pollute it, because it's important in Islam to look after what we're given. I don't focus on beauty standards, this stuff's no longer important, and it's like that with sexuality. The Catholic religion taught me that marital sex is for procreation only. In Islam, it's different. A wife is with her husband because it makes them happy. Even if they don't want to have kids ... we don't right now ... that's ok, if both spouses agree about that, [sex without procreation] it's ok, natural, and healthy. And not making a taboo out of it ... How we live, and how we do it, with contraception or without, it's our private business and I like that very much. I think of it as

a natural part of my life, and before talking about it was uncomfortable, I didn't want to talk about it. Now it's like eating, drinking, and it's totally ok. I don't mind talking about it. (Justyna)

Respondents' references to the intrusion of the Catholic Church into people's intimate lives are frequent and made with palpable distaste. In the past few years, scholars have drawn attention to the manner in which the Church (in collaboration with the conservative Law and Justice government) continues to exert social control over Poles, in particular women, by achieving a tremendous amount of control over their reproductive choices and sex lives at large. It enforced an almost full legal prohibition of abortion (Żuk and Żuk, 2019; Calkin and Kaminska, 2020), denied LGBTQ people's rights (Korolczuk, 2020; Mizielinska, 2020), and denounced the feminist movement (which it labelled "the gender ideology"; Odrowąż-Coates, 2015, Gwiazda, 2020). Less is known about the psychosexual effects of Catholic teachings on ordinary women who may identify themselves as Catholics; fragmentary data on Polish women's sexuality negotiation suggests that question of women's sexual satisfaction has been largely considered culturally unproductive and therefore inappropriate (Marody and Giza-Poleszczuk, 2000). Transgressions in relation to contraception use and divorce effectively put many believing Catholics in Poland outside the fold of the Church (Lamb, 2016; Mishtal, 2015). It is possible that Islam, by allowing contraception (Atighetchi, 1994) and divorce (Jaafar-Mohammad and Lehmann, 2011) is an attractive alternative for those who wish to practice religion but retain sexual agency related to these issues. Many of our interviews suggest this was true for the married and heterosexual respondents. For them, perceived Islamic sexual norms function as a useful "source of moral and social distinction from other religious groups as well as from the majority society," although in a different way than identified by Mossière and Le Gall in the Quebec context (2018, p. 105) or Beekers and Schrijvers (2020) in the Dutch context. In contrast to their findings, Islam was portrayed as significantly more open to female satisfaction, and therefore preferable to Catholicism. This narrative likely reflects the management of spoiled identity, as becoming Muslim is portrayed here as a pathway to greater female sexual agency, absent in Catholicism.

However, experiences of sex are not universally good among the married women we spoke with. Demonstrating tensions between religious prescriptions and lived reality of believers, Kornelia reflected on the challenges she experiences in relation to *wudhu*, the ritual ablution for purification required before prayer:

> One thing I find hard to accept in Islam is the requirement to wash yourself after intercourse to purify yourself before prayer. Sometimes we give up the sex, because we live in an old, cold, drafty building and ... sometimes the hot water pressure is just nonexistent. And I can't wash my whole body under cold water. Sometimes I miss just being able to cuddle and just fall asleep after sex. I could wash before *fajr* [the morning prayer], but try going to sleep knowing that you'll have to get up and take a cold shower. I have a bit of a [problem] with this and I'd change it, if I could. (Kornelia)

The narrative of Islam as naturally attuned to human nature was further complicated by accounts of unmarried respondents. Their situation was less compelling; several talked about their unfulfilled sexual needs but a lack of desire to get married solely for the purpose of gaining access to sexual intercourse. Maja, who was divorced, said:

> There was a time when I was alone, I didn't want a [new] relationship, because of the kids. When they grew up, I thought that maybe I'd like to ... I even considered becoming a second wife, as it's really just sex with no strings attached, but then I reconsidered. I'm just no good for a setup like this. I have to fall in love, create a relationship, sex on its own is just pure exercise. (Maja)

For Maja, the state of celibacy presented challenges; it was difficult to reconcile getting married while she still had young children in her custody. Her narrative suggests a dilemma related to having sexual needs which she could superficially address through marriage based on sexual attraction, but she simultaneously suggests that her sexual needs are bound up with emotional ones, and in reality, much harder to satisfy in absence of a suitable male partner. Imtoual and Hussein (2009: 27) note that the situation of women like Maja – "well past their teens, intellectually and morally mature" who have difficulty remarrying in a minority Muslim context – remains unaddressed. This challenge was also described by Suleiman (2013). Discourses about the affirmation of sexual satisfaction for both men and women are disconnected from and restrictive for their lived experience (Ali, 2006). Imtoual and Hussein (2009) point out that these women are trapped between the transgressive option of having sex outside marriage (and Maja did not even articulate this avenue) and celibacy, which is discouraged, as in Islam sex is seen as necessary for a healthy and fulfilled lifestyle. This situation is profoundly gendered, as many Muslim communities are more accommodating of men engaging in sexually transgressive behaviours such as sex outside marriage (Imtoual and Hussein, 2009). Two respondents we interviewed, Anna and Jowita, mentioned the institution of temporary marriage, variously framed as *mut'a* (Haeri, 2014), or a simply cycle of marriage/divorce, recognizing that it can variously reinforce or subvert gendered sexual norms. While commenting on the difficulty with finding an emotionally mature or compatible partner, Jowita suggested that seeking out purely sexual partners is permissible, as long as it is an intentionally temporary marriage:

> A female convert, if she wants to find a man, just to have a man [to have sex with], she'll find one. It's not a problem, you can find one every two months and get divorced later. It's not a problem … but if you want to find someone sensible [to have a steady relationship with], then there's a problem. (Jowita)

Polygamy is another topic that is imbued with tensions among the respondents; most accept it at the abstract level, but reject it at the personal level, often indicating that most men are not mature enough to practice it responsibly and fairly. Matylda commented:

> I think I would find it hard to accept. There are situations when it makes sense … there is [woman's name] who is able to find herself in it. I don't know if I'd find myself in it, I'm sure, personally, it would be difficult. I think a lot depends on the man, can he satisfy all his wives materially and spiritually? It's possible, but difficult. (Matylda)

In a similar vein, Kornelia suggested that polygamy may be a solution to an exceptional problem "but absolutely not as a general principle." As such, they did not represent what Rao (2015: 432) termed a "sacrificial disposition" in her study of American converts; unlike them, our respondents did not accept polygamy wholesale as part and parcel of the process of becoming appropriately gendered religious subjects (Rao, 2015, p. 432).

The view that men at large will inevitably seek out "another woman" at some point was also fairly common – the respondents considered the Islamic solution of a polygamous marriage in the open, where the man has to take the responsibility for the second family, as a much better solution than an underhand affair, which Joanna called "hidden polygamy." Alana said, for example: "For me, polygamy makes much more sense than a mistress on the side. At least the man is learning how to be responsible; if it's all about sex, then it has nothing to do with the teachings of Prophet Muhammad. Then, it's just a parody." Respondents criticized arrangements where the second wife is kept in secret – but tended to, in the abstract, accept polygamous marriages where the first wife knows and agrees to the existence of the second wife. Some women (Maja, Alana) we interviewed even described situations where the first wife sought out the second wife for her husband, wishing to have a say in who would join the household. Alicja, quoted below, was an exception. She lives in Poland, is married to an Egyptian man, but they do not live together.

> I wouldn't see a problem with it, because I will not give him children [according to her, due to age], and I know he would like to have one … I would be fine with a second wife, if he wants to feel fulfilled as a Muslim, because a real Muslim has to father a child. If he wants to, he'll cheat on me, and with a second wife, at least I'll know what's what. Why should he have to do something behind my back? (Alicja)

Alicja indexes male religious identity to sexual prowess and fatherhood to the point that she even accepts marital unfaithfulness as a possibility (illustrating the earlier point that male sexual transgressions are not treated nearly as seriously as women's). It is possible that she is more open to polygamy due to her frequent visits to Egypt, where her husband's family lives, and where polygamous marriages are accepted by over 40% of the population (Kramer, 2020).

Some reflections on polygamy were marked by a degree of fetishization and Orientalisation; Elżbieta said:

> We [Polish women] are Europeans, it is offensive to us … if you're from a family who practiced it for generations, then these girls are used to it … I would not accept that. Unless I got a prince from Dubai, I'd have my own palace, children, then … I'd reconsider [laughter]. I think every girl would, it wouldn't be a bad arrangement, huh? There would be some physical satisfaction, and if that was a handsome millionaire who would look after you, indulge you, well, then if he had another … our Polish man may also get another, but here, at least you'd live in luxury. (Elżbieta)

These conversations establish Polish female converts to Islam as an alternative collective interlocutor in the bifurcated discourse on sexuality in Poland that tends to contrast religious (Catholic) sexual norms (in particular the restrictive ones that prohibit contraception and decenter female sexual satisfaction[1]) with secular/liberal/Western sexual norms (in particular those that encourage

---

1 We recognize that there are discourses within Catholicism that do not disavow women's sexual pleasure; however, they are on the margins of the mainstream Polish sexual practices.

contraception, and female sexual satisfaction). Islamic sexual ethics was portrayed by heterosexual married respondents as natural, healthy, in harmony with the female body – but this narrative was simultaneously complicated by accounts of unmarried women. The women we interviewed – many of whom were practising Catholics prior to conversion – produce their religious selves by positioning their religious practice in contrast to Polish Catholics rather than the "secular Other" (Rao, 2015, p. 432). As such, the dichotomy of Islam and the secular Other is inflected by the presence of Catholicism, similar to Rogozen-Soltar's study of Spanish converts to Islam (2020). At times, they also position themselves against men in general (often, respondents would issue generic statements that seemed to encompass all men, regardless of faith). In doing so, they mobilise essentialist gendered discourse that positions men as full of lust and unable to control their instincts; this is seen particularly clearly in the next section where gender-segregated prayer is discussed. More often than not, even male Muslims are situated as "men," rather than "brothers" which highlights the problematic notion of benevolent gender relations in Islam (often contrasted with the "battle of the sexes" approach ascribed to secular gender relations).

## Embodied Prayer

Prayer featured prominently in the respondents' narratives as a central component of Muslim practice, a source of strength, and a special connection with God. In response to the interviewer's question: "What makes you a Muslim?", Maria answered: "Faith in God, prayer five times a day and being nice to society, to people, trying to be the best version of you." Intercorporeality (engaging in religious bodily practices that also establishes social and spatial relationships with others) is of paramount importance in cementing the religious identity for many converts. Iza commented: "Prayer at the mosque is important to me."

Several respondents implied that individual prayer helped them navigate various storms and crises in their lives. Alicja commented: "I think prayer is key, I feel that since I started to pray regularly, my life has drastically changed. For the better." Similarly, Anita said:

> Prayer is the biggest thing for me in Islam. I would have been broken by the stuff I had to go through and had serious depression, but I can survive this through … patience. Nighttime prayer is fantastic. I think after conversion, prayer makes you peaceful despite all the storms and life crises. You know you'll survive, and you're peaceful.

For Paulina, prayer was a coping strategy in response to a cancer diagnosis:

> Last year I found out that I had cancer. Having 3 young kids, this was a shock ... At first I was crying a lot, wondering what I'd do. I have to have an operation, and I have kids. I went to pray and I experienced peace, all the mental weight disappeared, I felt better right away. That's why praying five times a day is very important, because we're always so busy, and it's really easy to tie yourself up in knots, and it's too much. With prayer, we have five minutes off, leave everything, go, rest for a bit and we can carry on. So it's not just spiritual, as many people think. Islam is more than a religion. (Paulina)

Paulina suggests here that regular prayer has an overall beneficial effect on the human psyche, and is an example of Islam as a "way of life" rather than simply a set of beliefs and practices. Its obligations become a source of support and strength for those who are willing to accept it. Her quotation, as well as the one below, echo the notion of being "naturally Muslim," discussed in the previous section on sexuality. Eleonora described how prior to her formal conversion, she experienced spiritual, unprompted instances of "natural prayer":

> In any situation, even in an impure place, anywhere, in the street. I walked and I prayed, 100% for myself, nothing else exists, pure prayer, natural, without any knowledge, so it's what's within us, in every human's heart, what we feel. Every one of us knows it and remembers it when things get bad. Ever since I remember, I knew that God exists. (Eleonora)

Such moments of transcendence, she claims, are part of the shared human experience. For her, it was an experience that reflected a "natural disposition" to Islam. However, for converts, the bodily aspect of the daily Muslim prayer, *salat*, sometimes represents a practical challenge: textbook knowledge may be insufficient where body movements and flow are concerned. Ola decided to move the date of her wedding forward, so her future British Pakistani husband could teach her prayer through demonstration. She said:

> Learning stuff directly from him was one of the reasons why I got married. I wanted to live with him and observe. I already was a Muslim, I lived alone. I read books about ablution, prayer, and so on. But it's hard to figure out how to do these things, so it wasn't something I did from the beginning. I said: We could live together, you'll teach me all the things I can't do [laughter]. My first prayer happened after we married. I was

> doing only what I could imitate him. He was an imam, and I was imitating him, and slowly I started learning the verses by heart, and so on. (Ola)

At first, Magda needed a piece of paper to pray but was able to supplement this with observing other women during prayer:

> Sometimes I had to read from a piece of paper, until I learnt the basic stuff. I felt that I shouldn't read from paper, and I felt a bit strange, I felt I should learn faster. But recently I realised that it's better to pray from a piece of paper and try new stuff, than always stick to what we know … I learnt to pray through observation; in Dubai, every shopping mall has a prayer room. I was sitting in a prayer room and looking at other women. Finally, I joined them when they were praying collectively. (Magda)

There is social pressure on performing rituals correctly; Matylda was criticised by other converts, as some aspects of her prayer that were incorrect in their view:

> Interviewer: Did someone criticise you [at the mosque]?
> Matylda: Yes, for not wearing the hijab and having painted toenails. Also, I did not hold my feet together during prayer. Frankly … I didn't know. I used to pray, but nobody had told me that was the correct way.

Simply put, the bodily practice of prayer and dispositions that are formed in the process of learning how to pray are complementary aspects of habituation. According to Aristotle, the process of virtue-making "cannot be entrusted to merely intellectual instruction" as it is a process "of assimilation, largely by imitation and under direction and control." (Smith, quoted in Topal, 2017, p. 588) When the habituation process is complete, the subject gains a "growing understanding of what is done" and becomes socialised into the practice which now is no longer a burden. From then on, the subject has mastery of the practice and is able to engage in it "freely, willingly, and from within." (Smith, quoted in Topal, 2017, p. 588) In the examples given here, respondents observed, imitated, reproduced, and were corrected by others, as books could not communicate sufficiently the requirements related to the movements, the placement of the body in the sacred space, and the relationship to other believers' bodies.

While many of our respondents described themselves as Muslim feminists, they did not raise the issue of female prayer leadership or mosque management. However, they were often critical of male religious subjectivities. The following extract from an interview with Alana speaks to that blending of norms and expectations. Alana produces her religious self through communicating essentialist gender discourses regarding male congregants.

> I'll say this, as far as connection to God and prayer, I'm very much in favour of segregation. Because, unfortunately, women are ok, but men's minds are screwed up and they can't control themselves ... If they want to concentrate on God, they should do it in their own company, and not [among women] if they distract them. Because there are different women, there are women who like to focus on their own body and dress in such a way that they'll distract a guy ... I like it that in Judaism women and men pray separately ... and the Orthodox Jews have services for families. It's a different thing then. Mosques also should do it, promoting family prayer. They are trying to do it during Ramadan, eating together and so on. Here, it really annoys me, for *iftar* men and women eat separately. It's not always about sex, sometimes it's just celebrating with family. It's important to celebrate with your family, and not separately. I understand – when it's time for prayer and a focus on God, I'm in favour [of segregation]. But when it's mealtime, you celebrate with family. (Alana)

Again, the theme of men's lustful, uncontrollable nature resurfaces as a reason for solutions regarding specific ways of approaching religious practice. However, with strict enforcement of gender segregation, people are unable to celebrate iftar together, as families.

Some respondents reported difficulties regarding praying at specific times, especially at night. Jowita confessed that "It's hard to get up for *fajr*." Alana said "For me, the hardest part is the prayer. Five times at specified times. that's the hardest part for me." Maria commented: "I think the prayer five times a day is a particular challenge, especially at required times. I study, I'll be working and I don't always have the time to pray. So I get home and pray to make up. Often even in winter when the last prayer is at 4 PM. It's a challenge, but I've got used to it."

These narratives suggest what Shielke (2009, 2010) described as the need for acknowledgement and exploration of the complex lives of

> Muslims who – like most of humankind – are sometimes but not always pious and who follow various moral aims and at times immoral ones.... If we want to account for the significance of Islam in people's lives, we have to account for it in this wider context. (Schielke, 2010, pp. 2–3)

Pious lives are often marked by imperfection and various attempts to redress it, and these narratives about the hardship related to regular prayer, in terms of the need for incredible discipline, routines, and a context conducive to (non-Christian) religious practice highlight these circumstances.

### Food: Iftars, Fasting, Keeping Halal, and "Halalization" of Polish Traditions

#### *Iftars and Fasting during Ramadan*

The Holy Month of Ramadan is the ninth month of the Islamic calendar during which believers fast and abstain from bodily pleasures from sunrise to sunset, pray, and enjoy communal worship and celebrations. Observing it constitutes one of the five pillars of Sunni Islam, or the seven pillars in Shi'a Islam. Fasting is meant to have a deep spiritual meaning and arguably helps practitioners create and solidify a moral disposition (Winchester, 2008). For many Muslims, Ramadan is an opportunity to decorate their houses, increase charitable giving, and feel festive. However, for converts, especially those who do not have Muslim social networks, it may be a challenging time, as they may be unable to celebrate in a traditional way, with family, or communally. Double social alienation – from their previous traditions and the new faith community – has been described in reference to converts' experiences (Guimond, 2017). For some converts, "Ramadan is the loneliest time of the year" (Sacirbey, 2013, np). Many of our respondents described *iftars*, the evening meals eaten to break the fast, as solitary. Those who live in cities, celebrate in each other's houses, or involve their non-Muslim families. Alicja who lives in Poland, but regularly visits Egypt, reflected on the difference between the two contexts during Ramadan:

> I can't celebrate it here and my heart is breaking that I'm not in Egypt. There's this celebration in the air, the sense of a special time. People are much nicer and friendlier to each other, strangers sit down to *iftar*, spend time together. Here in Poland, I stay on my own, at home, and that's it. What kind of a celebration is it, meeting a few friends twice during that month? (Alicja)

Some respondents draw parallels between Ramadan and Christmas; Kornelia's comment illustrates cultural flow between the two contexts: "From the Christmas tradition, I have smuggled in little decorative trinkets, I always hang shiny crescent moons, and a lot of various decorations." For Loubna, religious

CONVERTED BODIES: INTERIOR LIFE AND EMBODIED RELIGIOUS PRACTICES 183

experience is a holistic one. In order for the body to become a site of religious experience, one has to mentally foreground its meaning. She explained this using the example of Ramadan fasting:

> If someone treats Ramadan as a diet, it must be horrible, it must be horrible and terrifying. But if Ramadan is purification and peace, then it's like salvation, the most beautiful time of the year. It's down to the attitude, as with everything. (Loubna)

Kornelia's account further highlights the importance of intentionality for Ramadan fasting:

> I fasted twice before I became Muslim. The first time wasn't about God, just curiosity and experience-seeking. I felt terrible at first, because it was not about spirituality but getting "an experience," so I walked around like a cyborg for a few days. I had awful headaches and felt really nasty. [One year later] I was already transforming and decided to fast in Ramadan for God, as thanks to Him, and I had no headaches, I was fine. That was a wonderful fast. I had a need for it. And the next year I was fasting as a Muslim. I always fast in Ramadan now, I always make up for the days I didn't fast [menstruating women are exempt – AP] plus six days, because if you do six days extra, it's like you're fasting the entire year. As my character is ... patchy, I try to fast extra to make up. It's my personal tradition that Ramadan's over, and I go back to fasting. (Kornelia)

It is poignant in this quotation how the intention with which one fasts is held central. The theme of the "right intention" cut across our data; the respondents recognize that difficult practices such as fasting, praying regularly, or wearing the hijab may be fulfilled for "wrong" reasons, mainly establishing one's position in the hierarchy of piety. In other words, fastidious practice may constitute social capital, and offer the individual recognition in their religious group on the basis of the high level of devotion to God. Kornelia's story reveals another striking aspect of practice – she bargains with God. Her extra fasting days are meant to make up for anticipated transgressions.

Maja talked about the embarrassment related to not fasting due to her period; in an attempt to keep the fact of her period private, she still fasted when in public during that time. This became so ingrained in her that, she said, she would not drink water on a train under those circumstances. Here, the stigma of the period (2011) led her to actually perform a difficult action that was not required by Islam; this highlights the process of incorporation of Islam into the daily life practices at multiple levels; this extra religious practice was operationalised to avoid being stigmatized for another reason.

### Intricacies of Keeping Halal

In contrast to Ramadan fasting during one month of the year, keeping halal is a whole year-long endeavour. Again, we see effects of habituation as respondents talk about self-regulation in regard to pork which is a popular choice of meat in Poland and a very common ingredient in a variety of foods. Maja commented on self-regulation regarding avoiding pork: "Pork … those restrictions become regulators of sorts, you start automatically feeling disgusted by pork, regardless of the context."

Interestingly, Maria indicated that checking for pork is somewhat derivative of checking for other ingredients:

> I do check labels, but not for gelatin, but milk powder, because I'm lactose-intolerant, so I have an excuse, when I check, it's for milk powder, but at the same time I can check for gelatin. Two in one. If both are absent, it's great. (Maria)

Checking for pork gelatin, in its own right, could single her out, checking for milk powder allows Maria to "pass" among others, and conceal the religious motivation for looking at the ingredient list; it gives her an opportunity to explain her actions in an intelligible way in a social context where pork is ordinary (she wears the headscarf intermittently, so it's likely that sometimes, she's unrecognizable as a Muslim in public).

While conversion usually leads to an ethical transformation of self, the boundaries set by some participants are less orthodox than others. They prefer to focus on internal aspects of experiencing Islam, and follow what they regard as common sense. Otylia, asked whether she keeps halal, said "Of course I eat meat. I don't eat pork. If the label says chicken sausage, I eat it. Some people say there's pork fat there. Yeah, there could be, but how much turkey meat can you eat?"

Interestingly, Małgorzata commented on eating non-halal meat (although, not pork) and occasionally drinking alcohol to maintain good relationships with her relatives:

> For me relationships, overall closeness are very important and I don't want anything to change in my family relationships. I like pork very much and it was difficult for me to give it up. I like pork chops, lard sandwiches, all of it. If my 83-year-old grandmother found out [about my conversion],

she would advise against it. But she'd also advise against me going vegetarian – this is about a deviation from the norm. [In Poland], there's no access to halal meat. I eat ordinary meat, usually it's poultry, fried chicken at my mother's. I do it inconspicuously, without confrontations. I give myself permission to drink some alcohol, a glass of wine, symbolically, to celebrate. But drinking on my own or getting drunk – no. But I allow for drinking to celebrate something, I always have done. I've never drunk a lot, sometimes wine with dinner. I can say no, I'm not drinking because I'm driving. So far, I've been able to avoid this topic in family interactions. I don't want to make a fuss on someone's birthday, come out with my conversion to Islam, if we meet once a year on that birthday. I'm trying to adjust slowly, so it all works for me. (Małgorzata)

Małgorzata's narrative about actions that for some, would represent a religious transgression, becomes revealing when she mentions that it's easier to maintain close relationships when social norms are shared – and in Polish families, eating and drinking together are ruled by particularly strong norms. In absence of strongly developed Muslim networks of support, retaining good family relationships may be important, especially for converts living in rural areas. She navigates the role of an "intimate stranger", who ultimately exposes the imagined intimacy in the family (Ramahi and Suleiman, 2017, p. 37). Here, a calculation becomes more clear: these occasional transgressions are the price Małgorzata is paying for decreasing tension involved in stigma related to becoming a Muslim in Poland in more intimate relationships or avoiding it altogether in other interactions. Goffman observed (1963, p. 124) that many individuals who bear stigma, are often at pains "keep the stigma from looming large. The individual's object is to reduce tension, that is, to make it easier for himself [sic] and the others to withdraw covert attention from the stigma."

### Islamic Dress among Polish Converts to Islam

The headscarf (hijab, called *hidżab* or *chusta* by our respondents) has captured popular imagination to such a degree that it has become the central framework through which the position of women in Islam has been considered from theological, cultural, and sociological perspectives. Khiabany and Williamson (2011, p. 173) assert that "it has become impossible to talk about Islam without reference to women, and impossible to talk of Muslim women without reference to the veil." This is in spite of the criticism that the unrelenting focus on veiling obscures more important issues affecting their lives, such as access to education, employment and political participation (Atasoy, 2003) However, veiling is undeniably enmeshed with these very aspects of life; in some contexts, veiled women report discrimination against them in education, the workplace, public spaces, as well as a variety of policies. In others, appearing unveiled may cause women to be harassed and belittled.

Among our respondents, we observed three approaches to dress practices. The first group stated that they did not wish to wear a headscarf. They often drew attention to the principle of hijab-as-modesty that encompasses behaviour as well as dress, which they see as more important than the headcovering itself. The second group wore a form of headcovering (headscarf, turban, hat), sometimes accompanied by an abaya (loose cloak) and a niqab (face veil) and considered it an important and enriching practice central to their pious subjectivities. The third group wore the headscarf dynamically – only in a particular country (the UK, Egypt), a religious space (mosque), or only among Muslims; they would take it off among non-Muslims.

Non-wearers' arguments were framed by their preference for private, interior religious practices that allow them to stay inconspicuous in public. This preference is likely to be related to hostile attitudes to Islam in Poland; the hijab is a stigma symbol; a marker of religious difference that is further implicated in unequal power dynamics in the interpersonal and structural sense. For example, Małgorzata's decision not to cover allows her to "pass" in the Polish society:

> I don't feel the need to go abroad and wear the hijab. I don't need to wear a noticeboard. For me, the change is internal, not external. If I lived in a country where most women wear the hijab, I'd wear it, because I wouldn't want to stand out. But I won't wear the hijab here. Perhaps if I travel abroad … but it's not my thing, I don't feel the need to wear it. (Małgorzata)

Maja has offered an alternative, contextual interpretation of the hijab based in Islamic law:

> I see Islam as a religion for people who are fallible, sometimes weak. It's not a task for [Muslim] women, or people generally to go out of their way to become martyrs. [For me] hijab is *muamalat*, social, not *ibadat*. How is it going to benefit God if people call me names and spit on me in the street? I don't think that God expects us to do things that could cause us or our families harm. (Maja)

Maja calls attention to the distinction between *muamalat* (civil dealings which allow considerably more room to develop and change the law to facilitate human interaction and promote justice) and *ibadat* (acts of ritual worship, not subject to innovation, Nasir, 1990). The categorization of the headscarf specifically as of *muamalat* type, as a negotiable expression of the general rule of modesty allows for adjustment of dress in regard to context. Maja's position on headcovering becomes even clearer in another part of the interview in which she extols the joy of wearing the hijab in the UK where she may remain more inconspicuous and safer, especially within the bounds of "Muslim areas" (Muhammad, 2013). Her preference is for headcovering; however, she sees the Polish context as too hostile to foster spiritual growth that can be achieved through this practice.

Paradoxically, sometimes *not wearing* the hijab in Poland may also present difficulties. The symbolism of hijab allows women to be recognised as Muslims which may be desirable in some situations, particularly in educational settings where women speak from a position of an insider expert on Islam. Conversely, not wearing a hijab means that Polish converts' identity as Muslims may be invalidated:

> My [academic] friend hosted a discussion about women in Islam [and had a guest speaker]. In the audience, there was a female Arabic studies student. The woman who took the questions was Polish, with blue eyes and blond hair, and does not wear the hijab. And the student in the audience accused her of not being a Muslim. (Daria)

In this case, the guest speaker appears to have been racialized due to her phenotype and the lack of hijab, as a non-Muslim. The racialization of Islam as a "brown" religion (Galonnier, 2017) in Poland has negative consequences for converts, as it results in being denied one's religious identity and experiences. Essentialist notions of Islam and Muslims are dominant in the Polish imaginary; Muslims, as the "Other," are expected to look different. The absence of hijab, a visual marker of Islam, led to an invalidation of the speaker's identity that in the context of an academic discussion led to confiscation of authority, which in this case relied on lived experience as a Muslim.

Even among those respondents who believed that headcovering was a religious duty, the journey to the headscarf was sometimes complex. Kamila commented on the lengthy process of incorporation of headcovering into her own practice and identity:

> When I began to study Islamic sources, it was clear to me immediately that hijab is a religious duty for women. But I only put it on when I went to university. For a few years prior, I was a Muslim and practiced Islam, but I didn't wear the hijab. [Embracing it] was gradual, but I knew that not wearing it was not in accordance with Islam. I always said it was something I should be doing but I wasn't ready and hoped that God would give me the necessary strength to do it, because it's a religious duty.

Wearing the hijab was initially the hardest challenge for Eleonora. Like Kamila, after conversion, she chose to focus on privatised emanation of faith, in particular the study of Islamic texts and commentaries. She would only wear the hijab when visiting the mosque, but she felt very uncomfortable wearing it in the street. However, the breakthrough came when she found scholarly arguments in favour of headcovering: she accepted this as God's will:

> When I found a passage about the hijab, something happened within me, that it's from God and whether I like it or not, I have to get over it. It's nobody's problem, but mine. It's my own challenge to change, to test myself if I really believe. So when I understood that that was it, something happened in my head, I couldn't think anything else than "wear the hijab, wear the hijab" ... I figured, OK, now's the time. I was alone at home, I watched a lot of YouTube videos and checked out different styles. I wanted to find something I really liked, something I'd feel comfortable in, and compliant with God's word at the same time. And even though nobody saw me, God saw me. And I got used to wearing it. (Eleonora)

The shift in perspective profoundly transformed her experience of the hijab. Previously an unwelcome burden, it gradually became a part of her daily practice. For her, shifting her attitude to headcovering became a part of religious formation of her new identity. It is striking how the intellectual acceptance was immediately coupled with the affective investment to find a style that suited her personally. By identifying and/or creating her own style of headcovering, she was able to create a feeling of comfort and peace.

Fatimah, one of the handful of niqab wearers, commented that the practice of face covering had become so ingrained and normalised for her that she would experience discomfort if she were forced to remove it.

> I like wearing the niqab very much and have got used to it. I would feel uncomfortable not wearing I, although I'd take it off if I had to, for

example at the airport. I wouldn't die if I took it off, right? But I really like it and feel good wearing it. (Fatimah)

Notably, the adoption of the hijab (in particular if it is accompanied by an abaya or a niqab) shifts that public perception. In Poland, members of the public and service providers are often simply at a loss when confronted with a situation requiring an atypical interaction. Another niqab-wearing woman recounted an encounter with a confused Polish border guard at the airport:

> [At the airport, the border guards] didn't know what to do about me, because I turned up and said: "Good morning gentlemen, I cannot show you my face, can I please be patted down by a female guard?", and the guy at the scanners said only "Eeeeeeeh....." He grabbed a phone, dialled and said to someone "listen I have this lady here, she is wearing a blanket [sic] and I cannot pat her down. Come on, get here quick." (Kinga)

Likewise, many participants commented that members of the public were often unsure how to interact with them. Despite the ubiquity of nuns wearing habits and headcoverings (in Poland, nuns usually present themselves much more traditionally than in the West, where nuns' attire is oftentimes informal) Islamic religious dress is immediately identified as out of the ordinary. Polish people often seem to lack a framework of reference to recognize the hijab, abaya, and the niqab as religious practices of Muslim women. In line with Goffman's reasoning (1963), Muslim converts are expected to explain themselves to strangers who feel it is their right to inquire about the visible difference; these invasions of privacy reflect the social control inherent in the process of stigmatization.

### *Practising Islam Outside of Poland*

Challenges encountered by many respondents related to communicating their faith in Poland to others – family, friends, the workplace, the public – are often absent in their emigration narratives. While they may still experience Islamophobic prejudice outside of Poland (from the majority British population as well as the Polish communities in the UK), overall, participants who have the experience of living in the UK temporarily or permanently reported that they did not feel as conspicuous in public settings there; they do not have to cope with charges of ethnic and national "betrayal" (Öyzurek, 2009, p. 107). Those accusations are particularly harsh against women who convert and marry Muslim men of other ethnicities (King and Perez, 2015). Not much is known about the experiences of migrant Muslim converts from Eastern Europe (Krotofil, 2011 and 2013) – but there was a distinct population of women who converted, or at least felt a strong pull of Islam, prior to their emigration.

As mentioned in Chapter 3, in the more diverse Western European environments, in particular in neighbourhoods characterized by strong Muslim and immigrant presence, such as Little Pakistan in Birmingham, converts can enjoy relative invisibility, as visible Muslimness is not so readily stigmatized. Moreover, topographies of such localities lend themselves to an Islamic lifestyle: easy access to mosques, halal supermarkets, and Islamic schools are unattainable in Poland. Justyna, who spent a year studying in London, described the impact of the Muslim spatiality (Mohammad, 2013) on her religious identity and experience:

> I accepted Islam in May, and in September I went abroad to study in London. I became very active, I wasn't afraid, because I was a complete stranger there, no one knew me, I had no problems [with practising]. My mosque was really close, it was wonderful, 5 minutes on foot. [It was] the Islamic Center on Holloway Road. And when Ramadan came, I could walk to pray tarawih. When I was out and about, and I felt like prayer, there was a mosque on every street corner. I could go to the mosque during lunch break, and sit in silence, read, pray. I felt way more connected to religion then than now, because we have this mosque, but it's really far from my house. (Justyna)

> All that time between accepting Islam and arriving in the UK, I spent on my own, gradually coming to the decisions regarding my behaviour and dress, and functioning ... [during that time] I did not wear the hijab. I dressed as always, more modestly of course, but I didn't stand out from the crowd. I started to wear the hijab after I came to England. (Agata)

For many participants, moments of transition out of Poland meshed with moments of religious significance. For example, Magda, who describes herself as "always very religious", and whose engagement with Islam began while she was previously working in Dubai, described an eye-opening experience of Islamic prayer upon her departure to the UK:

> When I was leaving Poland, I asked God to lead me, show me the way. And that was the first time I prayed with prostrations. I think it was my first prayer with prostration, as it's practiced in Islam. (Magda)

Magda had begun practicing Islam while still in Dubai, before she formally embraced it by saying the shahada (the declaration of faith). Her brief stay in Poland between her return from Dubai and departure for the UK demonstrated to her how difficult it would be to externalize her new faith in Poland and cement her new religious identity:

> I knew that in London wearing a headscarf would be completely normal. It would just be easier for me to find my feet. It would be easier to continue this identity, it wouldn't be denigrated everywhere I go. So other than going to the UK to university, I didn't want to settle down in Poland because I wanted to live in a multicultural environment, to practice my religion and today I'm proud that I cover. To me, it's a symbol of freedom of religion and conscience. I want people to identify me as a Muslim. I'm not ashamed; I want to embody diversity. (Magda)

Kornelia, who also converted to Islam before her emigration to the UK, said:

> [Here] I can practice my religion; I can go to the mosque, or wherever; since I came here, I only wear abayas, abayas are the most comfortable. In Poland, there's simply no opportunity to wear an abaya. I enjoy my lifestyle here so much more. (Kornelia)

In the narratives of Polish converts to Islam, the UK becomes a land of religious belonging and affordances. While by no means free of restrictions (many women talked about Islamophobic harassment they experienced also in the UK), the visible, unconstrained Muslim identity that they wish to cultivate is intelligible, and, in most places in the UK, at least grudgingly accepted. It is much easier to incorporate religious practices into daily, social life as illustrated by the following quotation from Maja who spent a period time in the UK:

> And it's wonderful in the UK ... wearing the hijab, meeting people and feeling a part of that community. It's mostly virtual, but it exists. It gives you a sense of belonging, I could do a lot: buy halal meat, go to the mosque, wear the hijab. Social life is very important, there's nothing possible without it. (Maja)

Emigration to the UK does not necessarily mean that Polish relationships, and norms with which they are imbued, are left behind. Recognizing that her religious identity is not salient or intelligible among her Polish friends, Elżbieta stated: "I'll put it this way: I do put the hijab on when I go out in public, but when I'm about to meet up with my Polish friends, I don't wear it anymore." She explained that she was not keeping her Muslim identity secret – "I often share articles or pictures related to Islam on my [Facebook] profile, I also post greetings during our [Muslim] holidays, so that's self-explanatory" – simply that she preferred to compartmentalise it at times. Her account challenges the theorization of Snow and Machalek (1983) who claim that for converts, the convert role is a "master" one that governs all situations and that "all role identities are subordinate to the identity that flows from the master role of the convert." (Snow and Machalek 1983, p. 278) Elżbieta is clearly comfortable with identity compartmentalization – she appears to see "being Muslim" and "being Polish" as distinct, but not mutually exclusive, in this context. Similar to Małgorzata, who occasionally sips wine, she works at preventing her stigma from "looming large". In the same vein, some of the women who wear the hijab permanently in the UK, take it off when visiting Poland. Agata, for example, admitted:

> when I go [to Poland], I go mainly to my family, to visit my family, not for any other purposes. And because we live in a village, and it is a really small village, I do not put the headscarf on. Instead, I wear a hat, or I use a hood to cover my head. (Agata)

Similarly, Ola said: "I didn't go to Poland straight away. I went there 3 years after my conversion. When I was in Poland, I was wearing a hat, not a headscarf." Wearing a more inconspicuous form of hijab is often motivated by the wish to protect the family from prying or ostracism, especially in smaller localities where diversity is brought an even sharper focus.

Moments of profound introspection undoubtedly play a role in the complex of identity reconfigurations faced by migrants. Similar to Pędziwiatr's findings (2017), some UK-based women we interviewed insisted on following Islamic practices with a distinctly Polish, individual flavour. Eleonora, cited earlier, ask God for a hijab style that would reflect her own identity:

> I know that I'm a Pole. Polish women are different from British ones. This also means something. Primarily, I'm a Muslim, but I'm also a Pole, so I won't adopt a style of another nationality. I'm an individualist, and I asked God, not just as a Pole, but as me, for my own style. Within seconds, I knew how to tie my hijab. (Eleonora)

This desire to create a style of practice that would reflect one's multi-layered identity was also observed by Shestopalets (2021) in his study of Ukrainian converts to Islam; some of his respondents insisted that the traditional Ukrainian female dress was compatible with the Islamic requirements of modesty. Paradoxically, the adoption of arguably archaic folk clothing (flowery handkerchiefs, embroidered shirts) by the Ukrainian converts bolsters the revival of traditional dress and results in appropriation of it by a non-Christian tradition (Shestopalets, 2021). In our dataset, we did not encounter a similar trend regarding Polish folk dress, but we observed that Polish converts tend to incorporate their practices into their social settings (Krotofil et al., 2022).

Studies conducted in various global contexts indicate that for many (but not all) Muslim women, veiling and modest comportment at large are considered to be religious obligations (Mahmood, 2005, p. 51). For others, it is a political statement signifying belonging to the Islamic community or a "passport" that allows them to move unhindered between different public and private spaces (Ruby, 2006). A small number of women we interviewed opted for the more concealing abaya and niqab; all of them had moved to the UK. Simultaneously, not veiling is a viable (and, as in case of many of our respondents, unavoidable) option for many Muslim women. They may prefer to remain modest in a more inconspicuous manner, thereby facing a different set of dilemmas: while avoiding stereotypes ascribed by mainstream society to veiled Muslim women, they often have to navigate expectations regarding their conduct within their communities (Ruby, 2006, p. 61). The ongoing need for making choices regarding self-presentation were clear in the narratives of women whose family and peer interactions remained strong following the conversion.

### *Complicated Norms and Realities of Modesty*

Some Muslims argue that Islamic modesty norms protect pious women from sexual objectification rife in the secular West (Gabriel and Hannan, 2011). In this narrative, which sometimes portrays the non-Muslim woman as a victim of the unattainable pursuit of patriarchally-defined beauty standards, the covered Muslim woman is free from such concerns and able to focus on her quest for piety. Anita suggested that modest dress signals personal confidence in the face of the lack of external validation:

> I think that someone who covers is confident, she does not feel compelled to show off her beauty, she doesn't have to reveal her body, "look at me, I'm beautiful." She knows she's beautiful so there's no difference if she wears an abaya, right? I feel good about myself. (Anita)

The discussion of embodied Islamic practices cannot be separated from a consideration of the gendered and regulatory quality of these practices (Stuart and Donaghue, 2011). Rigid understandings of Islamic modesty were variously accommodated and resisted by our respondents. Some indeed considered spiritual beauty as central to developing their ethical disposition (Mahmood, 2005) and distanced themselves narratively from mainstream prescriptions of female beauty. Others openly contradicted this view, arguing that it is impossible to overcome certain social demands, including that women participate in "regimes of beauty" such as makeup, diet, and exercise regardless of their religious belonging. Demands and restrictions of "normative femininity" (Bordo, 2004) do not simply cease upon conversion. Thus, instead of simply switching their focus from the "profane" to the "sacred" concerns, many of our respondents had to navigate, simultaneously, disciplining their ethical conduct (Mahmood, 2005) and physical bodies (Bordo, 2004). It is notable that moral valences are associated with successes and failings in both these self-projects (Bartky, 2003; Anwar, 2006).

Patriarchal regimes of beauty were occasionally reinforced by our respondents' Muslim and non-Muslim significant others; for example, Paulina's non-Muslim mother bemoaned her "terrible" post-conversion appearance, in contrast to her pre-conversion "pretty looks." Relatives bemoaned the concealment of conventionally attractive physical features: long hair, shapely legs, good teeth (in the case of niqab-wearers). Strikingly, even some respondents bemoaned "drab and unattractive" (Maja) appearance of other convert women in Poland, contrasting them with stylish and confident Arab women who, nevertheless, uphold Islamic modesty prescriptions.

Many of our respondents recognized the impact of these intertwined forces that blend modesty and beauty on their lives. Julianna commented: "In Islam the woman should be modest, and not beautiful, but let's not kid ourselves, the fair sex just wants to be fair." They attempted to navigate the paradoxes inherent in this situation; for example, Matylda said:

> I thought that my head wrapped in the hijab looked really small in relation to my oversize body. So I stuffed my hijab with a bunch of fabric, to give my head a more attractive shape. I knew that this wasn't the point of hijab, but ... (Matylda)

Expressing such a sentiment puts one at risk of being penalized for "not feeling beautiful" in a context where, in the words of another respondent, "beauty is achieved through modesty." Yet, as we saw earlier in the chapter, many women freely experimented with fashion and hijab styles, and enjoyed various beauty practices (makeup, nail art, body piercings). They did not interpret these preoccupations as religiously transgressive; instead, their concerns were in line with Tarlo and Moors' (2013, p. 13) conclusion that "the creation and wearing of fashionable styles [can be] a form and extension of religious action."

## Conclusions

The narratives discussed in this chapter demonstrate that spiritual and intellectual practices of Islam necessarily involve the body. Narratives of faith, as well as its affect, meaning, and form that together comprise a particular "grammar of concepts" (Mahmood, 2005, p. 188) are used by participants to communicate their experiences. The embodied aspects of faith, however, require a different kind of "tutelage." Learning, and associated ethical formation, involves disciplining the body, reconfiguring it into new positions, functions, and shapes; often, religious practices as discussed here involve discovering the body's new limits that are enabled by the pious intentionality. Conversion can be conceptualized as a process in which "technologies of self" (Foucault, 1988, p. 18) are applied with particular intensity, geared to

> permit individuals to effect by their own means or with the help of others a certain number of operations on their own bodies and souls, thoughts, conduct, and way of being, so as to transform themselves in order to attain a certain state of happiness, purity, wisdom, perfection, or immortality.

This dovetails with the keenness for ethical formation through education to agency "[which] is predicated upon [one's] ability to be taught, a condition classically referred to as 'docility'" Mahmood (2005, p. 29). The knowledge that one has complied correctly has spiritual benefits. It also helps cultivate it by creating a particular emotive state (Mahmood, 2005: 30) of peace, fulfillment and "rightness."

Simultaneously, the converts are faced with managing the spoiled convert identity. Those living in Poland are imbricated in cultural and social expectations that imply accommodation of norms inflected by Catholicism; accordingly, they are somewhat forced into a position where they need to actively seek connections between the Islamic tradition and the Polish culture (Krotofil et al., 2022) to be able to argue for the possibility of a Polish Muslim identity. They need to achieve that in a manner that minimises stigma in their relationships. Those living in the UK may practice Islam in visible ways, but are forced into a position of double marginalization, as Muslims and Polish immigrants. Additionally, the convert status may present difficulties in their interactions with some "born Muslims." These challenges are further highlighted by the experiences of those women who move between the two (or more) contexts; they are often in a state of flux, adjusting the form of their practice depending on the "audience." Respondents recognize the dynamic character of social contexts which they inhabit. Oyserman and James (2011, p. 120) argue that "contexts not only make a particular identity salient, they also shape the content and behavioural consequences of identities."

Analysis of the data in this chapter illustrates how particular modes of reasoning, performing and practicing Islam emerge locally. It also demonstrates the ambivalence inherent in lived religion, whereby the ideal of rigorous striving for purity is always confronted with often contradictory requirements of present circumstances where managing the spoiled identity remains at the forefront for many respondents. Working within the realm of ever-growing research on individual and privatized religion that embraces the lived religion approach, this chapter also accounts for those modes of religious engagement that do not fit the image of Islam as an idealized self-discipline project.

## References

Ali, K. (2006). *Sexual Ethics and Islam: Feminist Reflections on Qur'an, Hadith and Jurisprudence*. Oneworld Publications.

Anwar, E. (2006). *Gender and Self in Islam*. Taylor & Francis.

Asad, T. (2009). *Genealogies of Religion: Discipline and Reasons of Power in Christianity and Islam*. Johns Hopkins University Press.

Atasoy, Y. (2003). Muslim Organizations in Canada: Gender Ideology and Women's Veiling. *Sociological Focus*, 36(2), 143–158.

Atighetchi, D. (1994). The position of Islamic tradition on contraception. *Medicine and law*, 13(7–8), 717–725.

Bartky, S. L. (2003). Foucault, femininity, and the modernization of patriarchal power. In R. Weitz (Ed.), *The Politics of Women's Bodies* (pp. 25–45). Oxford University Press.

Beekers, D. and L. L. Schrijvers (2020). Religion, sexual ethics, and the politics of belonging: Young Muslims and Christians in the Netherlands. *Social Compass*, 67(1), 137–156.

Bordo, S. (2004). *Unbearable Weight: Feminism, Western Culture, and the Body*, University of California Press.

Butler, J. (2011). Is Judaism Zionism? In E. V. J. Mendieta (Ed.), *The Power of Religion in the Public Sphere* (pp. 70–91). Columbia University Press.

Byng, M. D. (2010). Symbolically Muslim: Media, Hijab, and the West. *Critical Sociology*, 36(1), 109–129.

Calkin, S. & M. E. Kaminska (2020). Persistence and Change in Morality Policy: The Role of the Catholic Church in the Politics of Abortion in Ireland and Poland. *Feminist Review*, 124(1), 86–102.

Delaney, C. (1991). *The Seed and the Soil: Gender and Cosmology in Turkish Village Society*, University of California Press.

Foucault, M. (1988). *Technologies of the Self.* In L. Martin, H. Gutman & P. Hutton (Eds.), *Technologies of the Self: A seminar with Michel Foucault* (pp. 16–49). The University of Massachusetts Press.

Gabriel, T. & R. Hannan (2011). *Islam and the Veil: Theoretical and Regional Contexts*, Bloomsbury Publishing.

Galonnier, J. (2017). *Choosing Faith and Facing Race: Converting to Islam in France and the United States* [Unpublished PhD thesis]. Northwestern University.

Goffman, E. (1963). Stigma: *Notes on the Management of Spoiled Identity*. Penguin Books.

Guimond, A. M. (2017). *Converting to Islam: Understanding the Experiences of White American Females*, Springer International Publishing.

Gwiazda, A. (2020). Right-wing populism and feminist politics: The case of Law and Justice in Poland. *International Political Science Review*. https://doi.org/10.1177/0192512120948917.

Haddad, Y. Y. (2007). The Post-9/11 Hijab as Icon. *Sociology of Religion*, 68(3), 253–267.

Haeri, S. (2014). *Law of Desire: Temporary Marriage in Shi'i Iran*, Revised Edition, Syracuse University Press.

Ibrahim, Y. (2019). Visuality and the 'Jihadi-bride': The re-fashioning of desire in the digital age. *Social Identities*, 25(2), 186–206.

Imtoual, A. & Hussein, S. (2009). Challenging the myth of the happy celibate: Muslim women negotiating contemporary relationships. *Contemporary Islam*, 3(1), 25–39.

Jaafar-Mohammad, I. C. & Lehmann (2011). Women's Rights in Islam Regarding Marriage and Divorce. *Journal of Law and Practice*, 4 (Art. 3). https://open.mitchell hamline.edu/lawandpractice/vol4/iss1/3.

Khiabany, G. and Williamson, M. (2011). Muslim Women and Veiled Threats: From Civilizing Mission to Clash of Civilizations. In J. R. Petley, & R. Richardson (Eds.), *Pointing the Finger: Islam and Muslims in the British Media* (pp. 173–200). One World Publications.

King, Y. & Perez, M. (2021). Double-Edged Marginality and Agency: Latina Conversion to Islam. In M. Logroño Narbona, P. Pinto & J. Karam (Ed.), *Crescent over Another Horizon: Islam in Latin America, the Caribbean, and Latino USA* (pp. 304–324). New York, USA: University of Texas Press.

Korolczuk, E. (2020). The fight against 'gender' and 'LGBT ideology': New developments in Poland. *European Journal of Politics and Gender*, 3 (1), 165–167.

Kramer, S. (2020). *Polygamy is rare around the world and mostly confined to a few regions*. Pew Research Center, https://www.pewresearch.org/fact-tank/2020/12/07/polygamy-is-rare-around-the-world-and-mostly-confined-to-a-few-regions/.

Krotofil, J. (2011). "If I am to be a Muslim, I have to be a good one": Polish migrant women embracing Islam and reconstructing identity in dialogue with self and others. In K. Górak-Sosnowska (Ed.), *Muslims in Poland and Eastern Europe: Widening the European Discourse on Islam*, (pp. 154–168). University of Warsaw.

Krotofil, J. (2013). *Religia w procesie kształtowania tożsamości wśród polskich migrantów w Wielkiej Brytanii.* Kraków Nomos.

Krotofil, J., Górak-Sosnowska, K., Piela, A. & Abdallah-Krzepkowska, B. (2022). Being Muslim, Polish, and at Home: Converts to Islam in Poland. *Journal of Contemporary Religion*, DOI: 10.1080/13537903.2022.2101714.

Krotofil, J., Piela, A., Górak-Sosnowska, K. & Abdallah-Krzepkowska, B. (2021). Theorizing the Religious Habitus in the Context of Conversion to Islam among Polish Women of Catholic Background. *Sociology of Religion*, 82 (3), 257–280.

Lamb, C. (2016, July 28). *Polish bishops vow to refuse communion to divorced and remarrieds.* The Tablet. https://www.thetablet.co.uk/news/5920/polish-bishops-vow-to-refuse-communion-to-divorced-and-remarrieds.

Mahmood, S. (2004). *Politics of Piety: The Islamic Revival and the Feminist Subject.* Princeton University Press.

Marody, M. & Giza-Poleszczuk, A. (2000). Changing images of identity in Poland: From the self-sacrificing to the self-investing woman. In S. Gal & G. Kligman (Eds.), *Reproducing Gender: Politics, Publics, and Everyday Life After Socialism*, (pp. 151–175). Princeton University Press.

McGuire, M. (2006). Embodied Practices: Negotiation and Resistance. In N. T. Ammerman (Ed.), *Everyday Religion: Observing Modern Religious Lives*, (pp. 187–200). Oxford University Press.

Mishtal, J. (2015). *The Politics of Morality: The Church, the State, and Reproductive Rights in Postsocialist Poland.* Ohio University Press.

Mizielinska, J. (2020). The limits of choice: queer parents and stateless children in their search for recognition in Poland. *Gender, Place & Culture*, 1–24. https://doi.org/10.1080/0966369X.2020.1845616.

Mohammad, R. (2013). Making Gender Ma(R)King Place: Youthful British Pakistani Muslim Women's Narratives of Urban Space. *Environment and Planning A: Economy and Space*, 45(8), 1802–1822.

Mossière, G. & Le Gall, J. (2018). Gender and Marriage among Religious Youth in Quebec: Sexual Ethics as a Source of Distinction. In P. Gareau, S. Bullivant & P. Beyer (Eds.), *Youth, Religion, and Identity in a Globalizing Context* (pp. 105–123). Brill.

Nasir, J. J. (1990). *The Islamic Law of Personal Status.* Springer Netherlands.

Odrowąż-Coates, A. (2015). Gender Crisis in Poland, Catholic Ideology and the Media. *Sociology Mind*, 5(1), 27–34. http://dx.doi.org/10.4236/sm.2015.51004.

Owe, J. R. (2017). *Media framing of Western female foreign fighters to ISIS* [Unpublished master's thesis]. University of Oslo.

Oyserman, D. & James, L. (2011). Possible Identities. In S. J. Schwartz, K. Luyckx & V. L. Vignoles (Eds.), *Handbook of Identity Theory and Research* (pp. 117–145). Springer.

Özyürek, E. (2009). Convert Alert: German Muslims and Turkish Christians as Threats to Security in the New Europe. *Comparative Studies in Society and History*, 51(1), 91–116.

Pędziwiatr, K. (2017). Conversions to Islam and Identity Reconfigurations among Poles in Great Britain. *Studia Religiologica*, 50(3), 221–239.

Ramahi, D. A. & Y. Suleiman (2017). Intimate strangers: perspectives on female converts to Islam in Britain. *Contemporary Islam*, 11(1), 21–39.

Rao, A. H. (2015). Gender and Cultivating the Moral Self in Islam: Muslim Converts in an American Mosque. *Sociology of Religion*, 76(4), 413–435.

Rogozen-Soltar, M. H. (2020). Striving toward Piety: Gendered Conversion to Islam in Catholic-Secular Spain. *Current Anthropology*, 61(2), 141–167.

Ruby, T. F. (2006). Listening to the voices of hijab. *Women's Studies International Forum*, 29(1), 54–66.

Sacirbey, O. (2013, July 8). *For some converts, Ramadan is the loneliest time of year*. Religion News Service. https://religionnews.com/2013/07/08/for-some-converts-ramadan-is-the-loneliest-time-of-year/.

Schielke, S. (2009). Being good in Ramadan: ambivalence, fragmentation, and the moral self in the lives of young Egyptians. *Journal of the Royal Anthropological Institute*, 15(s1), S24–S40.

Schielke, S. (2010). Second thoughts about the anthropology of Islam, or how to make sense of grand schemes in everyday life. *ZMO Working Papers*, 2, 1–16.

Shestopalets, D. (2021). There's More Than One Way to Tie a Ḥijāb: Female Conversion to Islam in Ukraine. *Islam and Christian – Muslim Relations*, 32(1), 97–119.

Snow, D. A., & Machalek, R. (1983). The Convert as a Social Type. *Sociological Theory*, 1, 259–289.

Stuart, A. & N. Donaghue (2011). Choosing to conform: The discursive complexities of choice in relation to feminine beauty practices. *Feminism & Psychology*, 22(1), 98–121.

Suleiman, Y. (2013). *Narratives of Conversion to Islam in Britain: Female Perspectives*. Centre of Islamic Studies, University of Cambridge.

Tarlo, E. & Moors, A. (2013). *Islamic Fashion and Anti-Fashion: New Perspectives from Europe and North America*, Bloomsbury Academic.

Topal, S. (2017). Female Muslim subjectivity in the secular public sphere: Hijab and ritual prayer as 'technologies of the self'. *Social Compass*, 64(4), 582–596.

van Nieuwkerk, K. (2009). *Women Embracing Islam: Gender and Conversion in the West*, University of Texas Press.

Winchester, D. (2008). Embodying the Faith: Religious Practice and the Making of a Muslim Moral Habitus. *Social Forces*, 86(4), 1753–1780.

Zine, J. (2020). Pandemic Imaginaries and the Racial Politics of Masking. *Topia: Canadian Journal of Cultural Studies*, 41. https://doi.org/10.3138/topia-004.

Żuk, P. & Żuk, P. (2020). 'Murderers of the unborn' and 'sexual degenerates': analysis of the 'anti-gender' discourse of the Catholic Church and the nationalist right in Poland. *Critical Discourse Studies*, 17(5), 566–588.

CHAPTER 7

# From a 'Salafi Bite' to the 'Middle Way'

*Beata Abdallah-Krzepkowska* | ORCID: 0000-0003-4370-8095
University of Silesia in Katowice

## Introduction

Information gathered from our respondents and participant observation indicates that many new Muslims encounter the Salafi version of Islam first. The popularity of the Salafi message among converts may be explained by its reluctance to leave anything for interpretation Such certainty is likely to be attractive to newcomers who sometimes struggle to find their own way through the labyrinth of the new religion. Another factor could be the ubiquity of the current achieved through intense missionary activity – lectures, meetings, courses, and popular websites (Shanneik, 2011; Inge, 2016). Further, as most Polish converts come from practising Roman Catholic families and were educated in Catholicism, a tradition that offers a uniform and highly organised message created by a centralised institution, Salafism seems an obvious current of Islam to embrace. Many scholars, such as Rambo (1993, p. 5) or Wohlraab-Sahr (2006, p. 75) acknowledge that conversion is influenced by events that an individual has experienced in earlier life. These are: socialisation, including religious socialisation, institutions, ideologies, and the social and political environments the convert has lived in. Another factor contributing to the attractiveness of Salafism could be the monoreligious character of Polish society and the lack of knowledge of other religious traditions. In this respect, however, many our respondents do not seem representative for the general population of Polish Muslims. Some of them had encountered other religious traditions, be it through university, travelling abroad, family connections, or one's own religious explorations. Nonetheless, little knowledge of Islam's traditions and its pluralistic character is not characteristic of converts' only. The same phenomenon has been observed in born Muslims who chose Salafism – although they had been raised in Muslim families and had received basic religious education, they were still unaware of Islam's diversity and its intellectual richness (Inge, 2016).

Irish converts, whose traditionally Catholic upbringing and cultural background was similar to that of Polish Muslims, were perceived by Shanneik (2011, p. 511), who studied them in the 80s, to have chosen Salafism as a reflection of the Catholic habitus acquired early in life. "The converts search for a univocal system that sets the norms and values of the individual on a daily basis. This pre-set plan of life that has parallels to the converts' former Catholic habitus that guarantees the correctness of their self-imposed identity of a true Salafi Muslim." (Shanneik, 2011, p. 512). Salafism fills the void left by a life organised by the Catholic Church – "Since social authority and pressure no longer play such a role in society, converts need to be constantly reminded of hell and salvation expressed in halal and haram. While in the past the converts were passive and oppressed followers of the rules and standards of the Church and community, they are now following their own rules and judge others according to their own set standards. Converts tend to use the univocal system of norms and values set by religion to construct a community that enforces rules on individuals and which acts as compensation for the lack of social pressure." (Shanneik, 2011, p. 513). Further she sees the Catholic habitus when converts "having experienced disorientation and instability, follow male authority figures who initiated them to Islam. The mentoring role of senior male figures (...) suggests a continuation of the Catholic habitus in its patriarchal form." (p. 513)

The picture presented by Shanneik may be applied not only to a description of Polish Salafi women activities, but also of the relations they enter into with male activists of Muslim organisations and imams of Polish mosques, which constitute a repetition of the Catholic priest-female parishioner relation. As Shanneik states, "Converts reactivate former social structures and religious control through the construction of a new form of religious habitus." (Shanneik, 2011, p. 513) While playing the role of a parishioner for the imam, the convert becomes a preacher for her fellow believers on the Internet. This is where she preaches 'her' truth *ex catedra* and chastises those who do not follow the rules she deems to be correct.

Polish Salafis are equally prone to following individuals (local imams, religious activists) or texts, especially ones found online (very often anonymous texts of unknown origin circulating on the Internet) and to granting themselves the right to their own, wholly arbitrary, interpretations of texts which they later impose on others. This is contrary to the Irish converts studied by Shanneik, whom she calls 'atypical' Irish converts, [who], however, avoid any individual engagement with Islamic texts and rely on "religious male authorities" (Shanneik, 2011, pp. 512–513). We also need to remember that the Muslims she studied in the late 80s would not have used the Internet.

We are inclined to think that the tendency to interpret Islamic teachings individually is intensifying. This phenomenon was described by Piela (2012), who studied English-language online groups dominated by mostly American converts. We believe that such behaviour is characteristic not only for Salafis, but also for beginner Muslims in general, who are 'unconscious Salafis'.

Our respondents say that the period of interest in Salafism is often characterised by the need to follow all religious rules, often described as 'restrictive', and enforce them on other Muslims. This attitude is often described in the interviews as 'radicalism'. Our respondents and forum users charge Salafis with embracing a Catholic-style cult of martyrdom and suffering. According to one user, they "turn life into some grim tomb without joy, music, celebration, colourful robes and beauty". Shanneik writes in a similar vein about the Irish Salafis. 'The converts believe that in order to reach salvation, a Muslim should sacrifice and devote him/herself to Allah through following strictly the Islamic sources' (Shanneik, 2011, p. 505).

The stories of conversion add up to form a sketch of a trajectory that consists of stages shared by many Polish converts. After the initial period of individual searching comes the stage of socialisation. It is common for the converts to join groups dominated by the Salafi discourse or simply to find it the most useful narrative from among those available. Salafis willingly engage in introducing new members, following the obligation of preaching to both existing and potential Muslims. Inge writes (2016, p. 8): "Far from hiding their beliefs, Salafis consider it an important religious duty to 'give *da'wah*' – that is, to proselytize – to those who in their view have not grasped 'pure' Islam, whether they are Muslim or not."

Not all converts have been through a period of Salafism, yet those who have not are usually either persons very independent in their theological searches or ones who converted to Islam in prior to the time in which Internet became widely available in Polish homes. 'The Salafi stage' of the conversion trajectory often ends with a crisis resulting in a dramatic departure from Islam or developing a middle position. It is also possible to remain a 'mature' Salafi, yet such cases do not seem to be numerous, and certainly not among Muslims residing in Poland. One ought to remember, however, that the time period covered by our research is very short. Most of the conversions span over 10–15 years, the longest-lasting one being 27 years and the shortest 2. Thus, speaking of 'remaining a Salafi' might signify a period of many years.

The story told by Patrycja and her own reflections pertaining to her trajectory seem very typical here. Following the events she discusses below, Patrycja completed a course in theology, which enables her to assess her initial choices not only from her personal perspective, but also from that of Islamic theology:

> Maybe now it is changing, but even ten years ago most religion classes and lectures were still (…) ones promoting a certain version of Islam and

it is usually that pure, puristic one ... (...) Such a version of purism, of this black-and-white attitude to life, which is not bad, but is not suitable for everyone at every stage. You need some knowledge to recognise (...) where the person who (...) is giving the lecture, where they are from. In this intellectual and geographical sense, (....) I was deeply fascinated by the Islam (...) I was listening to such things about which I did not know that they were not wholly suitable for me and there are multiple issues for a beginner, somehow, when she meets them suddenly, ones related to the social sphere, which might be quite problematic, such as being with non-Muslim family being *haram*, shaking somebody's hand being *haram*, (...) saying merry Christmas being *haram*. Everything, everything suddenly becomes *haram*. (Patrycja)

Anatolia, who has completed the whole journey from Salafism to Sufism (yet defines herself predominantly as Sunni) still highly values multiple aspects of Salafism, finding it a useful introduction to be utilised in teaching Islam to beginner Muslims due to the unambiguous character of Salafi teachings:

People give a lot of false information in all the discussions. I was initially convinced that all I was reading had to be true etc. Also, many of the sources I was reading at the beginning were Salafi ones I do not recognise as legitimate now. Not simply because I do not like them. (...) Rather, it is not my cup of tea anymore. But surely, what I do appreciate in Salafism is that those are such very concrete things. When there's the question of whether XYZ is allowed, the answer is: no, it isn't; or: yes, it is, because so and so; and not, as it is in the mainstream, that everything is relative etc. Yes, I think that for a beginner such concrete things, answers to questions, are needed to find some direction. (...) it did not discourage me personally. However, some of the things I was reading were radical to the point of being extremist, and that quite terrified me. But I could somehow (...) explain it to myself. (...) there was the famous (...) [one of the respondent's group's members], because his views were (...) so extremist, (...) it was terrifying for me (...) So, usually when he wrote something, I would rush to someone and ask whether it was true, because I don't believe it's true [laughter]. (Anatolia)

Sometimes, the 'Salafi agent' at the beginning of our respondents' paths was their husband, partner or an acquaintance introducing the convert to Islamic matters. Danuta's husband, born a Muslim, initially under significance influence of Salafi ideas, eventually became a follower of the Sufi version of Islam with her:

> I travelled such a path, I met the husband and his Islam, it is more Salafi. (…) But I thank him that he was searching as well and also became interested in Sufism, and because of that, we could achieve something together. (Danuta)

Even though (as our observations suggest) it seems that peak popularity of the Salafi current in Poland is already a thing of the past, it still attracts new Muslims. Respondents' first interactions with Salafi teachings happen predominantly in Salafi-oriented Internet groups. (Račius, 2011). Such a confrontation is often the beginning of a revision of one's attitude to Islamic teachings and its authorities, providing inspiration for one's own research. Those converts for whom encountering Salafism prompted a search for their own way, emphasise the role of rational thinking, an inner emotional compass and 'common sense' as the sole and ultimate signposts helping them navigate their religious dilemmas and searches among the wide offer in the Islamic market of ideas. Similar observations are made by Inge (2016) about British Salafi women, yet the criteria appear much simpler here. "They were often guided simply by what 'feels right' or 'wrong', as well as by how 'Islamic' a preacher appeared." Some of our respondents speak about the significance of common sense which made them feel impervious to the Salafi discourse.

For Anna, the 'inner compass' was vital follow from the very beginning of her conversion. She comes from an atheist family, but, to avoid social ostracism, she was sent to Catholic instruction classes, while simultaneously being told by her parents 'none of this is true'. Before Islam, she had experiences with other religions as well. She was attracted by the universalist and spiritual values of religion, while a deeper study of Islam was spurred by external motives – as a convert, she had to answer her friends' questions:

> I took what I liked (…), if something spoke to me (…) and that was, I guess, a kind of a healthy approach, and at some point, some 2 years after converting to Islam (…) I started investigating more and that didn't even come from within myself, it was just that when people around me were learning I was a Muslim, they would ask me about different things in Islam, about which I, quite naturally, didn't know, because my progress was, to an extent, based on my feelings, I also wanted to learn some things, I also didn't aim at immediately waking up as that 100% Muslim the next day. (Anna)

In the world of 'the chaos of Polish Islam' (a reference to the haphazard institutional organization of Muslim life in Poland made by another respondent, Beata), treating one's own intuition, feelings and rational thinking as guides in religious life is a warranty of a spiritual wellbeing and a sense of acting right and in harmony with oneself for the respondents:

> [Salafi prohibitions] are radical and hopeless, 'cause why should I change my life completely if I have been listening to music so far, (...) music helps me relax, I feel better, why should I give it up? Because somebody just thought I should? Photographs. And why shouldn't I have the photos? I don't pray to them after all, these are just photos of my child. (...) Oftentimes, girls who were converting would say I should burn or throw away all photos of myself or my family. (...) this is absurd to me. Never in my life will I agree with that (...). What else? (Małgorzata)

> At the beginning, I was young and callow. And then it proved that I was beginning to negotiate this Islam with myself to feel well, as not all solutions necessarily suit me (...) we, as converts, negotiate our Islam with those who were born Muslims, their culture and how they understand things. (Marysia)

Similarly to many other converts, Angelika describes difficult beginnings, when being 'bombarded' with prohibitions led to her experiencing pangs of conscience and a feeling of being 'a sinful and bad person'. Many narratives centre on particularly zealous Salafi converts, who, after a period of intensified efforts and attempts at reaching the ideal, reject Islam, oftentimes becoming its ardent critics.

> I know many converts have it that way, (...) first we are bombarded with all that we are not allowed to do: music – *haram*, (...) you must wear the headscarf or else you'll go to hell. (...) surely if somebody told me that alcohol had been being withdrawn throughput the 23 years of the Qur'an being revealed and it was actually only withdrawn completely in the last year, so it was a gradual change. So it is not that I become a Muslim and from that moment on I should not eat pork and listen to music. I don't believe that I should stop listening to music at all. (...) That would make living with that new religion of mine much easier. And here I got (...) the feeling that I keep doing something wrong, that I am imperfect, that everybody's saying what I should be like, and I am not like that, simply because I don't have proper conditions for that yet. If God allows,

> I will have them in the future, but now I don't or it is even that conditions in Poland don't allow applying them somehow on everyday basis, so normally. Now, I actually have a more relaxed attitude to my religion. (...) So, it was also that why I was feeling bad, because I read that I shouldn't do this, this, this, and suddenly I'm thinking, what a bad person I am. (Angelika)

The dissonance between the Salafi message and the reality of the ummah leads new Muslims to experience feelings of anxiety, chaos and uncertainty (Górak-Sosnowska, 2015; Inge, 2016; Račius, 2013). Beata converted to Islam in Poland, where she subsequently participated in the life of the Muslim community for some time. The dissonance between the observation of the practice of Polish Islam in Poland and the Salafi message was leaving her embarrassed and concerned:

> For many months, I was so lost that I didn't quite know which way to go. I was feeling Muslim, but it was all liberal in the mosque, and here I am, listening to scholars who are very restrictive, while I am somewhere in the middle, but I'm feeling bad about it and I don't know which way to choose. I was torn like that for very long (...) It seems to me (...) that maybe I embraced [Islam] a bit too quickly. Some do it quickly and handle it, but others do it too quickly and they simply have this kind of chaos in their heads (...) a fair number of such people later depart from Islam or become, for instance, very restrictive. (...) I kept balancing like that for a few months and it was hard for me. Well, but later, slowly, slowly, it got a little more normal. And since we came here, to England, it has actually been better. (Beata)

Maja feels that she is able to feel better and more secure as her views evolve:

> With time, my concept of God has broadened, it is less rigid, this concept of God has just become ... more appropriate for grasping various spheres of life. (...) when I visit the cemetery [on All Saints' Day], is that really a sin? I surely look at it less rigidly now. I am surely less afraid that something is *haram*. And the less you fear, the less you sin. I don't drink and I'm not affected by somebody drinking bear. We can sit at a table together. (Maja)

Noor, calling the phase a period of individualization, sees the converts as "agents who are making meaning of their everyday religiosity" (Noor, 2017, p. 91). She further states that "individualization tended to occur mostly among those interlocutors who had experienced religious pressure from communal norms of piety. Advancing age and a growing realistic assessment of their capacities and of the possibilities of the extent to which they could actually live according to Allah's rules' are also important factors" (Noor, 2017, p. 262).

It is very rarely that participants in online discussions define themselves as Salafis. This may result from a fear of criticism, as the irony and humour of new Muslims, both ones who have been through a Salafi period themselves and ones who have only encountered the discourse, is often aimed at the Salafi narration. The fear may also (or maybe primarily) pertain to being considered a radical, as Salafism has 'bad press' and is often identified with radicalism or even Muslim terrorism (Inge, 2016).

Another reason for an unwillingness to explicitly describe one's views as Salafi (even though this is clearly indicated by the views themselves and by one's selection of sources) might be unawareness of the fact that the current has its name and is actually a separate current or the convert's persuasion that it is the only real and possible Islam (a common slogan on the Polish Internet is *"islam jest jeden"* – "there is one Islam"). Some participants of the online discussions who represent Salafi views, when asked about their religious affiliation, claim that they are against Salafism, just as they are against "other sects". Can we, then, speak of 'unconscious Salafism'?

Several of our respondents from the UK expressed views which could be described as Salafi, yet none declared to be a supporter of the current. Most often, they identified as "simply Muslims", "Sunnis", "following the Qur'an and the Sunnah". Another reason for this act of "passing" can be related to the wish to avoid tribal stigma connected with being seen as a "fundamentalist Salafi" within the umma by "normal" Muslims and to decrease social stigma outside the umma where the more visible Salafis may be more discredited (Goffman, 1963).

Only one of our respondents, residing in Poland, declares to be a Salafi, yet, as she says, problems related to her family and her professional situation make it difficult for her to follow the ideal in practice. Thus, she is, in a sense, a 'theoretical Salafi':

> In this theoretical sense, I would be most inclined towards the Salafiyah, (...) but this everyday life. Somehow, I am not what I'd like to be, but that's what suits me, this clearer, rawer, I mean from those normal people's perspective, (...) Islam. I don't like those fractions, only this clear, basic, original, from the origins when there was the Prophet, as he was conveying it, 'cause even when there are schools, I couldn't fit into any school either. (Kornelia)

The clash between ideals and the necessity of functioning in a non-Muslim society, which is one of the reasons for disappointment with Salafism, pertains particularly to converts residing in Poland. For them, the need of acceptance from members of the various communities they belong to (family, colleagues, etc.), is much greater than it is for Polish converts residing in the UK. The latter emphasise the differences between practising Islam in Poland and in the UK, praising not only the well-developed Muslim infrastructure, or the opportunity for following one's faith fully and openly, but also the social culture which enables functioning of people of various cultures and religions. For some, the emigration became a *hijra*,[1] allowing them to practice their faith freely. Many of the women cannot imagine a return to their homeland. Even a holiday trip to Poland becomes a problem that disrupts everyday functioning, forcing one to make uncomfortable decisions related to eating *halal*, wearing the hijab, or performing the Muslim prayers. Our respondents also mention the significance of the distance between them and their Polish families for the sense of freedom of religious practice. These circumstances create pressure to find solutions to survive socially by managing spoiled identity.

Roald points out 3 stages of conversion: love, disappointment, and maturity. At the third stage, new Muslims 'start to formulate their understanding of Islam with the reference to their specific cultural context' (Roald, 2004, p. 347; 2001). For many migrant converts, however, the stage might be significantly delayed, because they are not very well "rooted" in society.

Marlena is planning to return from the UK to Poland, and therefore she finds it necessary to reformulate her understanding of religion:

> For a moment, I was fascinated by Salafism, as that somehow brings you closest to (…) the religion, close to the Prophet's times, but it is of little use today. Maybe you could live like that somewhere in the UK, but again I'd be alone in that, I'd need to join some group here, as the Salafism here is (…) so rigorous, harsh, to the point of being aggressive. So I removed myself from that a bit, because if I want to return to Poland, I have no chance of getting deeper into Salafism, as I wouldn't balance things, I think. In Poland, you need to adapt to the difficult reality. (Marlena)

---

1 Here, a metaphor for emigration that references Muhammad's withdrawal from Makkah in 622 AD and settlement in Medina. As that event also marks year 1 of the Islamic calendar, the use of this word can also symbolize a new beginning, a rebirth.

Maja, who now lives in Poland but has also spent several years in the UK, speaks of the differences in the extent to which it is possible to practise strict Salafism at home and abroad, as well as the conflicts it may engender:

> A few years ago, hard-line Salafism started to dominate Polish Internet, now it has calmed down a little, it could have been related to the fresh Polish migration to EU countries, mainly to the UK, but also to NL and DE. Those were Poles who had recently married and converted to Islam. It was a crowd mentality at times, the women from the UK would remove dolls' eyes, forbid their children to watch Peppa the Pig, their followers would all burn photographs and family memorabilia from their whole lives, which they now regret. That would sometimes spur conflicts in groups, in which we are together, after all. The foreign newbies accused us, residing in Poland, of not practising well, of seeking excuses. Obviously, it led to defensive reactions, as we have to simply live with other people here, with our families, neighbours, we have to make our living, we live in very traditional communities, not to mention the vitriolic Islamophobia. We were angry with them glorifying martyrdom for faith, meaning our martyrdom, of course. We responded that they were living in a comfortable bubble, in a welfare state. When you are an immigrant, your husband is an immigrant too, you don't work or you do manual labour, you do not come into contact with your diaspora, because you pretend not to be Polish when there are Poles around, you only know random Muslims, uprooted as well, you are far from your whole family, then you live in a social vacuum where you can happily be Mrs Nobody, and this is a very comfortable position. Meanwhile, I am Mrs Somebody, living in my social networks, with my own place on the social ladder and with no plans for being dragged down. I will not wear the hijab, not only because I fear physical violence. I also fear ostracism, falling out of those networks, that we won't get, me and my family, the minimum of respect that strangers are treated with. Maybe this is hypocrisy, but everyone must be bit of a hypocrite if they don't want to be perceived as martyrs or unhinged. (Maja)

In uncritical copying of the 'ancestors' generation's' behaviour, Patrycja sees a lack of realism which is detrimental for the *ummah*. Even though she corrects herself several times trying not to use the word "radicalism" (which other respondents do use in their accounts), she eventually deems attitudes that separate one from one's environment to be radical:

> [In their opinion] things are black and white. Nothing can be left uncertain. And that leads to great harm, because later they find out that life itself is the grey zone and this is the test for us and we need to get, to gather more knowledge. We need to look at how the Prophet actually lived, and not at what some only comment on his life, at the choices his first companions faced, (...) they were people of flesh and bone, they had certain weaknesses of their own and made mistakes and we should somehow learn from the mistakes. And if we use a mistake just to learn from it, it is a very nice thing. If we are, somehow, within the narrative of everything being, that golden age of Islam, the *sahabah*, who were almost angels, then we have the system which becomes black and white and also hard to follow. (...) it is radicalism of a kind, (...) a person looking at themselves only are radical too, as they don't listen to others. (Patrycja)

We are aware of the fact that these in-depth interviews do not reflect Polish converts' interest in various currents of Islam quantitatively. This is particularly significant given the disproportional numbers of respondents interested in the Sufi and Salafi currents. Based on participant observation, we estimate that the number of followers of Salafism is much greater, particularly among new converts, while the number of Sufis is small.

The stage of crisis, which emerges as a significant event in our respondents' stories, is also absent (or hard to see) from the online narrative. Crisis is much harder to gauge than zeal from posts on social media. In borderline cases, members of the community only see the result of the change, in the form of different dress, lifestyle or a transformed online image. The difference between the converts' online narrative and our interviews can be explained with a reference to van Nieuwkerk (2006), who notices two fundamental differences between converts' narratives offline and online. The first one is their purpose – online narratives are supposed to be a source of inspiration for others, while the second one is the context of production – on the Internet one can perform a desirable version of oneself. It is a space for finding one's place in the virtual *ummah* to which the new Muslim wishes to belong (van Nieuwkerk, 2006: 108–113). We may also add other factors. The first of these is the length of time for which a given person has participated online. The most active ones are the relatively fresh converts, who want to 'share the truth', thus identifying and articulating their own place in the *ummah*. Long-term converts are either not very active in discussions or refrain from participating. Another factor present in the realm of Polish Internet is the hostile atmosphere. All these factors render large online groups a platform for duels of 'truths' rather than honest reflection.

For Polish converts, Salafism is predominantly a transitionary stage. The absence of 'mature' Salafis, for whom embracing this current would result from their thoughtful reflection over several year, results from 1) the lack of an established Salafi environment or space that one could belong to, and 2) the difficulty of practising Salafism in Polish conditions.[2] Being a Salafi in Poland could mean alienation, both in the small Polish *ummah* and in the Polish society in general. They are doubly stigmatized and contact with them can be considered by some "normal" Muslims as "contagious" and increasing tribal stigma. Inge writes about the British Salafis who function in much more advantageous conditions than those present in Poland, that "[w]hile social networks were often crucial for the women to take the first steps towards joining a group that they might otherwise have avoided, becoming Salafi generally came at a social cost, rather than gain. They made some friends, but lost others – and many struggled to form attachments to fellow Salafis." (Inge, 2016)

### Polish and Global Inspirations

Outside the network of traditional transmission of knowledge, converts seek out knowledge in the global online *ummah*, where they can find a of variety preachers on YouTube or the popular site Halaltube. The only limitation is their English fluency – the only ones able to answer our question about inspirations from the epistemic 'stars' of global Islam were those with a good command of English (although some lectures had been translated into Polish).

The choice of favourite preachers and writers seemed unrelated to their popularity on the Polish Internet.[3] The one our respondents were most enthusiastic about was Nouman Ali Khan, while others held in high regard were also Tariq Ramadan, Omar Suleiman, Yasir Qadhi, Ahmad Deedat, Ismail Ibn Musa Menk/Mufti Menk, Yasmin Mogahed, Timothy Winter/Abdal Hakim Murad, Seyyed Hossein Nasr, Hamza Yusuf, Fadhlalla Haeri, Bilal Philips, Jonathan Brown and Yusuf al-Qaradawi.

While Ali Khan, Omar Suleiman and Yasir Qadhi are relatively well known on the Polish Internet, the results do not reflect the popularity of Ahmad

---

2  A small number of 'mature' Polish Salafi women live and practice outside Poland, but none of them accepted the invitation to participate in our study.

3  The preacher (who is oftentimes a writer as well, for example Tariq Ramadan) uses his personal authority, described by Pilger-Strohl as 'constructed through the acknowledgement of "subordinates"' and therefore 'must be earned, and repeatedly reconfirmed. (...) is dependent on trust, loyalty and integrity (...) has the possibility (...) to influence others' (Pilger-Strohl, 2014).

Deedat and Mufti Menk, who are currently popular among the Polish online ummah, or Bilal Philips and Yusuf Estes, popular several years ago. None of the respondents has mentioned Zakir Naik, who is enjoying a great deal of popularity on the Polish Internet.

While the Polish Internet is dominated by speakers from the circle of 'mild Salafism' (including Zakir Naik), with increasing presence of representatives of mainstream Islam, our respondents predominantly listen to theologians-specialists, whose narratives appeal to educated Western middle class, both with moderately liberal and moderately conservative religious views. Speakers remaining on the margins of our respondents' interests are 'niche' ones – Sufis, ones who are 'too academic', 'too Salafi', or whose message is oversimplified.

Our respondents also find inspiration in Polish and Western literature, both popular-scientific like Janusz Danecki, Marek M. Dziekan, and other Polish researchers working in the field of Arab studies and Islam; Karen Armstrong – mentioned twice, and purely scientific like Karolina Rak, a Polish researcher specialising in Arab feminism.

The following names were provided by our respondents as inspiring religious authorities working in the Polish *ummah*: the Shia theologian imam Arkadiusz Miernik (4), the Palestinian imam Ali Abi Isa (2), the Palestinian mufti of the Muslim League Nidal Abu Tabaq, the Syrian imam Nezar Charif, as well as Polish converts: the researcher and educator Blanka Rogowska, the researchers Mariusz Turowski and Jarosław Banasiak. Most of the individuals mentioned in the responses are not active in the public sphere any more – three of them have withdrawn from activity, one has passed away, and one has moved abroad.

Another significant fact is that the greatest number of positive opinions were given about Arkadiusz Miernik, who, as a member of Stowarzyszenie Jedności Muzułmańskiej [Association of Islamic Unity], represents a part of the Polish Shia minority. His popularity among some of the Polish Sunni Muslims is due to his educational activity in social media (a vlog, a FB page, and the Al-Islam magazine), which is both accessible and of high intellectual quality. As 'the only intellectual of the Polish institutionalised Islam' he is also perceived as 'Islam's ambassador in the out-of-ummah world' (Maja).

Other respondents agree with Maja and Faustyna that Miernik's charismatic personality, Polishness, religious inclusiveness and high competences render him a perfect representative of the Polish *ummah*:

> [as for] a Polish spiritual leader of sorts, I am closer to the Sunni than the Shia Islam, but he [Arkadiusz Miernik] seems so inclusive in what he

does and so Polish, it's a pity he's not here, he's sitting in England and we are lacking such characters, who simply aren't afraid to stir what's in the pot, to say, to stamp their foot and say, well, we want to eat our pierogi during the Ramadan. (Faustyna)

However, the Internet comments, as well as the number of views and likes of Arkadiusz Miernik's lectures, make it apparent that not everyone is interested in this type of message. His Shia-ness is an insurmountable obstacle even when the lectures pertain to Sunni Islam exclusively. A member of a Muslim group evaluates his activity as follows: "Just the love one another and do as you please kinda stuff, what's next, LGBT? A hippie Islam. Besides, Shiites are a sect, not Muslims."

### Polish Islam Is Full of Braggadocio

A common motive which returns in almost every conversation with a convert is a lack of willingness for an unrestrained discussion of religious matters and a fear of expressing one's opinion. A fear of being judged prevents many women from participating in meetings, which is why many Polish converts withdraw from the communal life of the *ummah*. Multiple respondents perceive the phenomenon as 'typically Polish':

> I would say that we Poles, we're full of braggadocio. Everyone is the wisest one (...) (Patrycja)

> those mutual attacks, I don't know whether I should blame it on Polish mentality, that "I know better and you don't, 'cause my Islam is this and that", and here it shows (...) that the person who keeps so showing off their knowledge doesn't know much as they only follow one particular school. (...) Born [Muslims] pass it [knowledge] from generation to generation, like the baton in a relay (...) converts want to show that they're better because they chose themselves and they wind themselves in the wrong direction (...). This is why I draw more from the born Muslims than from the converts. (Małgorzata)

> (...) there are the four schools, which generally shouldn't be in conflict and in international groups there are often the opinions that one school says this and another says that and you shouldn't argue with the person, while for example among Poles, there are, unfortunately, arguments. They

argue very often, there is often the viciousness (...) the Polish Muslim environment is a judgmental one, everybody is watching everybody else. (Beata)

According to Patrycja, the above is partially due to lack of knowledge about the diversity within Islam:

> I do not participate in any forums. Arguments as to whether someone is supposed to wear their socks for prayer, pluck their eyebrows or paint their nails. These are things which are not insignificant, as there are certain rules (...) but there's a lack of recognising priorities. What is more important (...), is that we do not argue or exchange our opinions in a respectful manner. Also, let us not discuss issues we are not knowledgeable about. These two things are priorities, and not, for instance, wearing socks, on which there is not a consensus among scholars. Since there is this lack of consensus among scholars, it means that both things are good, it is not that they took it from God-knows-where, but there are options. (...) And here one believer will be scratching another's eyes out because of that. (...) People often think like, now I am a Muslim and I shall be pure and cool, and they forget that they have the whole load of learnt behaviours, reactions, subconscious things, and all that remains and it is remains a task to address for the rest of your life. (Patrycja)

Anna is one of the persons who, after a longer initial period of 'lonely' Islam, decided to enter a 'communal' stage which, as in many other cases, was a difficult experience reorganising one's thinking about oneself as a Muslim:

> I was afraid that they would impose one style of being, rules, some group morality too much (...). At some point, I started mixing with different groups and watching what their Islam looked like and how other Muslims were practising it (...). Because, as I was very loose in that approach of mine and I had those Buddhist influences and different things, here I got really scared, and I didn't want to depart from Islam ... I had that inner dilemma, whether what I believe in is still Islam, or maybe I should rather follow what the Muslims are saying in order to be a good Muslim. I felt bad, terrible, and I had doubts, and I think that I am still in the process of departing from such thinking. I still feel that I haven't returned to the state from the time before I joined the groups. I am trying to return to that primary state, when I was doing it my way and feeling good. (Anna)

Maja experienced it in a similar manner when she entered the Muslim environment after years of being a 'lonely' unsocialised Muslim:

> I converted to Islam in the early 90s, I didn't know anyone because there wasn't anyone to know. I was practising that Islam alone, as an 'academic Muslim', rather from scientific books. And after several years, such a shock, Muslims! Of course, there were attempts to "straighten my ways" in many ways, only I am not interested in [others'] ideas for my life. Well, an academic background was also giving me confidence. For me, the environment of the ummah is very important, discussing things together is important, that's how the ummah is formed. It was thanks to meeting people, having discussions, reading books, and a perpetual dialogue with myself, people and books that I went a long way in Islam, learnt more about myself and my place. People avoid discussion for fear of *fitnah*, you're supposed to be nice, but there's nothing better to stimulate your thinking. (Maja)

Reproducing and producing knowledge on their own constitutes a significant part of life for the converts' communities (Stoica, 2011; Górak-Sosnowska, 2015; Noor, 2017), particularly in religious communities suffering from weak religious infrastructure (Górak-Sosnowska, 2015).

Van Bruinessen (2011) distinguishes two ways of producing knowledge in 'Western' Islam: one is the 'religious market model' which implies a hierarchical system: from 'teacher/preacher' to 'student.' In this model, religious specialists or movements/associations are producers of Islamic knowledge. Consumers can choose from a range of options. This model assumes a strict distinction between the producers and consumers of religious knowledge.

In the second model, everyone is involved in the production of religious knowledge. Through such activities as online discussions, but also, for instance, the activity of youth organisations, the Muslim tradition is reinterpreted and adapted to the conditions European Muslims live in. In such circumstances, these are particularly the Salafis who work intensively to transfer the 'right' knowledge that shapes fellow believers' views in the spirit of Salafism (*da'wah* and *tarbiyyah*) (Noor, 2017).

### "Islam Seems a Left-Wing Party to Me."

For many of our respondents, Islam is irrevocably connected with social and political views. Generally speaking, conversion can be a way of sacralising politics for already politically active people. Earlier political ideas survive conversion and are accommodated within an Islamic framework (Allievi, 1998).

Most of them identify as Muslim feminists or persons for whom issues of gender equality are extraordinarily important. Feminist awareness in this group is very high and it even seems to rise after conversion to Islam: "I might have even become a greater feminist than I had been before" (Alana). For some, their views on social equality are close to Islam. Several persons declare their views to be close to the left (which is not always precise, probably also in the specific understanding of the term on Polish political scene, we might expect that they mean cultural left). One identifies as a liberal Muslim (Daria) and one as a modernist (Angelika). Four persons identify as unequivocally left-wing (using the word 'lewacka', which is an appropriation of a right-wing slur directed at supporters of left-wing politics, roughly equivalent to the English 'leftie') and two as communists (which is very rare in Polish political discourse and, obviously, even rarer in the environment of the Polish *ummah*). For Anna, communist views, alongside a universalistic experience of spirituality, were the reason for choosing Islam as a religion closest to them. In Maja's case, her growing interest in socialism, and later communism, intertwined naturally with her interest in Islamic social thought. Alana puts it in a straightforward manner: "Islam seems a left wing party to me".

We may speak of an overrepresentation of persons with left-leaning views among our respondents compared with the Polish society in general. This, however, comes as no surprise – the discourse of the Polish right, xenophobic, exclusionary, and hostile towards Muslims in particular, cannot attract too many of them (although there are some supporters of the Law and Justice or Konfederacja parties to be found among Polish Muslims). Islamic ideas are also in conflict with nationalism. Allievi (1998) claims that the marginalization of many Muslims on both domestic and international level attracts some who incline to the left. Islamic ideas can be useful as a form of liberation theology offering an accessible language of protest to marginalized groups (Winter, 2000, p. 100).

For Maja, Mirosława, Daria and Danuta, Islam is connected with environmentalism. They relate their ethical choices and dilemmas, pertaining to issues such as animal rights, to their religion: "Islam regulates all the things which enable me to live in harmony with people, in harmony with nature, in harmony with the whole world surrounding me." (Daria) Mirosława finds it problematic to harmonise her feelings and thoughts on animal suffering and the ritual slaughter rule:

> When I converted to Islam, I accepted it all and only then did I begin to have some self-reflection. It was automatic then, and now I am beginning

to think about it deeper, for instance about the animal issues. And it absorbed me quite deeply and I started to read a lot on what it is like, on how animals feel (…), so when I read about those streets in Egypt washed with blood, I didn't feel good about it, and that is probably the main aspect that is controversial, this issue of halal slaughter (…). I always try to defend everything, and here I don't know. I know that this is best for us, that it is indeed meat without blood, pure and God-sacred, but I don't know … (…) this suffering. I have a problem with it, and this is the most burning issue [for me]. (Mirosława)

Similar reflection led Maja to vegetarianism and Danuta to veganism: "I am vegan. (…) That was also tragic for me how we can inflict suffering on others, (…), and be in any religion. For me, it was a shock." (Danuta)

It is also in this respect that we can observe dissimilarity between our respondents' narrative and the Internet discourse, the latter virtually completely disregarding it in discussions. Only a few dispersed texts and translations have appeared, and the general environmental awareness in the Polish *ummah* is still low. An exception to the rule was a blog published for years by a convert and largely devoted to eco-Islam (now already in an altered form http://polskaarabka.blogspot.com/). In 2020, the MZR launched the muzulmanie.pl website, intended to provide information not only about religious practices themselves, but also about such aspects of believers' life as environmentalism. The state of environmental awareness in the Polish *ummah* reflects the awakening of the Polish society in general.[4]

### The Crescent Surrounded by EU Stars

Most of our respondents appreciate European values, find them compatible with Islam and identify with Europeanness. One might risk the statement that Polish Muslims show pro-European sympathies to a degree larger than the average Polish citizen (which is also related to their greater interest in left-wing or liberal worldviews). For some, Europeanness is also a basis for Muslim identity. European Islam could be defined as "adapted to a Western setting, with its own local challenges and solutions", which means "that Muslim beliefs and practices and Muslims' modes of religiosity are transforming in western societies" (Noor, 2017: 89).

---

4 On the wide interest in environmental issue among Swedish converts, see Roald (2010, p. 332).

For Roald, it is obvious that the current Muslim religiosity is influenced by Western attitudes and that new Muslims play an important role in the blending of the various traditions (Roald, 2006: 66). Her studies of Swedish converts show that most of them (with a few exceptions) share their understanding of democratic ideas and human rights with the non-Muslim citizens of Sweden. (Roald, 2010: 325, 339) For Aleksandra, Faustyna and Mirosława, the idea of 'pure Islam' is a utopia which they replace with the idea of 'European Islam', compatible with fundamental European values. Aleksandra identifies predominantly as a European Muslim:

> What I like the most is the European option, that I am a European Muslim. As Tatars or Bosnians can say that they are European Muslims, why the hell can't I, as European values are very close to me. And, well, I think that European Islam makes sense. Muslims in Europe (...) are quite a large group already, one you can identify with. Of course, they will be completely different things in a Bosnian village and in a Polish Tatar's village, but they will still be close, as we have some set of common values, which are not necessarily related to Christianity, and it will still be closer than ideas from Pakistan, Malaysia or Indonesia. No, we have a completely different concept and also the completely different European approach to religious spirituality. I prefer the crescent surrounded by EU stars. I really like the fact that (...) we became united here in Europe. (Aleksandra)

Aleksandra thinks that it is possible to reconcile Islam with European values by interpreting the Qur'an in a post-enlightenment spirit. In the cases which she finds particularly problematic (such as Islam's attitude to homosexuality), she proposes to skip the inconvenient verses without unnecessary dispute and accept human rights:

> It was somehow possible to reconcile Judaism with homosexuality, even though the Old Testament is very spicy. Christianity can be joined with that, so why not Islam? It is enough to drop a few problematic pieces and accept the European concept of human rights. (...) [I would discard] "slay the idolaters wherever ye find them",[5] as The Sword Verse is very controversial (...) the European approach to religiousness is very close to me. I think that visitors from and residents of other countries might not understand it and deem us not to be Muslims, 'cause what does she look

---

5  Pickthall (1930).

like, what's she doing with the gays. In my opinion, this is not contradictory to religiousness at all. (Aleksandra)

Mirosława also finds the European identity and the ethical and cultural values related to it primary and believes that they are what European Muslims should shape their own European Islam in line with:

> Public flogging, (…) is also simply unacceptable for me (…) our European identity, the culture we were brought up in, shapes how we perceive certain things present in Islam, so violence and aggression (…) I don't quite agree with that. Talking to people, I hear some clinging to it and saying that it is necessary, that there is no other way. And others negate it and sometimes resign from being Muslims (…). And, to my mind, not all Muslims living in Europe are able to comprehend it [that contemporary life in Europe brings other challenges], and additionally, they also often justify that, saying: "you keep turning away from it, trying to find yourselves some comfortable solution instead of living according to the sunnah, as that's the way it was. And now we should show that the Prophet (peace be upon him) had such a terrible situation, so we shouldn't compare ourselves to him now." Obviously, it is impossible to compare, as it is a completely different context and a different story, which does not mean that our problems are of small importance. (Mirosława)

Faustyna feels a member of the progressive European ummah more than one of the Polish ummah. Although progressive Muslims are excluded by mainstream Muslims everywhere, being a progressive Muslim in Poland is even more difficult for her:

> I think that it is the same as everywhere globally, that progressive Islam is excluded by both sides – the mainstream *ummah* itself and the majority society, because who are they actually? Well, if you don't like mainstream Islam, the why are you even a Muslim, right? And when you go in the other direction, then, if you want to be a Muslim, then what is all that inclusivity about, and what is that, for instance, gay imam, or a woman leading a prayer about (…) I felt a little crushed, 'cause it was like, if I want to be in the ummah, it must be the way they want it, right? And I can't have a different approach. Not to mention acceptance for Muslims of homosexual orientation, right? Or even Muslim feminists, for that matter, as that was obviously not permissible, so I think, that again, we are somehow very much dispersed and not quite rooted yet, … that will be a

slow process, as you need to come out of the closet a bit, and coming out of the closet from a minority, that's a whole higher level. (...) (Faustyna)

Another position is that presented by Kornelia, for whom the overarching idea remains that of 'universal Islam', unconditioned socially or culturally: "I'm a sort of a spiritual caveman in this Islam, (...) I have a problem with fatwas, that it doesn't quite reach me, that they exist, that they pertain to Europe, to a certain situation." (Kornelia). Her position remains a minority one among our respondents, yet seems quite popular in the Polish *ummah*.

### *Pierogi* in a Mosque

Allievi calls the new Muslims' culture a 'do-it-yourself-culture' (bricolage culture), as the stage of conversion is followed by the phase of re-culturation, constituting a process of hybridisation occurring between various aspects of the local and the Muslim culture (Allievi, 1998, pp. 220–221).

Multiple researchers who have studied conversion write on the 'national' variants of converts' Islam. Roald mentions the 'Swedish Muslim', a mixture of Islamic and Swedish values regarded as the 'best Swede' and the 'best Muslim' (Roald, 2006, p. 58). Van Nieuwkerk reports on Dutch female Muslims calling themselves 'symbolic migrants' (van Nieuwkerk, 2006, p. 106), Nicole Bourque (2006) on Scottish Muslims, Özyürek on German ones, (2015, 2018), and Račius (2013) on Lithuanian ones.

Roald proposes to 'consider whether the rediscovery of the convert identity built on a merging of Scandinavian and Islamic values (...) is an instinctive reaction to (...) the downward step on the social ladder'. This way, they 'can distance themselves from the problems (..) weighing down the Muslim community and keep (...) the superior status (...) and gain relief from the sheer weight of the burden of the Muslim *ummah* (Roald, 2006: 66). Such a diagnosis might apply to some Polish female Muslims as well. While there are very few Muslim immigrants of low social status in Poland, the sheer disrespect for Muslims in Poland might be a cause for escaping into a 'Polish Islam'. It is a fact of no mean significance that these are educated and professionally active women from big cities who speak of 'Polish Islam'. They are the ones who do not want to stand out from the crowd, do not want to be associated with immigrants from Muslim countries, and do not want to be represented by activists of non-Polish origin.

For some of our respondents, 'Polish Islam' is a phenomenon either realised already or to become real in near future. They are mostly the converts residing in Poland who perceive it predominantly as a blend of cultural identity with being a Muslim. Özyürek in her study of German converts goes further, saying that being an European convert to Islam can 'simultaneously challenge and reproduce biological and cultural racisms as well as a homogenous understanding of a German and European culture.' Converts have a tendency to disassociate themselves from born Muslims, treating their 'wrong' Islamic cultural practices with suspicion. Born Muslims should be taught 'proper Islam'. Thus, converts reinforce a Europocentric attitude. (Özyürek, 2014)

Salafism can be another way for converts to distance themselves from born Muslims and to achieve a stronger position. Salafism presents itself as superior to any culture. It is well-adapted to globalization because it emphasises Islam's own deculturation and aspires to universal validity (Roy, 2008), tends to devalue nationalism and ethnicity as subordinate to religious identity (Zebiri, 2007, p. 96), placing new Muslims at the same level as born Muslims and, at least in theory, pushing aside cultural and ethnic differences (Özyürek, 2015, pp. 109–131).

Pirický writes about 'Slovakizing' and 'Bohemizing' variants of Islam dominant among Czech and Slovak converts. In his opinion, the reason for claiming to be a moderate, 'national' Muslim is 'a fear of expressing opinions that identify a person too closely with "foreign" variants of Islam' (Pirický, 2018). We believe that the same mechanism applies to Polish converts as well. While in the context of Western converts (as in the Swedish case described by Roald) one of the reasons is the fear of losing social status, in the case of Eastern Europe, the stakes are much higher – survival in society, or, at least, avoiding rejection or even physical aggression. Identifying with one's own nation is key to survival, both at the personal and the collective levels. It might be expected that the identification will be even stronger in the Czech Republic and Slovakia than in Poland, due to even smaller numbers of Muslims there and the absence of indigenous Islamic traditions such as the Polish Tatar Islam.

Maja finds it possible to create a culturally Polish 'Islam of our own' in the future, which, however, requires time and a certain 'critical mass'. She is critical about the 'bottom-up orientalisation' of Muslim practices:

> I'm dreaming of something where you can be yourself. Like Victorian Muslims, classical Victorians to the bone. For me, they are a model of blending one's own culture with Islamic ideas in Europe. Let us eat żur [traditional Polish fermented rye soup], only without the pork sausage in it. (...) Sure – a group needs certain self-identity elements, but let them be our elements – *bigos, sernik, makowiec* [three traditional Polish foods] as tradition for post-Ramadan holidays (not for Eid). And here we have

> Ramadan coming and everybody's buying oriental decorations from Amazon and sharing recipes for oriental dishes. Well, I understand that there's the lack of tradition and models, there's the cultural void, that many women have husbands from Muslim countries and draw inspiration from them, but maybe it is worth making the effort and taking something of our own? For me, Islam is *żur*, this everyday life respecting the values, not 'alhamdulillah', but 'chwała Bogu' [praise be to God]. (...) not some Scheherazade princesses (...) or [appropriations that look like] costumes. There is no religion without a culture, this is illusion, the only question is that of what we are going to dress the religion in – in a [traditional Polish] Łowicz headscarf, or in an abaya from the Persian Gulf. (Maja)

It is also according to Marysia that a 'pure' Islam, not culturally determined, does not exist and it is theoretically possible for a Polish Islam free from Arab cultural influence to arise in the future:

> Because Islam generally isn't uniform everywhere. The culture is diverse even though certain assumptions are common. Islam could Africanise and mill it through its calques, so why can't we and why should we pretend to be Arabs or anyone else? (Marysia)

Similarly to several other converts, Faustyna believes that Polish Islam is being 'Arabised' predominantly in the top-down direction, by the Muslim League which is supposed to be multicultural, but its practices are those of 'Arabising' the Polish *ummah*:

> And of course, it is obvious that there have never been any pierogi there, because that would of course be some heresy, right, to serve pierogi at a mosque? They must all be some Arab dishes, Turkish or Chechen ones. Well, and I have this feeling that, that the League is so powerful that those people who'd like to change something, converts in particular, give up at a certain point. They don't have any strength left. (Faustyna)

Another prerequisite for the existence of a Polish Islam for our respondents is the converts' power in decision-making processes and participation in organising the life of the Polish *ummah*. Faustyna is one of those who speak of a lack of a Polish voice in the League, an organisation which, according to Maja, 'has appropriated the space of Polish Islam':

> What I'm missing is, so to speak, a Polish section. This Polish section is simply Arabising in many fields and I think this shouldn't be. And nobody really allows it, there's no Polish [Islam]. (...) (Faustyna)

For Faustyna, who used to be an activist before, the cultural and religious Arabisation of Polish Islam is an obstacle which prevents her from working for the benefit of the community. She left because she had felt her voice did not count, 'due to the Arab men's behaviour (...) we were meant to be decorations' (Maja). Similarly to Maja, Aleksandra, Pamela, Franciszka and others, also having previously worked for the cause of Polish Islam, speak of their disappointment with inability to speak out in their own umma. Polish activists are only:

> 'pale faces' supposed to legitimise Muslim League's activity with their presence, but are not allowed to speak for themselves. All the intellectuals have left because they had only been used for editing texts in Polish (...) and women activists are used to make sandwiches and clean the mosque, like the ladies who decorate altars [in Polish Catholic churches], it also looks good on the outside, 'cause that's supposed to be equality. (Maja).

According to Faustyna, it is necessary for Polish Islam to 'cut the umbilical cord' from the Muslim League. The organisation, in her and other converts' (Aleksandra, Maja, Pamela) opinion is Arabising Polish Islam, curbing its development and not allowing anyone except the (Arabic) leadership, afraid of a plurality of opinions. Polish Islam should be part of European Islam and model itself on Western Europe, not the Middle East:

> (...) there are, I think, a few learned gentlemen, but (...) they are tightly restrained (...) by the League (...) and do not want to free themselves from the restraints. Until this changes, until there are women educated in this respect (...) And I'm not talking about being educated (...) in Arab countries, because (...) Islam is very much connected with the culture, (...) I don't know, maybe France or England (...) I think that at a certain moment there will be the critical mass, the fatigue, there will be the accumulation (...) of discontent and persons who will think, anyway, that this is not the way, and will want to implement a vision of Islam different from the Arabic one in their lives, and all that will pour out somewhere and maybe one more Islamic association will form. (Faustyna)

Angelika perceives the situation in Polish Islam from an entirely different perspective, finding the diversity of opinions in Polish Islam to be its weakness. In her opinion, a remedy for the 'theological chaos' of the Polish *ummah* would be a charismatic scholar or imam of undisputed authority, who has not appeared so far. Such a person would serve as a source of cohesion for Muslims of different affiliations and introduce common standards. Maja thinks it is difficult to create a community with such a small number of individuals, each of whom has their own highly individualistic approach to religious matters:

> What I can see (…) is lack of knowledge, (…) everybody enters, takes what they want and leaves. (…) It is better in England, because they can at least have some micro communities, some social contacts, religious authorities can form, while here it is all atomised, people are free electrons. (Maja)

The opinion of the 'chaos in Polish Islam' is also shared by Marysia. She describes the Polish *ummah* even more critically, as a concentration of exceptions to the rule:

> these are people who are all such exceptions to the rule, a concentration of exceptions to the rule, it is like: "Oh, you're here. Cool. Come join us then. Oh, you too, come on in then". Everybody's an exception, allegedly they're all the same, but in reality everybody's different. I have also met so many Muslims who were approaching their faith so differently that I doubt that there is such a thing as our Polish *ummah*. I do not think that such a thing exists, particularly since a large part of this *ummah*, in inverted commas, of ours are Arabs living here. (Marysia)

A growing number of Muslim immigrants, noted in particular by respondents living in Warsaw, complicates the image of Polish Islam seen as increasingly chaotic:

> Warsaw has got quite a few mosques now and horrible divisions have appeared with them, especially that Wilanów and the League in Ochota are places where anyone can go (…), but over time, a few national mosques have been established as well. There is the Turks' mosque, there is a mosque for those Caucasians, (…) and allegedly there are things said there that give you cystic fibrosis (…) I have never been there, but reportedly women are not allowed and bad things are happening there (…) (Aleksandra)

Another respondent who is sceptical about the feasibility of a Polish Islam is Patrycja. What appeals to her is the idea of an Islam above ethnic and cultural differences, a clear message addressed to a multi-ethnic mass of believers. Polishness, similarly to other forms of cultural expression, is but a nice addition:

> I think there is no Polish Islam. I think that there are Polish Muslims, who have their culture, there are Muslims who come here from different countries and also partially enter into this culture, but (...) also have their background. This is actually proof that Islam is super universal. It can look really differently and have different approaches like that. However, it is not a problem for us that we stand for prayer in one row and we are doing the same in the same language and that is what unites us at that moment. (...) Sometimes Polish Muslims like such gadgets with Polish folklore elements or some white-and-red hijabs for Independence Day, those symbols of the Kruszyniany mosque, i.e. a mosque which looks like a small wooden church etc. They don't have to eat chicken with rice as it's done everywhere in Asia (...) There is the question (...) of how much important the ethnicity is for them. (Patrycja)

Our respondents rather advocate for a Polish Islam to emerge rather than state that this has already happened. Nonetheless, many of them observe a definite discrepancy between the aims and lived experiences of Polish Muslims for whom blending into an imaginary, cosmopolitan *ummah* would be a road to nowhere.

### 72 Sects and Uber-Muslims

Discovering a diversity of opinions and currents leaves new Muslims anxious. Surprised by the theological richness of Islam, they set off in search of 'pure sources' "instead of settling for one of the many cultural expressions born Muslim term Islam" (Roald, 2004, p. 113). One of the converts' problems is not being rooted in the network of Muslim teachings and education, which could be analysed as 'a westernisation of Islam' consisting of 'fragmentation of religious authority and the pluralization of Islamic knowledge' (Noor, 2017, p. 94). This pluralisation is caused not only by authorities (whom to deem such an authority remaining a most disputable issue) but also by the Muslim community as a whole.

If a new Muslim does not have earlier knowledge of the diversity of Islam derived from academic or popular-scientific sources (Aleksandra, Pamela, Maja, Marysia), initially she will usually treat the first interpretations of Islam she encounters as the only and binding ones. Then, there is the stage of learning about the multitude of currents within Islam. One of the reactions is discarding this diversity and accepting the attitude expressed in the call for "one Islam", an incredibly popular view on the Polish Internet, which usually constitutes a shutdown of any discussion, used by those who wish to exclude all opinions except their own.

It is difficult to establish to what extent Polish Muslims lack knowledge about the diversity of currents and opinions, and the functioning of Muslim law and legal schools. This is because our respondents do not constitute a representative group – they are individuals possessing substantial knowledge about their religion and willing to expand it. However, the observation of Internet discussions suggests that the ideas of diversity of opinions and the lack of a central authority are not commonly known. Suffice it to say that one of the attitudes observed with high frequency is treating fatwas as final legal verdicts.

Not moving beyond the stage described above and the bullying-like pressure young converts are subjected to are the primary obstacles for further religious development:

> The Prophet says that there are 72 groups and only one of them is going to go to paradise, but this is just one group and this narrative is so terribly (...). This narrative used by certain groups is so strong that it seems that only their vision is such a vision of pure Islam, and a person who has [just] accepted Islam is just so susceptible. She wants to live well, she doesn't quite know how yet, wants to take on a lot from the start, well, and this vision, that there is just this one straight road and the only true one is just like that ... and if such a person enters into this narrative at the very beginning, then it will be difficult for her to open up to new things. I was entering into such a narrative because it seemed the only thing [available]. It is so available on the net, in such a prevailing amount, that it seems that it is just the truth. (Patrycja)

Some of our respondents represent the group of converts who deny the existence of schools and currents, which we estimate to be quite a large one. They identify as "simply Muslims, following the Qur'an and the Sunna". According to Roald (2010, p. 113), numerous Scandinavian Muslim women rejects legal schools, wanting to follow the Qur'an and the Sunna exclusively. In her view, this is "a consequence of their being faced by a multitude of Islamic expressions" and "this methodology is used by new Muslims of various trends but with different results due to differences in outlook" (2010, p. 114).

> I know there are different schools, but (...) I wouldn't describe myself as a follower of any of them. I follow the Qur'an and the Sunna, I listen to scholars, but to ones from various schools. So I'd go for saying that I'm rather [just] a Muslim (...) not to go astray somewhere, not to encounter a bad source (...) I am just a Muslim. (Ewelina)

> Well, I mostly follow what the Qur'an says. Then I reach (...) for what there is in the Sunna and (...) After all, the Prophet (may God's blessing be upon him) was also explaining, giving some kind of fatwas, also explaining the Qur'an, so this is what I follow. What is most important for me is one of the hadiths, not to be too radical in religion, because that doesn't lead to anything good either, right? So I choose what I feel is good (...) I think that I'm simply a Muslim, I do know that Muslims are divided into the Sunni, the Shia and so on. (Cecylia)

> (...) frankly speaking, when I ask anyone who they are, they say they're just Muslims and I like such an approach, and actually I don't know anything about schools. When I'm reading about something, if something is based in the Prophet's Sunna or in the Qur'an, if it is logical, I accept it, and if not, I keep searching and I just try to, kinda engage my own thinking. If something doesn't suit me, then, if it's some fatwa that we don't have to stick to, I reject it then, and that's it, so I think I'm just a Muslim. (Angelika)

Maria, who lives in the UK, clearly perceives the diversity of Islam in negative terms, finding it rather a burden for the faithful stemming from cultural and regional differences:

> the issue of various mosques (...) It's not even about the background, but about the sects and factions in Islam. For example, here we have Sunni Muslims, but there are 4 schools, so one mosque follows the Hanafi one, another mosque follows the Shafi'i one, (...) now everybody goes to their own mosque because the teachings are a little different. They pray differently, there aren't many differences, but there are the small ones, and you just won't find yourself in a mosque where they're doing everything differently. These are such things that it's difficult to get over them and then you sometimes begin to get lost. For example, is it me who is praying

> the wrong way, or them? If you haven't spent some part of your life studying Islam and the differences between the *madhabs*, (…) this is terribly confusing, very. (…) then there are still again the stupid divisions into sects, (…) it's often about where they came from. (…) I think that it's quite a cultural and denominational mix, because there are terribly many of those factions when you start reading about how this Islam is divided. (…) There's so much of it that you can go mad. Especially in England, there are such mosques that it's just a different Islam, it's a shock. (Maria)

In Aleksandra's view, such an attitude signifies negating a complex reality and yielding to an illusion of simplicity and clarity.

> There are people who are saying that they are some kind of uber-Muslims and that the division into the Sunni and the Shia and all the derivatives is a later one and that the Prophet and his companions only had one Islam. You need to discover and perform your role in anything and anywhere yourself. (…) a large part of converts would like to create such a niche for themselves and enter into such a role. Because this is very simple, (…) the illusion that the world may be simpler. (…) such a longing for a community, isn't that the same? Because now you have some 20 types of cereals to choose from at the shop and you don't know which to choose, and there used to be just one and people were happy. (Aleksandra)

A diversity of opinions is perceived as a potential trigger for conflicts and source of *fitnah*:

> I used to try to explore the four schools, but I would find different things suiting me in each of them. I also don't listen to speakers, as each has some other position and this kinda messes with my head. It was the same when there were quarrels among sisters, in some discussions (…) because few people are able to have a discussion, it often finished with some quarrel, because nobody could respect another person's opinion, because somebody listens to a different speaker, somebody follows a different school, when someone else is different, this is bad. So, all in all, I try to keep such things that I like for myself. (Franciszka)

> When you want to push your opinion forward as the only one and shut others' mouths, or keyboards, you will shout that there is one Islam and you can't make *fitnah*. A multiplicity of opinions – it scares people! (Maja)

According to many of our respondents, the Muslim League, a religious organisation converts belong to, not only fails to educate new Muslims about the diversity of Islam, but also pushes forward the idea of 'one Islam' in various ways.

> They all keep saying that there is one Islam, but it is diverse after all, so I'd like to learn in Poland how I am to join this religion with being a Pole, and not just draw from Arab culture. Why should a bearded Saudi man be telling me about the things he knows partially from a customary and cultural perspective while this is not a religious approach? (Franciszka)

> An Islam from the sacristy, remnants of Catholicism. The patterns of, you know, the parish priest, this rather unequal relation, a hierarchical one. (…) Many people also have no idea of what authority in Islam looks like, so that imam, some scholar etc. they're quite unfortunately mistaken for the priest. (…) There's a kind of court arising from that. (Maja)

The anxiety resulting from lack of centralised authority and multiplicity of opinions forces the new Muslim either to undertake the time-consuming effort of learning about the differences or, which might seem a more 'economical' option, to accept one interpretation as the only right one. A dose of distrust seems justified in such context: "On the Internet, you don't know who it really is. There are various sects publishing [content] out there. (…) I am just a Muslim. I don't like sects." (Daria)

Similar to individuals who are against defining their religiousness in a manner more precise than 'Muslim', Anna, who chose Islam for its 'simplicity, universalism and spirituality', finds it difficult to define herself:

> I wouldn't like to choose a label, but I'd rather go for it than say I'm a Sunni. I generally identify with Islam simply more than with Sunnism. I used to say I am a Sunni, but rather because I am not a Shi'a. However, I later decided that I did not need the label. I prefer to describe myself as a Muslim generally, rather a progressive one, but I am also interested in Sufism, it is closer to me. (Anna)

### Sufism

Unlike in Poland, in Western countries the road for Sufi Islam, and sometimes for Islam in general, was paved by the so-called 'Western Sufism', which originated in the late 19th century as a result of changes in European religious life and mores (Sedgwick, 2016). An influx of immigrants helped transplant branches of traditional Sufi orders. These were subsequently joined by converts, making their first step towards Islam in general (van Niewkerk, 2006; Poston, 1992; Yarosh, 2018). Interest in Sufism and its popularisation in Western societies intensified with the coming of the 'Age of Aquarius', with its search for Oriental spirituality, when thousands of young people headed for the East seeking the meaning of life. According to Dutton (1999, p. 163), Sufism is "(...) one of the main points of entry to Islam, especially to contemporary European and Americans".

Jawad claims that "Sufism, as the core of Islam, encompasses what is the most attractive for converts to Islam. She states that Sufism 'has contributed to the process by which Islam is made (...) acceptable (...) way of life." (Jawad, 2006, p. 154). Sufism is particularly significant in conversions of women from the Western world. According to Jawad, Sufi orders' adepts in Western countries are in particular women belonging to the higher classes, drawn to Islam by the spiritual values which Sufism has espoused. It speaks through emphasising the feminine side of spirituality and the womanly/maternal aspects of God and God's relations with humans (Jawad, 2006, pp. 154–160).

Poland, which was part of the Eastern bloc at the height of the Age of Aquarius, was either bypassed by all the above processes entirely, or affected by them only to a minimal extent. The interest in Buddhist and Hinduist traditions was extremely niche, while the popularity of the hippie culture was much smaller than in the West (Karczewski, 1992; Kosior, 1997; Krajewska, 2013; Kubiak, 1992, 1997; Tracz, 2012, 2014, 2018; Libiszowska-Żółtkowska, 2003; Sipowicz, 2015).

Although there are no more obstacles precluding effective cultural communication nowadays, the share of the Sufi current in Polish Islam is very modest. It has only been within the last few years that we have been able to speak of a presence of Sufi elements in popular culture (popular Turkish historical drama series *Ertugrul*; in 2015 the Barbelo publishing house began publishing a Polish translation of the *Masnavi* poem by Jalal ad-Din Rumi, with two volumes published so far; memes quoting Rumi's poetry began appearing on Facebook).

The only form of Sufi organisation has been the activity of Andrzej Saramowicz and the Polska Fundacja Sufich im. Dżelaladdina Rumiego [Jalal ad-Din Rumi Polish Sufi Foundation] he founded in 2012. Andrzej Saramowicz learnt about the Sufi movement during the time he spent in the West. He is a student of sheikh Hazrat Azad Rasool from India and the master of a branch of the Naqshbandiyah order. In spite of the activity and efforts the Foundation put into spreading knowledge about Sufi mysticism, as yet the idea of Sufi Islam has not become a popular one in Poland. The Foundation failed to reach Polish Muslims, many of whom were critical or sceptical about its activity, deeming it a non-Muslim group. The above situation was largely caused by the founder himself, who said publicly that he and his family were also practising Catholics and criticised Polish Muslims women wearing hijabs. As for those members of the Polish *ummah* who were searching for new spiritual paths, the Foundation helped them learn about Sufi practices and systematise their knowledge of the topic.

Thus, the influence of the Foundation's activity on Polish Muslims and their attitude to Sufism remains minimal. The influence on the non-Muslims participating in the meditation meetings organised by the Foundation might not be of much greater significance. The persons who accept Islam during the meetings rarely join the Polish *ummah*. Their interactions usually remain limited to the meditation group and they themselves remain 'ephemeral' converts.

The last 30 years of sociocultural changes in Poland has also resulted in a departure from traditional religion and an interest in new forms of spirituality typical for New Age. 'Enlightenment seekers shopping for different religious alternatives' (Yarosh, 2018) in Poland might arrive at the Zachodni Zakon Sufi w Polsce, branch of the Inayati Order, related to Hazrat Inayat Khan. Officially active in Poland since 1989 and registered in 1991, the group does not identify as an Islamic one, but as a secular one, open for everyone regardless of their religion.

The last few years of interest in new forms of spirituality has also resulted in (very chaotic, to be precise) mentions of Sufism in various online publications concerned with broadly understood esoterism.

The decades-long fascination with Sufi spirituality experienced by masses seeking their own way in the Western world is quantitatively different from the less-than-modest interest in Sufism in Poland. However, one factor they seem to have in common is the relatively low number of converts to Islam whose interest began with Sufism compared with other Islamic movements. Descriptions of this disproportion in the Western world can be found in Smith (2009), Hermansen (2000) or Yarosh (2018).

The absence of Sufism in Polish Islam results not only from lack of a lively tradition, but also from a specific discourse arising from Salafi ideas. This discourse has led to Sufi practices being associated with such concepts as *shirk* or *bid'a*. Due to constant repetition, the associations are now at work even in persons unaffiliated with the Salafi movement. Because of inadequate translation of the term from English, Sufism is also called *sekta*, Polish for 'sect' on the Polish Internet. Even though the dictionary meaning of the term in Polish is 'a faction of a religion; also: a group of people concentrated around a leader, with their own religion', its meaning implied in colloquial Polish is 'a dangerous and organised group of heretics', with strong negative connotations, thus closer to a cult. Another term used to refer to Sufism on the Polish Internet is *dewiacja*, Polish for 'deviation'. Its negative connotations are just as strong as those of *sekta* and, even though its dictionary meaning is 'a significant departure from norm in behaviour, actions or thinking', it is predominantly used in the meaning of sexual deviation. Sufi practices are condemned by Internet users as non-Muslim, also due to their alleged sources in other traditions (Persian or Indian) and religions (Buddhism, Hinduism, etc.).

We have learnt that there are several women practising Sufism who follow particular *tariqas* and several individuals interested in Sufism among Muslim Internet groups users. Nonetheless, their experience is absent from the online discourse, which might result from their fear of criticism or being misunderstood. Most of them had moved abroad permanently and came into contact with Sufi practices during their stay in Muslim or Western European countries, sometimes drawing inspiration from practising husbands and their families. As Salafis, they may experience tribal stigma inside the umma but they can use their affiliation as a means of managing the spoiled identity with non-Muslims to lessen to stigma of being Muslim.

So it was in Danuta's case. Her biography, family history and interests were connected to a pluralistic understandings of faith. Raised in a family of Catholics who actively participated in the life of the Church, she also came into contact with Judaism and Protestantism in her extended family and neighbourhood. Her further studies and religious searches revolved around Judaism and Hinduism. She came into contact with Sufi practices during her stay in India and Muslim countries, before she accepted Islam. Interaction with Andrzej Saramowicz allowed her to organise her knowledge about various forms of Sufism ("There are so many sectarian factions here"). When she moved to the UK after converting to Islam, she began practising moderate Salafism together with her husband. However, she began to gradually lean back towards Sufism. The doubts she had originated from anxiety about both her own motivations and the opinion about Sufism common among Muslims, yet she eventually found mystic Islam to meet her needs best:

> While I was reading, I already knew that Sufism was closest to me [because of earlier religious experiences]. And I was a little afraid. And I was afraid because of my husband. Sufism is not popular among Muslims, because

it is a very spiritual and mystical version of Islam. And mysticism is often considered sinful because it adds even more variations. And this growing up to Sufism, am I really so mystical or do I [just] want to pretend to be a saint. But I decided that if I don't try and if I'm not honest with myself, I'll never find it out. And I'll keep searching and be mistaken. Nothing will be perfect for me, so I'm saying OK, I know my limitations, some of those earthly things that are tying me up, but I want to and I will strive for that. (...)

[People] will expect that you behave in this way or that. I want to be above it. I have one aim, and it is the aim of finding God. And I would like my life to be devoted to this aim, as Sufism has it. This is also taken from Hinduism, I heard it in some lecture somewhere, (...) that we are here, in this woeld, there are multiple diseases, and there is a suitable medicine for each disease. And religions are also those medicines. (...) This is something I take from Hinduism, because I think that we all are souls. And because we identify with different things, ideas, various problems arise. We must accept ourselves as souls. A soul which wants to find God. And what others are doing does not interest me at all. I have chosen my way, I am going to God. And this exactly is Islam for me. (Danuta)

Living in Poland, Maja had certain theoretical knowledge about Sufism, yet she never found it interesting until a certain moment. She surprised herself when she suddenly developed the interest in what she had earlier perceived as 'esoteric nonsense'. Her doubts were caused by theological issues. After a certain time, practising in Poland was no longer sufficient for her and later she had the opportunity of participating in one of the orders' practices during her stay in the UK.

After so many years (...) it came to me in life, as if of itself. (...) my Islam (...) was evolving, I had this lightly Salafi approach. (...) and I became interested in this Sufism somewhat suddenly (...) There were the two basic obstacles (...) I've been reading quite a lot about it, I'm about 80 per cent convinced. The theological obstacle, because all the time I had been troubled by the issue of whether *wasila*, i.e. the Prophet's intermediacy, is possible, and whether certain elements really aren't *shirk*. It is also difficult for me, as a person of left-wing views, to accept the political quietism and the rather right-wing inclination common among Sufi orders. (...) There is also the issue related to psychology, it is difficult to overcome, because (...) there is the master, so something I had run away from. (...) (Maja)

Engaging in Sufi practices also means an opportunity of satisfying one's aesthetic needs related to religious practices:

> I listen to music, I love music, I couldn't live without music. Poetry is important to me as well. And here's another nod towards Sufism. Sufism is simply above it all, it allows you to rejoice, also in culture, and I need it. This is so this-worldly, but I like it. In another dimension of Islam, you aren't supposed to listen to music. (Danuta)

Living in Poland, Anna had no opportunity of meeting anyone from Sufi circles. However, similarly to Danuta, thanks to her spiritual interests and earlier religious experiences (her own Buddhist ones and those reported by people she knew), she began practising Islam from *dhikr* and meditation:

> The way I meditate is that I like to sit down, listen to *dhikr* and repeat (...) *dhikr* was my first form of prayer, that was my salat. Because that was actually what my Islam came from. From Sufism, and not from something else. I think that it was proceeding rather parallelly. I converted to Islam for rather universalist reasons. (Anna)

Danuta had an insight into the everyday aspect of Sufi practices thanks to her family relations and attempted to approach the topic of Sufism in an unbiased manner. She justifies her rejection of the idea using both rational and emotional reasons. As it was in Maja's case, there are certain theological and psychological issues which make her hesitate:

> I have used various sources on Islam. I tried, for example [to learn] about Sufism (...) The way X [a member of the respondent's family living abroad] was acting, what she is telling, what hadiths she quotes, that was just a tiny bit unbelievable for me, and this Sufism reminds me a tiny bit of Christian mysticism. It also reminds me that there's the sheikh, whom you entrust with your life and your decisions and it just makes you think of a Catholic priest. So, I just don't have trust in this path in Islam. I'd rather prefer those Wahhabis, who want to follow a straight path without those human additions, and in my opinion this Golden Chain in Sufism is kinda far-fetched. (Danuta)

Sufis among our respondents are overrepresented in comparison to the estimated proportion of Sufis in the Polish *ummah*. Moreover, the narratives of

Sufism in the online *ummah* are different from those from the interviews with our respondents. The difference between the Western and the Central European experiences makes it difficult to speak of a parallel between the Polish and the Western interest in Sufism. In Poland, Sufism is an intermediate stage or a final one, arrived at after many years, rather than a point of departure. The low popularity of Sufism and the relatively low popularity of Salafism (particularly of the radical version), the two currents representing opposite ends of the orthodoxy spectrum, might result not as much from lack of sources as from lack of a social background – both are difficult to practise alone or in a small group. Therefore, Polish converts interested in Sufism are most likely to learn and practise this form of Islam abroad.

## Conclusions

Presented here problems with affiliations highlight strategies of managing spoiled identity. In most cases, Polish converts to Islam follow a path which leads through a usually unconscious interest in Salafism. The 'unconscious' Salafism results from a lack of knowledge about the traditions and diversity of Islam. The ideal quoted by many converts is 'pure Islam', free from 'cultural additions' which ostensibly define born Muslims' faith. There are multiple factors contributing to the popularity of Salafism in the initial phase of conversion. Some of them are the active presence of Salafi missionaries on the Polish Internet and the clarity of the current's message, the latter particularly appealing to those whose first religion was Catholicism. The confrontation of the radical new rules with the (lack of) opportunity for their application in everyday life often ends with a crisis. We can observe differences between Polish converts living in their homeland and those who immigrated to the United Kingdom (more about Polish Muslims in the UK in Chapter 3). For Muslims living in Poland, this stage comes rather quickly. This is because due to the small number of Muslims in Poland and the resulting lack of a support group one could belong to, the homogenous character of the Polish society, and the widely spread Islamophobia. In these conditions, the new Muslims quickly observe the inadequacy of Salafism in the Polish reality. Of a significant importance might be the fear of rejection and breaking family and friendship bonds, and losing sense of security and social position. For many women, a true breakthrough comes with a stay in the UK, where they can learn how diverse Islam is and how different British Islam is from the 'theoretical' Islam they know from Poland. Some of the converts living abroad remain Salafis not only because of the significantly greater ease of practice, but also because of the freedom they experience thanks to the social void they find themselves in as immigrants, far from their families and compatriots.

Such crises are nearly absent from the narratives to be found on social media, Polish *ummah's* main meeting place. This indicates the largely self-made character of the converts' online discourse. Despite the immense role it plays in the life of the Muslim community, the Internet is perceived as a hostile space where the main activity consists in power play and judging others. It is for the fear of the above attitudes that the converts who have already been through the initial stage of infatuation with purist Islam avoid sharing their views or doubts online. Thus, many groups become places where new converts are trying to proselytise to popularise Salafi rules. They are commonly venues for fierce arguments about the 'accurate' understanding of Islam. It is common for the whole *ummah* to be described as 'judgmental', hence many converts speak of sharing their experiences and religious realisations only in a circle of sisters they are close with.

If the crisis does not end with rejection of Islam, the first option, more common in converts residing in Poland, is finding oneself in one's own version of Islam, which is an 'Islam of the centre', adjusted to the needs defined by living in the Polish society ('potato Islam'). Another option, which is generally less common and found predominantly among emigrants, is moving to the position of a 'mature Salafism'. The attitude of the converts living in Poland who find themselves in the Islam of the centre does not require the support of a group. It can be practised individually and does not collide with their social roles. Some of the converts postulate the existence of a Polish or European Islam, which would combine Islamic ethical values with European human rights and/or Polish cultural traditions, to emphasise their separateness from the Muslims of Arab descent residing in Poland.

Several respondents interested in politics or social issues merge their views with Islam after conversion. Most of our respondents' views could be (quite broadly) described as left-wing-liberal. Most women identify as Muslim feminists, while interest in environmental issues is quite niche. Several respondents also speak of inclusive Islam, which includes various traditions and currents. Progressive Muslims constitute a small percentage, and their views make them feel quite estranged from the Polish *ummah*. Those interested in Sufism constitute a similarly niche group, as Polish Muslims have no opportunity to engage in Sufi practices due to lack of such tradition. Some respondents are also uninterested in Sufism due to the ubiquitous Salafi message which excludes the Shia' and the Sufi. It was only a stay abroad or their own research that led a handful of our respondents to become interested in Sufism.

## References

Allievi, S. (1998). *Les convertis à l'Islam: les nouveaux musulmans d'Europe*. L'Harmattan.

Bourque, N. (2006). How Deborah became Aisha. In K. van Nieuwkerk (Ed.). *Women embracing Islam. Gender and conversion in the West* (pp. 233–249). University of Texas Press.

van Bruinessen, M. (2011). Producing Islamic Knowledge in Western Europe: Discipline, Authority, and Personal Quest. In M. van Bruinessen & S. Allievi (Eds.). *Producing Islamic knowledge: transmission and dissemination in Western Europe* (pp. 1–27). Routledge.

Dutton, Y. (1999). Conversion to Islam: the Qur'anic paradigm. In. Ch. Lamb & M. Darroll Bryant (Eds.) Religious conversion: Contemporary practices and controversies (pp. 151–165). Bloomsbury.

Goffman, E. (1963). *Stigma – Notes on the Management of Spoiled Identity*. Simon and Schuster.

Górak-Sosnowska, Katarzyna. (2015). Between Fitna and the Idyll. Internet forums of Polish female converts to Islam, HAWWA. *Journal of Women of the Middle East and the Islamic World*, 13(3), 344–362.

Hermansen, M. (2007). Hybrid Identity Formations in Muslim America: The Case of American Sufi Movements. *The Muslim World*, 90(1–2): 158–197.

Inge, A. (2016). *The Making of a Salafi Muslim Woman. Paths to Conversion*. Oxford University Press.

Jawad, H. (2006). Female conversions to Islam. The Sufi paradigm. In K. van Nieuwker (Ed.). *Women embracing Islam. Gender and conversion in the West* (pp. 153–171). University of Texas Press.

Karczewski, Leszek (1992). Buddyzm japoński i tybetański w Polsce. *Przegląd Religioznawczy*, 163(1), 79–95.

Kosior, K. (1997). Buddyzm w Polsce, *Nomos*, 18–19, 189–198.

Krajewska, M. (2013). Dżinsy, t-shirt i mnisie szaty. O recepcji buddyzmu w Polsce. *Humaniora. Czasopismo Internetowe*, 2(2), 123–132.

Kubiak, A. E. (1992). Wspólnota świadomości Kryszny w Polsce. *Przegląd Religioznawczy*, 163(1), 97–116.

Kubiak, A. E. (1997). *Delicje i lewa ręka Kryszny. Kreacja i ewolucja ruchu Hare Kryszna w Polsce*. IFiS PAN.

Libiszowska-Żółtkowska, M. (2003). *Religijność konwertytów nowych ruchów religijnych*. Wydawnictwo UMCS.

Noor, S. (2017). *Creating a Female Islamic Space Piety, Islamic knowledge and religious authority among Born-Muslims and converts to Islam in the Netherlands and Belgium*. Doctoral diss. Radboud University.

Özyürek, E. (2018). Giving Islam a German face. In K. van Nieuwkerk (ed.). *Moving In and Out of Islam* (pp. 107–129). University of Texas Press.

Özyürek, E. (2015). *Being German, Becoming Muslim. Race, Religion, and Conversion in the New Europe*. Princeton University Press.

Pickthall, M. M. (1930). *The Meaning of the Glorious Koran. An Explanatory Translation*. Alfred A. Knopf.

Pilger-Strohl, M. (2011). Authority. In: K. von Stuckrad (Ed.). *The Brill Dictionary of Religion*. Brill.

Pirický, G. (2018). Merging Culture with Religion: Trajectories of Slovak and Czech Muslim Converts since 1989. In K. van Nieuwkerk (Ed.). *Moving In and Out of Islam* (pp. 107–129). University of Texas Press.

Poston, L. (1992). *Islamic da'wah in the West. Muslim missionary activity and the dynamics of conversion to Islam*. Oxford University Press.

Račius, E. (2013). A 'virtual club' of Lithuanian converts to Islam. In T. Hoffmann & G. Larsson (Eds.). *Muslims and the New Information and Communication Technologies. Notes from an Emerging and Infinite Field*, (pp. 31–47). Springer.

Rambo, R. (1993). *Understanding religious conversion*. Yale University Press.

Roald, A. S. (2001). *Women in Islam: The Western Experience*. Routledge.

Roald, A. S. (2004). *New Muslims in the European Context: The Experience of Scandinavian Converts*. Brill.

Roald, A. S. (2010). Multiculturalism and Religious legislation in Sweden. In H. Moghissi & H. Ghorashi. *Muslim Diaspora in the West: Negotiating Gender, Home and Belonging* (pp. 55–72). Ashgate.

Roald, A. S. (2006). The Shaping of Scandinavian "Islam". Converts and Gender Equal Opportunity. In K. van Nieuwkerk (Ed.). *Women embracing Islam. Gender and conversion in the West* (pp. 48–70). University of Texas Press.

Sedgwick, M. (2016). *Western Sufism: From the Abbasids to the New Age*, Oxford: Oxford University Press.

Shanneik, Y. (2011). Conversion and Religious Habitus: The Experiences of Irish Women Converts to Islam in the Pre-Celtic Tiger Era. *Journal of Muslim Minority Affairs*, 31(4): 503–517.

Sipowicz, K. (2015). *Hipisi w PRL-u*. Cyklady.

Smith, J. I. (2010). *Islam in America*. Columbia University Press.

Stoica, D. (2011). New Romanian Muslimas. Converted women sharing knowledge in online and offline communities. In K. Górak-Sosnowska (Ed.). *Muslims in Poland and Eastern Europe. Widening the European discourse on Islam*. University of Warsaw.

Tracz, B. (2012). Katowicka ścieżka Zen, *CzasyPismo*, 1(1), 146–157.

Tracz, B. (2014). *Hippiesi, kudłacze, chwasty. Hipisi w Polsce w latach 1967–1975*. Oddział IPN w Katowicach & Wydawnictwo Libron.

Tracz, B. (2018). Zen na poddaszu. Przyczynek do recepcji buddyzmu w Polsce. *Polska 1944/45–1989. Studia i Materiały*, XVI, 203–225.

van Nieuwkerk, K. (2006). Gender, Conversion, and Islam. Online and Offline Conversion Narratives. In K. van Nieuwkerk (ed.). *Women embracing Islam. Gender and conversion in the West* (pp. 1–16). University of Texas Press.

Winter, T. (2000). Conversion as nostalgia: Some experiences of Islam. In. M. Percy (Ed.). *Previous Convictions: Conversion in the Present Day* (pp. 93–111). SPCK.

Wohlrab-Sahr, M. (2006). Symbolizing Distance: Conversion to Islam in Germany and the United States. In K. van Nieuwkerk (Ed.). *Women Embracing Islam. Gender and conversion in the West* (pp. 71–92). University of Texas Press.

Yarosh, O. (2018). Religious authority and conversions in Berlin's sufi communities. In K. van Nieuwkerk (Ed.). *Moving In and Out of Islam* (pp. 179–203). University of Texas Press.

# Conclusions

*Anna Piela, Joanna Krotofil and Katarzyna Górak-Sosnowska*

All of our participants relayed their unique stories where the joys they experienced are intertwined with the sacrifices they had to make. The limitations of academic writing and methodology we employed for this study prohibit us from doing justice to the individual trajectories and presenting these stories in their rich entirety. The re-moulded story presented in this book emphasizes the common threads and shared experiences.

The Polish converts to Islam who participated in our study have embraced and continue to practice a religion that results in attribution of stigma in the Polish society. The difference is neither objectively given, nor complete; rather, it is constantly negotiated and shifting. It is constructed and enacted in discursive and embodied practices. The religious beliefs are compared and juxtaposed with Catholic teachings which represent the heritage religion of most converts and the religion of the Polish majority. In the process the similarities are identified and cherished in the quest for biographical continuity, but the differences are also firmly stated. The moral proscriptions adopted with the new religion are identified, adopted and cultivated with great effort and dedication. They also reinforce the difference palpable in everyday life. In contrast to people around them, the converts refrain from drinking alcohol, adhere to different diet and dress codes, limit their interactions with opposite sex, etc. The practices are effected through bodies and language undergoing reflexive recalibration and adjustment. Some (but not all) Polish converts adopt voluntarily the religious attributes such as the *hijab* that are considered discrediting from the point of view of the normative framework of a modern culture, or, alternatively, a Polish Catholic culture. For them, the embodied habitus is carried into the realm of the political (Göle, 2003, p. 811). For others, it remains strictly private, or becomes creatively blended with the Polish tradition in a process that Wohlrab-Sahr (1999, p. 351) called 'religious syncretism', which lays the foundation for a 'new Polish Islam', different from the immigrant Islam or the indigenous Tatar Islam. Through these practices they often contest what they perceive as the dominant trends in the mainstream culture, although their narratives strongly indicate that Polish Muslim converts transcend the binary oppositions between liberal and conservative views.

Converts to Islam are aware that their individual experiences are shaped by the dominant socio-political framings of Islam. Some of them have experiences of living in the UK, where as part of the multiculturalism policy, Muslim enjoy better political representation and have more established status than in Poland. Although many women in that group agree that Poland is a difficult place to live in for Muslims, they also maintain multiple connections with their home country. They openly challenge Islamophobic discourses and many engage in grassroots work aimed at promoting a positive image of Islam. This task is performed in casual encounters with strangers, as well as in relationships with significant others (including close friends, parents, siblings).

One type of coping strategy stands out as part of the effort to manage challenges resulting from the 'spoiled' Muslim identity – having the support of and sense of belonging gained upon establishing relationships with fellow converts. Although many women have limited opportunities for regular face-to-face interactions with other female converts, occasional gatherings (for example, the weekend gatherings for women organized at mosques and Islamic centres, the Muslim League camps, or smaller meetings in private homes) as well as online interactions provide important source of emotional support, practical advice and guidance. In these groups individual converts are no longer "different", but form a community of shared experience and orientation.

Simultaneously, the converts are faced with navigating ambiguous realities of Polish women who became Muslim. We have found that not only is conversion to Islam in Eastern Europe different than in the West – we also pointed out that Poland is the "odd one out" in Eastern Europe as a conversion context because it is so intensely Catholic. The arcs of conversion are much more anchored in pre-existing faith in (one) God than in more secularised contexts. This has an important implication for "lived" Islam of converts who, as Muslims, often display patterns of behaviour and thinking developed in their earlier lives as practising Catholics, especially in relation to understanding religious authority hierarchically. Those living in Poland are imbricated in cultural and social expectations that imply accommodation of norms inflected by Catholicism; accordingly, they are somewhat forced into a position where they need to actively seek connections between the Islamic tradition and the Polish culture (Krotofil et al., 2021) to be able to argue for the possibility of a Polish Muslim identity. Those living in the UK may practice Islam in visible ways, but are forced into a position of double marginalization, as Muslims and Polish immigrants. Additionally, the convert status may present difficulties in their interactions with some "born Muslims." These challenges are further highlighted by the experiences of those women who move between the two (or more) contexts; they are often in a state of flux, adjusting the form of their practice depending on the "audience." Respondents recognize the dynamic character of social contexts which they inhabit. Oyserman and James (2011, p. 120) argue that "contexts not only make a particular identity salient, they also shape the content and behavioural consequences of identities". Thus, we argue that the Polish Islam is shaped by the pragmatic and creative stance adopted by the majority of our respondents who integrate Polish cultural practices with their new religion, deftly negotiating the meanings of those practices. As one of our respondents aptly pointed, the ways of practicing Islam exist on a continuum, from the invisible, private 'potato Islam' (the potato being the Polish staple food) to 'the Scheherazade complex' (the most visible and externally apparent way of embracing Islam), with many variations in between.

No matter how visible or private their religion, converts continue engaging with the non-Muslim in many social contexts. The women interviewed for this study provided numerous examples demonstrating that converts are not 'all about Islam'. They are able to draw on their citizenship rights, cultural knowledge and linguistic skills to fully participate in the Polish society. Polish Islam is, therefore, the product of developing inclusive identities containing both local and global loyalties, as summarized by a post in the Facebook group 'Islam for Poland': "I am European, I am Polish, I am Muslim and I am very proud of it." As we have demonstrated in our analysis, the creativity and agency are manifest in a whole range of practices, including the 'halalisation' of food and the traditional Polish festive practices, the incorporation of Arabic vocabulary into Polish language and even creation of a hybridised religious language, and offering a vision of Islam as a religion compatible with the Polish culture.

Although concepts such as 'Polish Islam' cannot really escape the double epistemological impasse in research on Islam in Europe highlighted by Fadil (2019), it is an appropriate tool for exploring how particular modes of reasoning, performing and practising Islam emerge locally. "The dual imperative to account for dominant social structures and individual resistance" (Fadil & Fernando 2015, 59) is a long-standing problem in sociology and one that is not easy to overcome. By using the concept of Polish Islam and placing convert's experiences in a particular, dynamically approached socio-cultural and historical landscape, we demonstrate the agency and resistance manifest in converts' efforts to embed their religion in the Polish context. This approach advances the reflection on the relationship between agency and local structures operating in the religious field and offers a more localized understanding of Islam.

To conclude, this book offers the findings of the first systematic study of the lives of Polish female converts to Islam. It documents a religio-social trend, conversion to Islam, in a culturally monolithic country where national identity is sacralised as immutably Catholic, and religion is racialized. Poland is riven by 'platonic Islamophobia' (high levels of hostility to Muslims despite only a small number of Muslims living there; Górak-Sosnowska, 2016), and yet, conversions to Islam are on the rise. Therefore, while on the face of it, the book is about conversions, it also provides a prism for debates on national identity, culture, citizenship and belonging in a unique context of an Eastern European country. The significance of this book is multifold: it consolidates and extends sociological research on Polish Islam; it contributes to bridging the research gap on Eastern European Islam, an entity that still remains largely unaddressed; and pushes the boundaries of conversion theory, taking into account intersecting cultural, former religious, and national backgrounds.

## References

Fadil, N. (2019). The Anthropology of Islam in Europe: A Double Epistemological Impasse. *Annual Review of Anthropology*, 48(1), 117–132.

Fadil, N. & Fernando, M. (2015). Rediscovering the "everyday" Muslim. *Journal of Ethnographic Theory*, 5(2), 59–88.

Göle, N. (2003). The Voluntary Adoption of Islamic Stigma Symbols. *Social Research*, 70(3), 809–828.

Górak-Sosnowska, K. (2016). Islamophobia without Muslims? The case of Poland. *Journal of Muslims in Europe*, 5(2), 190–204.

Krotofil, J., Piela, A., Górak-Sosnowska, K. & Abdallah-Krzepkowska, B. (2021). Theorizing the Religious Habitus in the Context of Conversion to Islam among Polish Women of Catholic Background. *Sociology of Religion*, 82(3), 257–280.

Oyserman, D. & James, L. (2011). Possible Identities. In S. J. Schwartz, K. Luyckx & V. L. Vignoles (Eds.), *Handbook of Identity Theory and Research* (pp. 117–145). Springer.

Wohlrab-Sahr, M. (1999). Conversion to Islam: Between Syncretism and Symbolic Battle. *Social Compass*, 46(3), 351–362.

# Glossary

‘ayn (*‘ayn*)   The evil eye. A traditional belief that individuals can harm other people, animals or objects by looking at them.

Abaya (*‘abāya, ‘abā'a*)   A loose, long-sleeved women garment covering the whole body except the head, feet and hands. Originally worn in Arab countries, nowadays popular amongst Muslim women all around the world.

Adhab al-qabr (*‘aḏāb al-qabr*)   Punishment of the grave. According to some Hadith, sinners are punished in the grave by two angels.

Ahl al-bayt (*ahl al-bayt*)   the smaller of the two major branches of Islam, the Shi‘ah, or the family of prophet Muhammad.

Alhamdulillah (*al-ḥamd lillah*)   literally 'praise be to God', usually used as 'thank God'.

Allah yubarik fik (*Allāh yubārik fik*)   'God bless you', sometimes used as say 'thank you' or as a reply to *mabrook* 'congratulations'.

Allahu a‘alam (*Allāh a‘alam*)   'God knows best', is an Islamic phrase that finds frequent usage in Islamic texts (legal opinions, *tafsirs*, etc.), meaning that only God is all knowing.

Aqiqa (*‘aqīqa*)   tradition of the sacrifice of an animal seven days after a baby is born.

Arkan al-din (*Arkān ad-dīn, Arkān al-islām*)   'Pillars of Islam' the five religious duties: the profession of faith (*šahāda*), prayer 5 times a day (*ṣalā*), the alms tax for benefit the poor and the needy (*zakā*), fasting during the month of Ramadan (*ṣawm*), pilgrimage to Mecca (*ḥaǧǧ*).

Ar-Rahman ar-Rahim (*Ar-Raḥmān ar-Raḥīm*)   '[God] the Most Gracious, the Most Merciful'.

Ashura (*‘Āšūrā'*)   a Muslim holy day observed on the 10th of the month of Muharram. For Sunnis, Ashura is a commemoration of the day when the Red Sea was parted for Musa and his people. This holiday is especially important for the Shi‘ah, as the commemoration of the Battle of Karbala.

Assalamu alaykum wa rahmatullahu wa barakatuhu (*as-salam alaykum wa raḥma Allāh wa barākatuhu*)   'Peace be upon you and God's mercy and blessings'. A Muslim greeting.

Bid‘ah (*bid‘a*)   any innovation that does not originate from the Quran and Sunnah. Modern Islamic movements are particularly invested in popularising this concept as prohibited.

Dabbat al Ard (*Dābbat al-arḍ*)   'The Beast of the Earth', one of the signs of the coming of the Day of Judgement.

Dai (*dā‘ī*)   a person practising Islamic proselytism (*da‘wā*).

Dars (*dars*)   lesson.

## GLOSSARY

**Dawah** (*da'wā*)   the act of calling people to embrace Islam. For some fundamentalist and purist movements within Islam, dawah is considered as one of the most important aspects of their activity.

**Dhikr** (*ḏikr*)   'remembering God' by reciting prayers or litanies (God's names, ritual expressions) practised aloud or silently. *Dhikr* plays a central role in Sufi practices and each Sufi brotherhood has established its own particular *dhikr* to be recited in solitude or during community gatherings.

**Dua** (*du'ā'*)   a prayer of invocation, supplication or request.

**Eid** (*'eid*)   Islamic festival.

**Eid al-Adha** (*'Īd al-'Aḍḥā*, called also *al-'Īd al-Kabīr*)   one of the two main Muslim holidays, celebrated on the 10th day of Dhu al-Hijjah. It marks the culmination of the pilgrimage (*ḥaǧǧ*), and is a commemoration of Ibrahim's sacrifice. During the festival, animals are ritually sacrificed, then the meat is divided equally among the poor.

**Eid al-Fitr** (*'Īd al-Fiṭr*, also called *al-'Īd aṣ-Ṣaġīr*)   one of two main Muslim holidays. Eid al-Fitr marks the end of Ramadan, the month of fasting, and is celebrated in the month of Shawwal.

**Fajr** (*ṣalāt al-faǧr*)   the dawn prayer, one of the five mandatory prayers.

**Fi sabili Allah** (*fī sabīl Allāh*)   'in the path of God', used also in the meaning 'in the cause of God', 'for the sake of God'.

**Galabiyya** (*ǧalābiyya*)   a traditional Egyptian male garment, the term is now used for any loose and long garment worn by Muslim men.

**Ghusl** (*ġusl*)   the major ablution, performed in a state of major ritual impurity, it entails the washing of the entire body.

**Hadith qudsi** (*ḥadīṯ qudsī*)   'holy hadith', a special category of Hadith, whose content is attributed to God but the actual wording is credited to Prophet Muhammad. This category of Hadith enjoy elevated status between Quran and the regular Hadith.

**Hajj** (*ḥaǧǧ*)   the pilgrimage to Mecca, the fifth of the Pillars of Islam which every adult Muslim who is physically and financially able to do, must perform once in a lifetime. It begins on the 7th and ends on the 12th day of Dhu al-Hijjah.

**Halal** (*ḥalāl*)   permissible acts, as opposed to *haram* (forbidden) acts. In common usage, the term is particularly associated with Islamic dietary laws and animal slaughter.

**Hamza** (*hamza*)   a letter in the Arabic alphabet, representing the glottal stop.

**Hanafi** (*ḥanafī, maḏhab Ḥanīfa*)   one of the four Sunni schools of law, with the largest number of followers.

**Haram** (*ḥarām*)   the term means 'forbidden' and may refer to either something sacred and forbidden to access or to an anything evil and forbidden as sinful. In Islamic jurisprudence, *haram* is any act forbidden by God.

**Hasanat** (*ḥasanāt*)    Good deeds, weighed up against believer's bad deeds.
**Haya** (*ḥayā'*)    modesty.
**Hijab** (*ḥiǧāb*)    is a veil worn by certain Muslim women in the presence of any male outside of their immediate family or sometimes by men. It covers the head and chest. Its second meaning is that of more broadly understood modesty that encompasses clothing and behaviour. In the Quran, the term *hijab* is used to refer to a curtain, rather than a headscarf.
**Hijabi**    A woman who wears the Islamic head-covering (*hijab*).
**I'tikaf** (*i'tikāf*)    a practice of a period of staying in a mosque for a certain number of days, spending time praying and reading the Qur'an, especially during the last 10 days of Ramadan.
**Ibadat** (*'ibādāt*)    a part of Islamic jurisprudence – practices concerning the relations between God and humans.
**Iftar** (*ifṭār*)    the evening meal ending the daily Ramadan fast at sunset.
**Ijaz al-Quran** (*i'ǧāz al-Qur'ān*)    the doctrine of inimitability of the Quran, holding that it has a unique, miraculous quality in content and form.
**Imam** (*imām*)    (here) one who leads Muslim worshippers in prayer.
**Iman** (*imān*)    faith.
**Inna lillahi wa ilayhi raji'un** (*inna li-llahi wa ilayhi rāǧi'ūn*)    'Verily, we belong to God and verily to Him do we return'. The phrase used by Muslims upon hearing news about someone's death.
**Inshallah** (*in šā' Allāh*)    'if God wills', 'God willing'. Used by Muslims when talking about the future.
**Jahanna** (*ǧahanna*)    hell.
**Jahiliyya** (*ǧāhiliyya*)    the period preceding the revelation of Islam.
**Janaza** (*ǧanāza*)    funeral.
**Janna** (*ǧanna*)    Paradise.
**Jazaka Allahu hayran** (*ǧazāka Allāh ḫayran*)    'May Allah reward you' Islamic expression of showing gratitude or thanks.
**Jihadi brides**    women who travelled to Syria to live as wives of ISIS combatants in the 'Islamic State' established in Syria in 2013.
**Jumu'ah** (*Ṣalāt al-ǧumu'a*)    the Friday congregational prayer.
**Kafir** (*kāfir*)    a person who disbelieves in God. The term has been understood differently by classical Islamic scholars and modern Islamic movements.
**Khutbah** (*ḫuṭba*)    religious narration, usually this term refers to Friday sermon.
**Kufr** (*kufr*)    an act of unbelief.
**Laylat al-Qadar** (*Laylāt al-Qadar*)    'Night of Power' or 'Night of Destiny'. The night on which the Quran was revealed. It is believed to have taken place on one of the final 10 nights of Ramadan, but the exact date is unknown.

## GLOSSARY

**Masdar** (*maṣdar*)   an Arabic verbal noun.

**Mashallah** (*mā šā' Allāh*)   literally 'what God has willed', a phrase used to express a feeling of awe or beauty and to wish for God's protection from the evil eye.

**Masjid** (*masǧid*)   mosque.

**Mawlid** (*mawlid, mawlid an-Nabī*)   the birthday of the Prophet Muhammad, celebrated on the 12th day of the month of the Rabi' al-Awwal.

**Muamalat** (*muʿāmalāt*)   that which guides the relations between humans. Generally, all aspects of *fiqh* that are not *ibadat* (acts of worship).

**Mufti** (*muftī*)   an Islamic legal scholar who gives a private, legal opinion (*fatwa*) in answer to an inquiry.

**Muhasaba** (*muḥāsaba*)   the retrospection of one's deeds and anticipation of the Last Judgment through self-assessment.

**Munafiq** (*munāfiq*)   a hypocrite in a religious sense.

**Mutah** (*nikāḥ mutʿa*)   a temporary marriage contracted for a limited period. This kind of marriage is practised only by the Twelver Shi'ah.

**Nafs** (*nafs*)   translated as 'psyche', 'ego', 'self' or 'soul'. Contemporary popular understanding of this term is based on the Sufi doctrine, in which *nafs* is considered as the lowest dimension of human soul and identified by believers as the 'ego'.

**Nikah** (*nikāḥ*)   Islamic marriage.

**Niqab** (*niqāb*)   a veil covering the face, worn by some Muslim women, reflecting their interpretation of modest Islamic dress.

**Radiya Allahu anhu/anha** (*raḍiyā Allāh ʿanhu/ʿanha*)   'May God be pleased with him/her', an expression mainly used while mentioning the Companions of the Prophet.

**Rahimahu(ha) Allah** (*raḥimahu(ha) Allāh*)   'May God have mercy on him/her', an expression used while mentioning righteous deceased Muslims.

**Ramadan** (*Ramaḍān*)   the holy month of fasting, the ninth month of the Muslim calendar.

**Sabr** (*ṣabr*)   patience.

**Sahabah** (*Aṣ-ṣaḥāba*)   the companions of the Prophet Muhammad.

**Salafi**   a member of the Salafi movement (*Salafiyya*), whose doctrine is based on the return to the beginnings of Islam, to the traditions of the 'ancestors' (*salaf*), the first three generations of Muslims to practice the ostensibly unchanged, pure form of Islam.

**Salam alaykum** (*as-salām alaykum*)   'Peace be upon you', Islamic greeting.

**Salat** (*ṣalā*)   the daily ritual prayer, one of the five pillars of Islam (*arkan al-Islam*). Five obligatory prayers: *salat al-fajr* (dawn), *al-dhuhr* (midday), *al-ʿasr* (afternoon), *al-maghrib* (sunset), and *al-ʿisha'* (evening).

**Salat al Eid** (*ṣalāt al-ʿĪd*)   Holy Holiday prayers.

**Salat al jumuah** (*ṣalāt al ǧumʿa*)   the Friday congregational prayer.

**Salla Allah alayhi wa sallam** (*ṣallā Allāh alayhi wa sallam*)   'blessings of God be upon Him and grant Him peace', an expression used by Muslims after mentioning the name of the Prophet Muhammad.

**Shafi'i** (*šāfiʿī, maḏhab al-šāfiʿī*)   one of the four Sunni schools of religious law.

**Shahadah** (*šahāda*)   the first of the five Pillars of Islam (*arkan al-Islam*), the Muslim profession of faith: 'There is no god but God; Muhammad is the Prophet of God.' The only thing required to become a Muslim is a sincere recitation of the *shahadah*.

**Sheikh** (*šayḫ*)   Arabic term signifying honourable, middle aged or elderly people. The title can be held by chiefs of tribes, villages and town quarters. In the religious sense, it can be applied to Islamic scholars (*ʿulamaʾ*), heads of religious orders and people who memorized the entire Quran.

**Shia** (*šīʿī*)   member of the less populous of the two major branches of Islam, the Shiʿah (*ahl al-bayt*).

**Shifa** (*šifāʾ*)   healing.

**Shirk** (*širk*)   denial of the oneness of God (*tawhid*), the association of God with other deities, worshipping anything besides God. Both concepts are of special interest for contemporary fundamentalist movements. For some, they became synonymous with any belief or practice not accepted as 'truly Islamic' by a particular sect.

**Subhana Allah** (*subḥāna Allāh*)   'May He be praised', an expression used after mentioning the name of God.

**Subhana wa ta'ala** (*subḥāna wa taʿālā*)   'May He be praised and exalted', an expression used after mentioning the name of God.

**Sufi** (*ṣufī*)   a Muslim practising Sufism (*taṣawwuf*), mystical Islam. Believers seek to know God on the path of love and personal experience.

**Sunni** (*Sunnī*)   member of Sunnism, the larger of the two branches of Islam (Sunnism, *ahl al-Sunna wa al-ǧamāʿa*).

**Ta marbuta** (*ta marbūṭa*)   a variant of the letter *tāʾ* used at the end of a word, mostly marking grammatically feminine gender.

**Taghut** (*ṭaġūṭ*)   concentrating on worship of an entity other than God. In the modern usage, the term can be associated with worshipping tyrannical power.

**Tajweed** (*taǧwīd*)   rules of Qurʾanic recitation.

**Takfir** (*takfīr*)   accusing another Muslim to be an apostate. This concept was broadly discussed by classical Islamic scholars, representing different opinion in this topic. At the end of 20th century using *takfir* became a tool used by some individuals and organizations against political and ideological opponents. The radical 'takfirism', has been utilised by extremists, terrorists, and jihadist organisations.

**Talaq** (*ṭalāq*)   divorce.
**Taraweeh** (*tarāwīḥ*)   special prayers performed in congregation during Ramadan nights. They involve recitation of the Quran and performing many *rakaṯs*.
**Tarbiyyah** (*tarbiyya*)   pedagogy.
**Tawhid** (*tawḥīd*)   the oneness of God, the central concept of Islam, reinterpreted differently by different movements within Islam.
**Ukht** (*uḫt*)   sister.
**Umm al muminin** (*umm al mu'minīn*)   'Mothers of the Believers', the title given to the wives of the Prophet Muhammad.
**Ummah** (*umma, umma al-Islām*)   the collective, global Muslim community.
**Wa alaykum assalam** (*wa alaykum as-salām*)   'and unto you peace', a response to *salam alaykum*.
**Wa iyaki** (*wa iyāki*)   'and to you too', response to *jazaka Allahu hayran*.
**Wasila** (*wasīla*)   in religious contexts, the *tawassul* is the use of an intercession to arrive at or obtain favour of God. The concept has a special importance for Sufi practices.
**Wudu** (*wuḍū'*)   ritual ablution consisting of washing the face, arms, head, nose, ears and feet.
**Zina** (*zinā'*)   fornication.

# Index

Afterlife   139, 201
Alcohol
   abstinence from   59, 111, 117, 171, 205, 240
al-Fatiha   139, 140
Arab
   culture   152, 222, 229
   Muslim activist in Poland   223
   Muslims in Poland   224, 236
Arabic language   25, 136–140, 143, 147–164, 242
Arabisation   161–163, 220–223
Association of Islamic Unity   41, 42, 212

Belonging   72, 81, 89, 96, 152, 210, 235, 243
Biographical continuity   97, 240
Birt, Jonathan   75, 77, 81, 83
Body   25, 169, 170, 171, 240
Boundaries
   cultural   73
   ethnic   73, 82, 84, 90
   religious   73
Bucholtz, Mary and Hall, Kira   135–136
Buddhism   171, 214, 230, 232, 234

Catholicism   2, 34, 73, 94, 137–138, 140, 164, 171–174, 155, 165, 166, 200, 201, 202, 204, 223, 229, 231, 232, 234, 235, 240, 242
Christianity   145, 147, 154, 218, 234
Church   76, 118, 137, 138, 140, 155, 201, 223, 232
Converts to Islam
   and Catholic Church   2, 57, 76, 106, 113, 200–202
   as agents in Polish Islam   161, 201, 222–223, 242, 230–233
   as cultural agents   218, 220
   as everyday explainers   52, 104, 106, 107, 128, 204
   as migrants   1, 4, 23, 24, 45, 54, 72, 79, 82, 93, 94, 97, 241, 206–210, 227–228, 235–236
   demographic profile of   52–57
   family reactions   86, 90, 110–112
   history   43, 163

In Eastern Europe   8, 235
In the West   7, 8, 9
Islamic knowledge (re)producers   201–202, 204, 213–215, 228
   number of   34, 51, 73, 105
   political views   65, 215–216, 233, 236
   position in Muslim organisations   43, 159, 201, 222, 223
   relation to other Muslims   61, 63, 82–87, 205, 241, 218, 220–228
   social activity   1, 3, 60–62, 128

Danecki, Janusz   9, 64, 212
*Daʿwah*   109, 146, 202, 214
Deedat, Ahmad   211–212
*Dhikr*   138, 234
Diet   59, 205, 240
Discredited person   77, 80, 91, 207
Diversity   72–80, 84, 88
Dziekan, Marek   9, 64, 65, 76n, 212

Embodied religious practices   25, 169, 170, 178, 193, 195, 240
Environmentalism   216–217, 236
Ethical and moral self   169, 170, 172, 173, 194
Ethnic minority   74, 77, 86
Europeanness   217–220, 236

Feminist views   12, 15, 16, 26, 56, 57, 65, 77, 174, 212, 216
*Fitnah*   215, 228
Food   59, 117, 121, 124, 169, 170, 181, 184, 185, 191
   Abstaining from   181, 183
Foucault, Michel   169, 195, 197

Goffman, Erving   3, 5, 6, 7, 23, 24, 73, 77, 78, 80, 91, 97, 152, 159, 185, 207
Gender   175, 178, 180

Habitus   200–202
Hadiths   64, 139, 141, 227
*Halal*   181, 184, 185, 190, 191, 201, 208
*Haram*   201, 202, 205, 206

Hijab
    as headscarf   25, 59, 81, 91, 106, 108, 109,
        110, 124, 146, 164, 170, 171, 172, 185, 186,
        187, 188, 189, 191, 192, 194, 205, 208, 231,
        240
    not wearing of   59, 111, 117, 146, 164, 172,
        186, 187, 188, 192, 209
    as modest dress   170, 171, 186, 191, 193
    as modest behaviour   25, 169
Hinduism   171, 230, 232, 233
Holidays   58, 66, 91, 116
Honorifics   137, 150, 152

Identity
    conflict   95, 159–161
    constituting   152
    cultural   71, 152
    denied   162
    essentialized   83
    ethnic   90, 94
    European   217, 219
    inclusive   242
    intersecting   72, 84, 88, 192, 195
    language   159–162
    national   94–97, 242, 163, 220, 221,
        222, 225
    politics   83
    religious   76, 80, 91, 96, 147, 221, 241
    Self-imposed   201
    social   5, 6, 7, 159
    spoiled   1, 46, 71, 78, 96, 152, 159, 166, 174,
        195, 196, 208, 235
i'jaz al-Qur'an (untranslatability of the
    Qur'an)   137, 138
Imam   160, 162, 201, 212, 229
Integration   74, 75, 162, 165
Internet   61, 62, 64, 64, 106, 159, 160, 163, 202,
        204, 207, 209, 210–212, 217, 226, 230,
        232, 235–236
Intersectionality   14, 18, 24, 78, 81, 89, 92
Islam
    diversity   200, 210, 222, 224, 235
    European   218, 219, 223
    lived   72, 81, 84, 96, 241
    mainstream   212
    Polish   205, 206, 213, 240, 242, 243,
        220–225, 230

progressive   219
"proper"   221
"pure"   218, 222, 225, 226, 235
as idealised tradition   210
western   214
"westernisation of"   225
Islamic
    authorities   204, 206, 211–213, 224, 227,
        229, 231–234
    borrowed vocabulary/loan words   136,
        137, 142–161
    dogmas   141, 145, 217
    ethics   137, 141, 145
    knowledge   63–65, 145, 200, 202, 204,
        213, 214, 225, 226, 229
    law   141, 226, 227
    practice   145, 162, 202, 208, 213, 214, 217
    teaching   201, 202, 204, 211–214, 221, 225,
        226, 229
    values   80, 81, 215, 220
Islamophobia   24, 77, 103, 159, 186, 189, 146,
        241, 242
    and national identity   94, 104, 114, 162,
        164, 241
    and the refugee crisis   119, 120
    as microagressions   105, 119
    as violence   119–122
    at school   117, 118
    coping strategies   124–128, 159, 163, 164,
        235, 241, 209, 221
    institutionalised   116
    rural vs. urban   108–109

Judaism   181, 218, 232

Khutba   160, 161, 162

Left-wing   26, 215, 217, 233, 236
Liberalism   26, 215, 217, 236
Linguistic
    anthropology   135
    camouflage   165
    communication   24, 164
    Integration   165
    practices   137, 142
    skills   242
    socialisation   138
    sociocultural   136

Mahmood, Saba   18, 169–170, 193–5
Markowski   143, 144, 145, 147
McGhee, Derek   75, 77, 81, 83
Menk, Ismail Ibn Musa /Mufti Menk   211, 212
Methodology   11–23
Miernik, Arkadiusz   212, 213
Modood, Tariq   74–76
Mogahed, Yasmin   211
Moral
  community   86, 93
  panics   75, 77
Mosque   87–89, 97, 152, 160, 162, 201, 206, 220, 224, 227, 241
Multiculturalism   24, 74, 75, 77, 78, 81
  everyday   72
  failure of   75
  ideology   77
  lived   71, 74, 86, 208, 220–222, 227–228
  political   83
Multicultural
  project   75, 92, 96
  policy   240
Muslim
  feminists   180, 216, 219, 236
  League   40, 41, 42, 51, 159, 161, 212, 222, 223, 224, 229, 241
  Religious Union   34, 40, 42, 159, 162, 217
  scholars   141, 142, 206, 229
Muslims
  number of   34
  hypervisibility of   86
  of migrant origin
    and converts to Islam   39–40
    and Tatars   38, 162
    as newcomers   33, 103, 159
    history of   38
  progressive   219, 229, 236
*Muamalat* (civil dealings)   186, 187

Niqab   111, 170, 188, 189

Orientalism   44, 114, 221
Otherness   104, 107, 146, 159, 171
Ottoman Empire   44, 45

Pędziwiatr, Konrad   73, 74, 76–78
Philips, Bilal   211, 212
Polish Muslim organisations   62, 143, 157, 158, 201, 212–213

Polishness   162, 163, 212, 225, 236
Polygamy   176, 177
Post-colonialism   74, 75
Power relations   84, 87, 94, 229
Prayer   58, 112, 138, 139, 169, 170, 174, 175, 178, 179, 180, 181, 190, 208, 225, 227, 234

Qur'an   63–64, 227
  Interpretation   218
  quotations   141, 156
  reading   139
  recitation (tajweed)   138, 139, 140, 141
  translations   135, 145, 147, 153, 159
  vocabulary   138, 143, 161

Racialization   84, 92, 94, 113–115, 187
Racism   75, 96, 74, 221
Ramadan (month of fasting)   182, 183, 213, 221
Ramadan, Tariq   64, 211
Rambo, Lewis   3, 200
Religious
  activists   200, 201
  authority   146, 201, 241
  imagination   165
  Infrastructure   165, 214
  language   135, 136, 137, 138, 144, 146, 147, 149, 154, 159, 165
  socialisation   202
  tradition   163, 166, 214
Right-wing   215, 233
Ryan, Louise   73, 82, 93, 94
Rzewuski, Wacław   44, 45

Salafism   4, 26, 142, 200–214, 221, 232, 233, 235–236
Salvation   201, 202
Saramowicz, Andrzej   230, 232
Secularism   76, 96
Sexual practices   141, 172, 173, 174, 175, 176, 177, 178, 181
Shia   42, 43, 149, 154, 212, 213
*Shirk*   231, 233
Social
  authority   201
  equality   216
  exclusion   164, 235–236
  hierarchy   151, 220, 221, 229
  networks   208–211

Social (*cont.*)
   pressure   201–207, 235
   relations   151
Sufism   142, 203, 210, 212, 229–236
Stigma   24, 26, 78, 92, 93, 104, 152, 159, 166, 170, 171, 195, 207, 211, 232, 240

*Tariqah* (Sufi order)   230, 232, 233
Tatars   9, 23, 136, 159
   and converts   36, 162, 240
   as Polish diaspora   45
   as the established Muslims   33, 35, 40, 76, 77, 162, 163, 218, 221
   ethnic mobilization   37
   history   34–35, 163
   identity   34–37, 40, 162

Ummah   214
   English-speaking   165
   European   219
   Global   25, 146, 148, 165, 211, 225
   Imaginary   225
   Local   160, 206, 207
   Polish   10, 24, 148, 159, 165, 209, 211, 212, 215, 217, 219, 220, 222, 224, 231, 232, 234, 236
   virtual   135, 141, 147, 159, 210, 211, 212, 234

*Wudhu* (ablution)   174, 175, 179

Zebiri, Kate   82, 87, 89